ADVERTISING: DEVELOPMENT AND ISSUES IN THE DIGITAL AGE

MEDIA AND COMMUNICATIONS – TECHNOLOGIES, POLICIES AND CHALLENGES

Additional books in this series can be found on Nova's website under the Series tab.

Additional E-books in this series can be found on Nova's website under the E-books tab.

BUSINESS ISSUES, COMPETITION AND ENTREPRENEURSHIP

Additional books in this series can be found on Nova's website under the Series tab.

Additional E-books in this series can be found on Nova's website under the E-books tab.

MEDIA AND COMMUNICATIONS – TECHNOLOGIES, POLICIES AND CHALLENGES

ADVERTISING: DEVELOPMENTS AND ISSUES IN THE DIGITAL AGE

WILLIAM L. POULSEN

EDITOR

Nova Science Publishers, Inc.

New York

NOTICE TO THE READER

The Publisher has taken reasonable care in the preparation of this book, but makes no expressed or implied warranty of any kind and assumes no responsibility for any errors or omissions. No liability is assumed for incidental or consequential damages in connection with or arising out of information contained in this book. The Publisher shall not be liable for any special, consequential, or exemplary damages resulting, in whole or in part, from the readers' use of, or reliance upon, this material. Any parts of this book based on government reports are so indicated and copyright is claimed for those parts to the extent applicable to compilations of such works.

Independent verification should be sought for any data, advice or recommendations contained in this book. In addition, no responsibility is assumed by the publisher for any injury and/or damage to persons or property arising from any methods, products, instructions, ideas or otherwise contained in this publication.

This publication is designed to provide accurate and authoritative information with regard to the subject matter covered herein. It is sold with the clear understanding that the Publisher is not engaged in rendering legal or any other professional services. If legal or any other expert assistance is required, the services of a competent person should be sought. FROM A DECLARATION OF PARTICIPANTS JOINTLY ADOPTED BY A COMMITTEE OF THE AMERICAN BAR ASSOCIATION AND A COMMITTEE OF PUBLISHERS.

Additional color graphics may be available in the e-book version of this book.

LIBRARY OF CONGRESS CATALOGING-IN-PUBLICATION DATA

Advertising : developments and issues in the digital age / editor, William L. Poulsen.
p. cm.
Includes index.
ISBN 978-1-61761-783-6 (hardcover)
1. Advertising. 2. Internet advertising. I. Poulsen, William L.
HF5823.A1686 2010
659.1--dc22
2010036378

Published by Nova Science Publishers, Inc. † New York

CONTENTS

PREFACE

The advertising industry is a major sector of the U.S. economy, employing hundreds of thousands of workers and accounting for about 2% of the nation's annual output. Advertising campaigns by large firms and small businesses provide consumers with product information and generate crucial income for newspapers, television and radio stations, magazines and other ventures. The advertising industry is in the midst of a fundamental restructuring, however. The deep recession has depressed ad spending. At the same time, the industry faces longer-term challenges as consumers migrate from traditional media to digital platforms such as websites, cell phones, mobile e-readers, and gaming networks. The emerging digital market offers great advantages including lower distribution costs, the ability to target ads to individuals rather than broad groups, and more precise tools to measure ad impact. This book explores current advertising developments and issues in the digital age.

Chapter 1- The advertising industry is a major sector of the U.S. economy, employing hundreds of thousands of workers and accounting for about 2% of the nation's annual output, according to some estimates. Advertising campaigns by large firms and small businesses provide consumers with product information and generate crucial income for newspapers, television and radio stations, magazines, and other ventures. The advertising industry is in the midst of a fundamental restructuring, however. The deep recession has depressed ad spending. At the same time, the industry faces longer-term challenges as consumers migrate from traditional media to digital platforms such as websites, cell phones, mobile e-readers, and gaming networks. The emerging digital market offers great advantages including lower distribution costs, the ability to target ads to individuals rather than broad groups, and more precise tools to measure ad impact. But the rise of cut-rate online advertising has hurt media companies and businesses that depend on ad revenue. The changing structure of the market is also forcing changes in ad presentation and content, with implications for consumer privacy, Internet regulation, and media profitability.

Chapter 2- To produce revenue, websites have placed advertisements on their sites. Advertisers will pay a premium for greater assurance that the advertisement they are purchasing will be seen by users that are most likely to be interested in the product or service offered. As a result, technology has been developed which enables online advertisements to be targeted directly at individual users based on their web surfing activity. This practice is widely known as "behavioral" or "e-havioral" advertising.

This individual behavioral targeting has raised a number of privacy concerns. For instance, questions have been asked whether personally identifiable information is being collected; how the information collected is being protected; and whether current laws are being violated if data are being collected without the consent of the parties involved. It is often unclear whether current laws, such as the Electronic Communications Privacy Act and the Communications Act, apply to online advertising providers that are collecting data through click tracking, capturing search terms, and other methods. However, it is likely that in many cases these laws could be held to apply to such activities and that these methods of data collection would be forbidden unless consent is obtained from one of the parties to the communication. This chapter will examine the application of these statutes to online behavioral advertising in more detail.

Chapter 3- A phenomenon that has become more and more important over the last decade, direct-toconsumer (DTC) advertising has grown from about $800 million in 1996 to over $4.7 billion in 2007. Its supporters point to more informed consumers who then visit their doctors and become more involved in their own treatment, leading to better and earlier diagnosis of undertreated illnesses. The critics believe that industry's presentation of the balance of drug benefit and risk information may encourage the inappropriate use of advertised products and lead to higher than necessary spending. In addition to concerns with accuracy and balance, health professionals point out that DTC ads rarely mention alternative treatments, such as other or generic medications or non-drug interventions.

Chapter 4- This chapter provides a brief overview of federal law with respect to six selected advertising issues: alcohol advertising, tobacco advertising, the Federal Trade Commission Act, advertising by mail (including junk mail), advertising by telephone, and commercial e-mail (spam). There are numerous federal statutes regulating advertising that do not fit within any of these categories. As random examples, the Food, Drug, and Cosmetic Act requires disclosures in advertisements for prescription drugs; the Truth in Lending Act governs the advertising of consumer credit; and a federal criminal statute makes it illegal falsely to convey in an advertisement that a business is connected with a federal agency.

This chapter provides a brief overview of federal law with respect to six selected advertising issues: alcohol advertising, tobacco advertising, the Federal Trade Commission Act, advertising by mail, advertising by telephone, and commercial email (spam).[1] There are numerous federal statutes regulating advertising that do not fit within any of these categories. As random examples, the Food, Drug, and Cosmetic Act requires disclosures in advertisements for prescription drugs[2]; the Truth in Lending Act governs the advertising of consumer credit[3]; and a federal criminal statute makes it illegal falsely to convey in an advertisement that a business is connected with a federal agency.[4]

Chapter 5- Chairman Inouye, Vice Chainnan Stevens, and Members of Committee, I am Lydia Pames,[1] Director of the Bureau of Consumer Protection at the Federal Trade Commission (the "FTC" or "Commission"). I appreciate the opportunity to appear before you today to discuss the Commission's activities regarding online behavioral advertising, the practice of collecting information about an individual's online activities in order to serve advertisements that are tailored to that individual's interests. Over the past year or so, the Commission has undertaken a comprehensive effort to educate itself and the public about this practice and its implications for consumer privacy. This testimony will describe the Commission's efforts, which have included hosting a "Town Hall" meeting and issuing for public comment FTC staff's proposed online behavioral advertising principles.[2]

The Commission's examination of behavioral advertising has shown that the issues surrounding this practice are complex, that the business models are diverse and constantly evolving, and that behavioral advertising may provide benefits to consumers even as it raises concerns about consumer privacy. At this time, the Commission is cautiously optimistic that the privacy concerns raised by behavioral advertising can be addressed effectively by industry self- regulation.[3]

Chapter 6- CDT recognizes that advertising is an important engine of Internet growth. Consumers benefit from a rich diversity of content, services and applications that are provided without charge and supported by advertising revenue. However, as sophisticated new behavioral advertising models are deployed, it is vital that consumer privacy be protected. Massive increases in data processing and storage capabilities have allowed advertisers to track, collect and aggregate information about consumers' Web browsing activities, compiling individual profiles used to match advertisements to consumers' interests. All of this is happening in the context of an online environment where more data is collected – and retained for longer periods – than ever before and existing privacy protections have been far outpaced by technological innovation.

Chapter 7- (a)   The Guides in this part represent administrative interpretations of laws enforced by the Federal Trade Commission for the guidance of the public in conducting its affairs in conformity with legal requirements. Specifically, the Guides address the application of Section 5 of the FTC Act (15 U.S.C. 45) to the use of endorsements and testimonials in advertising. The Guides provide the basis for voluntary compliance with the law by advertisers and endorsers. Practices inconsistent with these Guides may result in corrective action by the Commission under Section 5 if, after investigation, the Commission has reason to believe that the practices fall within the scope of conduct declared unlawful by the statute.

The Guides set forth the general principles that the Commission will use in evaluating endorsements and testimonials, together with examples illustrating the application of those principles. The Guides do not purport to cover every possible use of endorsements in advertising. Whether a particular endorsement or testimonial is deceptive will depend on the specific factual circumstances of the advertisement at issue.

(b) For purposes of this part, an endorsement means any advertising message (including verbal statements, demonstrations, or depictions of the name, signature, likeness or other identifying personal characteristics of an individual or the name or seal of an organization) that consumers are likely to believe reflects the opinions, beliefs, findings, or experiences of a party other than the sponsoring advertiser, even if the views expressed by that party are identical to those of the sponsoring advertiser. The party whose opinions, beliefs, findings, or experience the message appears to reflect will be called the endorser and may be an individual, group, or institution.

(c) The Commission intends to treat endorsements and testimonials identically in the context of its enforcement of the Federal Trade Commission Act and for purposes of this part. The term endorsements is therefore generally used hereinafter to cover both terms and situations.

(d) For purposes of this part, the term product includes any product, service, company or industry.

(e) For purposes of this part, an expert is an individual, group, or institution possessing, as a result of experience, study, or training, knowledge of a particular subject, which knowledge is superior to what ordinary individuals generally acquire.

In: Advertising: Developments and Issues in the Digital Age   ISBN: 978-1-61761-783-6
Editor: William L. Poulsen   © 2011 Nova Science Publishers, Inc.

Chapter 1

ADVERTISING INDUSTRY IN THE DIGITAL AGE

Suzanne M. Kirchhoff

SUMMARY

The advertising industry is a major sector of the U.S. economy, employing hundreds of thousands of workers and accounting for about 2% of the nation's annual output, according to some estimates. Advertising campaigns by large firms and small businesses provide consumers with product information and generate crucial income for newspapers, television and radio stations, magazines, and other ventures. The advertising industry is in the midst of a fundamental restructuring, however. The deep recession has depressed ad spending. At the same time, the industry faces longer-term challenges as consumers migrate from traditional media to digital platforms such as websites, cell phones, mobile e-readers, and gaming networks. The emerging digital market offers great advantages including lower distribution costs, the ability to target ads to individuals rather than broad groups, and more precise tools to measure ad impact. But the rise of cut-rate online advertising has hurt media companies and businesses that depend on ad revenue. The changing structure of the market is also forcing changes in ad presentation and content, with implications for consumer privacy, Internet regulation, and media profitability.

U.S. advertising spending declined in 2008. Deeper reductions are forecast for 2009. The sharp drop in ad dollars has prompted advertising agencies and media companies to lay off tens of thousands of workers and curtail production. Though the market is projected to gradually stabilize, some ad-dependent businesses like newspapers and magazines may not see revenues return to pre-recession levels for years, if then.

Online advertising has slowed during the recession, though it is expected to claim a growing share of the market over the longer term. Internet advertising has nearly doubled since 2005, to about 12% of the market, and some forecasts call for it to more than double again by 2014. Digital advertisers are experimenting with a variety of approaches to reach consumers, who are not only dispersed among a multitude of Web pages, games, and social networks, but have more power to screen content using pop-up blockers or video recording devices. Firms are using "behavioral advertising" (tailoring ads to individuals based on technology that tracks their Web activities) or, increasingly, marketing on their own websites or through bloggers. The most successful approach to date is "search" advertising—where companies like Google and Yahoo sell ads as part of consumer-initiated information queries on their browsers. Search advertising, dominated by a few large firms, accounted for nearly half of digital ad revenues in 2008. The online market is generally compressed, with the top 10 digital ad firms garnering 71% of online revenue in the second quarter of 2009.

Congress has long regulated advertising to protect consumers and ensure fair competition. Lawmakers are now debating whether, or how, to update advertising laws for the Internet age, without stifling growth or unduly hurting media outlets dependent on advertising revenue. House members are mulling legislation to enhance privacy rights, which could limit the growth of behavioral advertising. The U.S. Food and Drug Administration (FDA) is examining pharmaceutical marketing in social networks and recently set policies for online marketing. The Federal Trade Commission (FTC) has released guidelines calling on bloggers to disclose paid product reviews. Other potential issues include looking at advertising in online games and online political advertising.

INTRODUCTION

Congress has a long history of regulating advertising to ensure fair competition, shield consumers from unfair or misleading messages, limit the exposure of children, and restrict promotion of products such as tobacco and liquor deemed morally or physically harmful.[1] Policymakers face new challenges as the advertising industry enters a period of far-reaching change brought about by the economic downturn and structural shifts as consumers move to the Internet and other digital platforms for news, entertainment, and socializing.

Federal oversight of the advertising industry is intensifying as regulators and lawmakers try to keep pace with shifting technology and consumer habits. In just the past several months, the Federal Trade Commission (FTC) has updated guidelines for product endorsements to cover online bloggers.[2] The U.S. Food and Drug Administration (FDA) has announced hearings to examine web-based pharmaceutical marketing[3] and the Federal Communications Commission (FCC) is assessing protections for children in the digital sphere, including online advertising.[4] In Congress, lawmakers have introduced legislation to limit the deductibility of advertising for pharmaceutical marketing.[5] Representative Rick Boucher, chairman of the House Energy and Commerce subcommittee on Communications, Technology, and the Internet, has announced plans to introduce legislation setting tighter standards for online privacy, which could limit some forms of targeted advertising.[6] House and Senate committees have held hearings on the state of the newspaper industry, which is in financial distress due to eroding ad revenue.[7] This chapter is intended to provide context and background for the emerging regulatory debate.

Like other economic sectors, the advertising sector has been affected by the recession. Ad spending declined in 2008 compared to 2007, and fell another 15.4% in the first half of 2009 as companies pared advertising budgets, according to Nielsen Company.[8] Other media analysts say media spending also declined in 2007.[9] Forecasters expect gradual improvement, starting in 2010. Putting the decline in context, advertising has not fallen for three consecutive years since the Great Depression, according to some analyses.[10] While the market is expected to gradually rebound, some traditional media outlets—newspapers, magazines, and radio—may not see revenues rebound to pre-recession levels even over a five-year horizon.[11]

Advertising firms across the country have imposed layoffs and, in some cases, shut down as ad spending has weakened. The number of people employed in advertising and related industries such as public relations and marketing fell to 416,300 in August 2009 from a recent peak of 478,600 in October 2007.[12] Job losses are not confined to the advertising sector. Newspapers, magazines, radio, and television outlets that depend on advertising for most, or in some cases nearly all, of their revenues have fired workers and scaled back operations in response to the advertising declines. Newspapers alone have shed about 30,000 jobs since January 2008.[13]

Even as the advertising industry grapples with the immediate impacts of the recession, it must adapt to structural changes as consumers migrate from traditional media to online platforms. Internet advertising has been the fastest-growing segment of the market, rising to $23.4 billion in 2008, from $4.6 billion in 1999.[14] The digital arena, loosely defined, includes video, text, and "display" advertisements placed on business and media websites, within social media like My Space and Facebook, on iPhones and digital readers. Internet advertising declined by 5.3% in the first half of 2009 compared to the same period in 2008, according to the Interactive Advertising Bureau (IAB). During the next five years (2009-2014), however, consulting firm Forrester Research expects digital advertising, now about 12% of the U.S. advertising spending, to reach a 21% share, with revenues rising from $26 billion to about $55 billion.[15] The Internet has grown nearly twice as fast as cable television did in its infancy, for instance, measured in terms of ad revenues[16] and with the advent of new technologies allowing long-form video on the Web, has the capacity to emerge as a substitute for television as it presently exists.

The online market potentially offers major opportunities for advertisers. Smaller businesses can place their ads in front of millions of people at a low cost. Technology makes it possible to measure the effectiveness of ads by counting the number of consumers who click on online offerings or watch online videos. Cell phones and other mobile devices give advertisers more access to more consumers for more hours of the day.[17] Companies have increased ability to fine-tune ad strategies, with many now buying and adjusting media on a weekly or daily basis, rather than at set intervals during the year.[18] Firms can also directly tout their products online, which has helped spur growth in so-called below-the-line marketing such as corporate websites, blogs, and e-mail solicitations. Below-the-line marketing appears to be crowding out some above-the-line spending, the term generally used to refer to media-based advertising.[19]

Despite the myriad of websites and blogs, the online market is compressed. The top 10 ad-selling firms accounted for 71% of total online advertising revenues in the second quarter of 2009, according to the IAB.[20] Search advertising alone accounted for 47% of digital ad revenues in the first half of 2009, the IAB data show.[21] Under search, an advertiser bids, via an ongoing auction process, to have his or her ad displayed when a consumer types a query into a search engine using a given keyword. The search market is dominated by Google and Yahoo (now in a partnership with Microsoft, which has the Bing search engine).

At the same time, the vast proliferation of ad-supported websites, online videos, blogs, and other offerings has created more supply than can be readily sold, helping to depress advertising rates in both online and in conventional media markets. "The Internet hurt traditional media by not only increasing its share of consumer time spent, but also by further weakening the ad-pricing power of traditional media," according to an analysis by Catalyst Investors.[22]

Advertisers also are discovering that it can be challenging to connect with online consumers, who have more power to screen content via pop-up blockers, digital recording devices, and other technologies. "With digital consumers increasingly in control of their media experience and advertisers shifting their spend to more interactive, measurable formats, companies must move beyond traditional advertising," IBM Global Services analysts wrote in a recent report.[23]

Firms are experimenting with new tools. Advertisers have long used demographic and other data to target audiences, but the Internet, with its veritable wealth of information about consumer behavior, is moving this practice to a new level. Advertisers are using behavioral advertising (targeting ads using data collected as individuals browse the web, register for websites or sign up for promotions) in conjunction with search and other strategies. Companies are also aiming to become part of ongoing digital consumer conversations, tapping into social networks, creating mobile phone applications and working with popular bloggers.[24]

ADVERTISING AND THE ECONOMY

Advertising—the use of images, sounds, and slogans to communicate a message that will spark consumer interest in goods or services—is deeply ingrained in America's market-based economy. Advertising allows businesses to promote products or burnish corporate reputations, politicians to connect with voters, the military to boost recruitment and advocacy groups to raise public awareness.

Advertising has been part of the U.S. economy since Colonial times. The first known ad published in the United States was a 1704 announcement in the *Boston News-Letter* seeking a buyer for an Oyster Bay, New York estate. Investor and diplomat Benjamin Franklin's *Pennsylvania Gazette*, which began production in 1729, included pages of advertisements.[25] (See Box, page 8.)

Today, advertising is so intertwined in the nation's daily business that consumers may not realize how constantly they are bombarded with product pitches. By one accounting, the average American is exposed to 500-1,000 advertisements daily.[26] In 2005, for example, a one-hour broadcast television program included anywhere from 16 to 22 minutes of commercials. Ads—ranging from a grainy line of text to sophisticated video—are everywhere from cell phones to gas pumps, billboards, television, newspapers, magazines, and movie screens.[27]

Advertising can improve market efficiency by providing consumers and businesses with information about products or services that increase competition and reduce prices.[28] The online market potentially offers even more advantages by reducing costs and allowing closely targeted messages.[29] The ad industry has also been assailed by critics, however, including some economists, who say advertising increases business costs by making it more expensive for new entrants to compete against established brands.[30] Consumer groups have condemned advertisers for exploiting public fears and aspirations to push products that can be unnecessary or harmful.[31]

Advertising plays another important role in the United States: providing a subsidy for "free" broadcast television and radio, low-cost newspapers, and magazines. U.S. newspapers have traditionally garnered about 80% of revenues from running advertisements, consumer magazines 55%, and some specialty publications such as business trade magazines up to 100%.[32] Broadcast radio and television depend on advertising for the vast bulk of their earnings. The longstanding ad-based media model is now breaking down due to the recession and emergence of the Internet, with implications for specific businesses and, more broadly, for dissemination of news and information.[33]

Scale of the Advertising Industry

Advertising makes up a larger slice of economic activity in the United States than in other countries, which is not that surprising considering that ad spending tends to be higher in wealthier, consumer-driven nations.[34] According to one longstanding measure, the advertising industry accounts for about 2% of annual Gross Domestic Product, the broadest measure of goods and services produced in the United States.[35] (See Figure 1.)

Estimates of the size of the advertising industry vary, depending on the type of data and precise market definition used. Some measures encompass advertising and marketing. Advertising refers to specific messages designed to pique consumer interest in a brand, institution or service, while marketing is the broader practice of researching, planning, and buying advertising.[36] Other industry definitions include public relations and other services.

The advertising industry for decades relied on estimates by Robert Coen of advertising firm Universal McCann (now part of MAGNA, which is owned by industry giant Interpublic). His estimates were also cited by government agencies. Coen, who retired this year at age 86, began working in advertising in 1948. He compiled data based on agency billings, production and proprietary information. Coen also tracked advertising fluctuations against changes in overall GDP. In his last published forecast, for 2008, Coen pegged U.S. ad spending at $258.7 billion.[37]

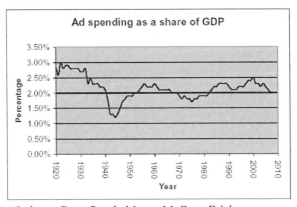

Source: U.S. Advertising Industry Data, Purple Motes, McCann Erickson.

Figure 1. U.S. Advertising and the Economy

Coen's successor at MAGNA, Brian Wieser, has taken a different approach that measures advertising by focusing more on revenues than on billings, includes different underlying sources for determining the volume of Internet advertising and lower revenues for direct mail than Coen, for example. Wieser expects U.S. advertising to reach $161 billion in 2009.[38] Wieser says his data show advertising spending is most sensitive to fluctuations in consumer spending and manufacturing output, rather than overall changes in GDP.[39]

According to the Census Department, advertising and related service firms had $84 billion in revenues in 2008. For the first six months of 2009, such firms had revenues of $38 billion, a more than 8% decline from the same period in 2008.[40] Other media and advertising consulting firms that provide forecasts and estimates include the Nielsen Company, TNS Media, eMarketer and Veronis Suhler Stevenson.

Though forecasters differ on bottom-line numbers, their trend lines are generally similar. Total advertising spending is forecast to decline this year, largely due to the recession. The online sector is not immune, though it is projected to fare better than many other segments, such as print newspapers and broadcast television. (See **Table 1**.)[41]

The Nielsen Company estimates that U.S. ad spending fell 15.4% in the first half of 2009, compared to the same period in 2008.[42] Analysts at Barclay's Capital forecast that total 2009 U.S. ad spending will shrink by 13% from 2008.[43] Over the longer term, Wieser expects advertising spending to recover, with a compounded annual growth rate of 1.2% between 2009 and 2014.[44]

One big reason that ad spending has taken a nosedive has been the distress in the U.S. auto industry, a huge national advertiser. Car companies sharply curtailed ad spending as their sales cratered and General Motors and Chrysler went through bankruptcy. Still, many businesses in highly competitive sectors of the economy have tried to keep their ad budgets constant in recent months, or increase them, to protect market share. In 2008, the top 100 U.S. advertisers reduced spending by a collective 2.7%, according to *Advertising Age*. But half of the top 100 advertisers increased total ad spending, seeking to hold on to or increase sales and name recognition.[45]

Table 1. U.S. Advertising Revenues by Select Media, 2009
Projected ad spending for 2009, compared to 2008, in billions of dollars

Type of Media	Projected 2009 Revenues	Percentage Change
Television[a]	$47.7	-14.4%
Newspapers	$28.5	-29.5%
Online total	$23.0	-2.2%
Direct Mail	$19.2	-11.2%
Magazines	$15.7	-18.3%
Radio	$14.0	-21.0%
Directories	$12.1	-10.5%
Outdoor	$6.1	-12.9%

Source: MAGNA Media Advertising Forecast, July 13, 2009.
a. Television category does not include cable.

U.S. ADVERTISING HISTORY

The modern ad industry traces its roots to the 1800s, when advances in photography, magazines, the telegraph and other technology brought about national communications, mass production and mass marketing.[46] Volney Palmer, a Philadelphia businessman, formed the first U.S. advertising agency in the 1840s when he began buying large chunks of ad space from newspapers and reselling them to clients at a higher price.[47] At the close of the 19th century, advertising agencies had moved from merely brokering sales to creating advertising content. The industry became more professional and more persuasive.

In the 1920s, the J. Walter Thompson advertising agency hired noted psychologist John Watson, a leader in behaviorism, which explains human action in terms of stimulus and response.[48] George Gallup, later of the famous Gallup polling firm, joined ad agency Young and Rubicam in 1932.[49] Advertising expanded with the growth of radio. Advertising firms backed radio programs such the Fleischman's Yeast Hour, with crooner Rudy Vallee, and the Lucky Strike Dance Hour; two of the top-rated evening radio programs of 1930-31 season.[50]

With the advent of television in the 1940s, advertising was again transformed. As with radio, advertisers initially supported programs— Milton Berle's Texaco Star Theater and Kraft Television Theater are examples—but costs became prohibitive. Advertisers moved from backing entire programs, to buying one- or two-minute blocks of time. They still had influence over programming, but networks had say over content.[51]

The advertising industry hit creative highs during the 1950s and 1960s. Chicago ad firm Leo Burnett created product icons like the Jolly Green Giant, Pillsbury Dough Boy and Marlboro Man. [52] Ad firm Doyle Dane Bernbach's "Think Small" promotion campaign for the Volkswagen Beetle—which created wide consumer acceptance for a runty foreign car that looked like nothing on American roads—is rated by many as the most influential ad campaign in U.S. history.[53]

In the 1970s and 1980s prominent ad firms—some with competing clients—were merged or taken over. The ad sector is now dominated by large holding companies such as Publicis Groupe and Omnimedia. The recession of the early 1980s changed advertising patterns as advertisers began relying more on promotions via coupons and direct marketing. By 1990 the advertising industry had lost 25% of its share of business marketing budgets to other forms of marketing communications. Additional changes meant the loss of 13,500 advertising jobs in three years.[54]

By the mid-1990s, advertising budgets were again growing at double-digit rates. The industry took another hit when the dot.com bubble burst in the late 1990s.[55] In recent years smaller, edgier firms have gained prominence. New companies focus on digital advertising and marketing. New ad networks are springing up on the web.[56]

Other large U.S. advertisers, by dollar value, are home products firms like Proctor & Gamble, and retailers like Macy's.[57] (See Table 2.) The most-advertised U.S. brand in 2008 was Verizon with $2.2 billion in measured media spending, followed by AT&T, with just under $2 billion, according to TNS Media Intelligence.[58] Pharmaceutical spending has become a major category, with direct-to-consumer advertising of prescription drugs rising from about $800 million in 1996 to more than $4.7 billion in 2007.[59]

Advertising Employment

The advertising industry is now dominated by large, multinational holding companies. Four of the biggest, Omnicom Group, the WPP Group, the Interpublic Group of Companies, and Publicis Groupe, accounted for 54% of the $31.1 billion earned by U.S. ad firms in 2007.[60]

"The holding company concept was pioneered by the Interpublic Group of Companies as a means of circumventing the longstanding industry norm which precludes an advertising agency from serving competing clients in the same market. To respect this requirement, holding companies are organized into separate sub-groups or "networks" of affiliated units offering more or less similar mixes of services but that operate independent of one another and that often compete with one another for client accounts," Harvard professors Alvin Silk and Charles King III wrote in an analysis of the industry.

Their paper examined data from the late 1970s through most of the current decade to test whether the market was overly concentrated.[61] It found that, using the Herfindahl-Hirschman Index (HHI), a benchmark measure of industry competition, the advertising and market services industry was not overly concentrated at the general level. The four largest holding companies had between a fifth and a quarter of total industry revenue, a share that was stable from 2002-2006.

Table 2. Top Advertisers, First Half 2009
Dollar amounts in millions

Product Category	Q1-Q2 2009	Q1-Q2 2008	% Change
Automotive	$3,681.2	$5,363.6	-31.4%
Fast Food Restaurant	$2,200.7	$2,093.4	5.1%
Pharmaceutical	$2,148.0	$2,421.2	-11.3%
Wireless Telephone	$1,871.4	$1,847.1	1.3%
Motion Pictures	$1,709.0	$1,680.7	1.7%
Auto Dealers - Local	$1,688.5	$2,288.3	-26.2%
Department Stores	$1,565.8	$1,637.2	-4.4%
Direct Response Products[a]	$1,260.1	$1,181.1	6.7%
Restaurants	$834.6	$867.7	-3.8%
Furniture Stores	$773.8	$802.9	-3.6%
Top 10 Product Groups	$17,733.1	$20,183.1	-12.1%

Source: The Nielsen Company.

a. Direct Response refers to products sold via infomercials or home shopping networks including such products as Snuggie Blankets, Rosetta Stone Computer Software or Video Professor Computer Software Data excludes business-to-business magazine ad spending.

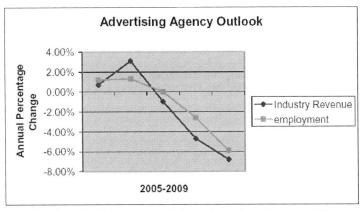

Source: Real Growth Numbers, IBIS World, *2009 Advertising Agencies in the U.S.*

Figure 2. Advertising Agency Economic Conditions

Holding companies offer such services as account management and ad production and placement. Boutique firms, which can be independent or part of a larger company, generally focus on one aspect of marketing or advertising.[62] Advertising firms are found across the country, though about 20% of advertising businesses, and more than a quarter of the industry's workers, were located in California and New York in 2006.[63]

The composition of ad agencies is changing as digital advertising assumes a more important role. Online advertising, as compared to traditional ad campaigns, is more data-driven, based on information about consumer preferences, website popularity, clicks per ad and mathematical formulas used by Google and other ad sellers to determine price and placement of ads. "Advertising strategies, campaigns and distribution are increasingly based on predictive algorithms, spreadsheets and math. Marketing and math have intersected," according to a Booz & Co. report for major U.S. advertising groups.[64]

Advertising agencies have been focusing on higher-growth non-advertising business, including market research, media planning, interactive media and customer relationship management. Companies are deriving a larger share of revenues from non-advertising sources.[65]

There were 416,300 people employed in advertising and related industries in August 2009. That was down from a recent peak of 478,600 in October 2007 according to the Labor Department. Looking at a narrower slice of the industry, advertising agencies employed an estimated 163,300 workers in August 2009, compared to a recent peak of 189,700 in October 2007.[66] According to 2002 economic census, there were about 38,000 advertising, marketing, public relations and related establishments in the United States. The U.S. Census Department data include workers who write copy, create drawings, photos, paintings and video, perform market research and executive ad buys in various media.[67] The industry is labor intensive, with wages equaling about 44% of total revenues.[68]

U.S. advertising agencies traditionally charged clients a 15% commission for their work. Such pricing continued to be the industry standard for years, even after courts in the 1950s ruled against advertisers in a series of antitrust cases. In those cases, magazine and newspaper publishers charged that the commission system limited their ability to directly bargain with advertisers.[69] Industry compensation has changed significantly in recent decades. In 2003, just

10% of large national advertisers relied on commissions, while 74% used fee-based models according to one study.[70]

ADVERTISING AND MEDIA

The shifting ad market, in conjunction with reduced ad spending due to the recession, has had a dramatic impact on traditional media. In the past year, newspaper publishers such as the Tribune Company, which publishes the *Chicago Tribune*, *Baltimore Sun* and *Los Angeles Times*, have declared bankruptcy.[71] Publishers have pulled the plug on venerable magazines like *Gourmet*, which had been in operation since 1941.[72] Radio and television revenues have plunged.

In one example of the market shift, consulting firm Borrell Associates expects advertising in the Yellow Pages (print telephone directories of local businesses), newspapers, radio and direct mail to decline by nearly 20% during the next five years. Local online search advertising is expected to surge by nearly 40% during that period.[73]

Media companies are struggling to craft new business strategies, developing extensive online operations as their readers, viewers and listeners move to the web. Some media firms now have online properties that pull in millions of consumers each month. But revenues have not grown in proportion to the digital audience, for several reasons. Most news organizations chose to offer content for free online, under the theory they would generate higher advertising revenues by increasing their consumer base.[74] Another factor is proliferation of websites, which has pushed down the price for some types of ads, especially as demand has waned during the recession.[75] Newspapers, for example, may be able to sell an ad in their physical ink-and-paper product for $20 per thousand, but for less than $1 on their website.[76]

Media companies are taking on some of the functions of marketing and advertising firms as they reposition themselves. Media outlets are providing marketing services to potential advertisers based on their own internal data about subscribers, their Web reach and other information. Newspapers are banding together to combine their content or are working in concert with Internet ad giants like Yahoo.[77] A number, including *Newsday*, are starting to charge for online content.[78]

News Corp. Chairman Rupert Murdoch recently said the ad environment is improving or at least leveling out.[79] But earnings reports by large newspaper companies show that the advertising environment continues to be challenging. Gannett Co. reported that advertising revenues at its newspapers were down 28.4% in the third quarter of 2009, compared to a year earlier.[80] That is a slight improvement from the second quarter, when revenues were 32% below year-ago levels. Still the company eked out better-than-expected profits by slashing expenses.

Even if online advertising does double by 2014, as some forecast, traditional media is expected to have the lion's share of the market. Television is expected to remain the dominant advertising choice, given the ease of reaching huge audiences on broadcast and cable stations. Still, there is no question that some areas of the media, particularly print media, face financial stress due to the current, troubled ad market:

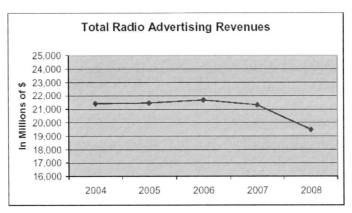

Source: Radio Advertising Bureau.

Figure 3. Broadcast Radio Advertising 2004-2008 Includes Network, National, Local and Off-Air Revenues

- Daily newspaper revenues have declined to about $38 billion in 2008 from $49.5 billion in 2005.[81] Print ad revenues plummeted 30% in the second quarter of 2009, compared to the same period a year earlier. Online newspaper ad revenues, which had been growing, declined 16% during the period.[82] Newspapers have attracted millions of online readers, but earn only about 10% of their revenues from digital operations.[83] Newspapers have lost lucrative classified advertising to online sites such as Craigslist that charge very few fees.[84] Borrell Associates predicts newspaper advertising revenues will rise by 2.4% in 2010, and by low single-digit increases for several more years after that. By 2014, newspaper ad revenues will be 8.7% above 2009 levels, though still remaining well below previous peaks. The firm admits what it terms a positive projection "equates to a dead-cat bounce more than anything else."[85]
- Magazine advertising totaled $9.1 billion in the first half of 2009, a 21% decline from the previous year, the Publishers Information Bureau reported in July. The number of ad pages was down 28% during that period. [86] The impact was clear in early October, when publisher Conde Nast closed four magazines—including *Gourmet*. The company also imposed 20-25% cost reductions on many remaining publications.[87] Longer term, analysis firm Zenith Optimedia says magazines have a brighter outlook than newspapers, since reading a magazine is less easy to replicate on the Internet. The firm predicts magazine advertising will return to 1.5% growth in 2011, though it will be 22.4% below 2007 levels.[88]
- Broadcast radio, which makes nearly all its money from advertising, saw a 9% increase in digital revenues in the second quarter of 2009.[89] Radio revenues declined about 25% in the first half of 2009, according to the Radio Advertising Bureau.[90] Radio stations are moving aggressively into the digital marketplace, offering radio streaming applications for iPhones and creating their own websites. Some radio firms have been buying Internet-based companies. In the United States, radio advertising peaked at nearly 13% of the market in 2002 and is now down to about 10%.[91]
- Television broadcast ad revenues fell 12.8% in the second quarter of 2009 compared to the same period in 2008, according to the Television Bureau of Advertising, which

based its analysis on TNS Media Intelligence data.[92] Still, even though the audience has become more splintered among hundreds of cable channels, television has the broadest scope and is the easiest platform to use to reach a mass audience. The industry is expanding its digital offerings. Hulu.com, a free Internet site (supported by advertising) where people watch episodes of broadcast and cable programs like "Family Guy or "Desperate Housewives" has attracted millions of viewers. Some industry leaders are questioning whether programs that cost millions of dollars to produce should be offered for no cost.[93]

AD PRICES/ADVERTISING STRATEGIES

In some ways, the digital world is very similar to the traditional ad market. Newspaper and magazine websites run display ads that are placed along the sides or across the top of websites, in much the same way ads are posted in a physical magazine or newspaper. Radio and television websites impose audio and video ads in the midst of online programming, as in conventional broadcasts. Many ad prices are quoted in cost per thousand viewers or readers, like in traditional media.

But in a number of vital ways, the markets are far different. One example is competition. A print newspaper may be the dominant source of information in its local market, but on the Internet that same newspaper is up against hundreds or thousands of websites, bloggers and Twitterers offering general news, information and opinion. The huge supply has made it tougher for media outlets, and other ad-dependent businesses, to charge premium prices online unless they have reached major scale, can sell unique content or have a desirable market niche/demographic.

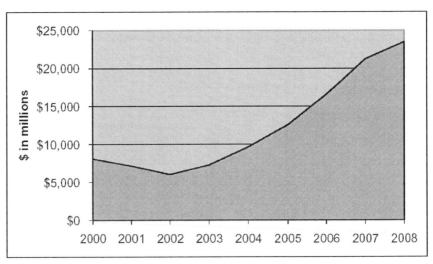

Source: Interactive Advertising Bureau and Price Waterhouse Coopers.
Notes: Internet advertising revenues were $10.9 billion in the first half of 2009.

Figure 4. Internet Advertising Revenues 2000-2008

Another difference is the fact that despite the multitude of websites and other digital locations, the online advertising market is compressed, with just the top 10 companies accounting for 71% of ad spending in the first half of 2009 and the top 50 for 89% of all online advertising.[94]

Benjamin Edelman, an assistant professor at Harvard University, has proposed a Bill of Rights for Advertisers, saying the concentrated market places them at a clear disadvantage.[95] Edelman says large ad companies should be more transparent about ad placement and pricing, advertisers should have easy access to data about where ads are placed, more detailed billing information and more control over the use of data generated by search advertising."[96] "It's a very high burden for the advertiser to figure it all out," Edelman says.

Measurability

One major difference between established and emerging markets is the development of more advanced tools to quantify consumer response. Advertisers for decades have used various measurements to determine where to place ads and to glean insight into consumer response. Nielsen offers data on television viewership through consumer panels and special measurement devices. Arbitron Inc. is a leader in radio audience measurement. The Audit Bureau of Circulations measures sales of newspapers. Companies may supplement these audience measurements with other qualitative research on consumer demographics and behavior, as well as separate surveys designed to measure return on investment.

In the digital world, advertisers have access to faster, more granular measurements. Digital advertisers can count the number of people who click on an ad, forward an email or view a video. "One of the primary benefits of digital advertising is that it lends itself to quantitative analysis. Companies can easily track ad impressions, click-throughs, unique visits and time spent on each page. Drawbacks of online advertising are that … many consumers ignore passive ads, in part because they often had no relevance to what the consumer was viewing," according to an advertising case study published by Dartmouth's Tuck School of Business.[97]

Most online ads are sold on the basis of consumer response. According to the IAB, 38% of online ads sold in the second quarter of 2009 were priced on cost per impression (the number of times viewers saw an ad), with 58% sold on a performance-based model such as cost per click.[98] The rest were sold on a hybrid basis.

There are questions as to the accuracy of such metrics. comScore, a leading U.S. firm measuring consumer digital behavior by tracking behavior of a million U.S. consumer volunteers, says only about 16% of Internet users clicked on an ad in March 2009, and just 8% of Internet users accounted for nearly 85% of all clicks.[99] "Today, marketers who attempt to optimize their advertising campaigns solely around the click are assigning no value to the 84% of Internet users who don't click on an ad. That's precisely the wrong thing to do," the company said in a press release.[100] Another ongoing problem is click fraud, a practice whereby companies or individuals manipulate the numbers to make ads look more popular or to draw clicks to their websites and away from competitors.[101]

Whatever the imperfections, the new gauges have pushed other media toward more finely tuned measurement tools. For example, technology company TRAnalytics has developed a measurement system that will combine information from monitoring devices placed atop televisions, household purchase data gleaned from scanners in stores and from advertisers, and demographic data.[102] Other firms are trying to go beyond clicks to things such as "dwell time"—the amount of time a consumer spends with a promotion including watching video, expanding the size of an ad or forwarding it to friends.[103]

Search/Ad Networks

A vexing challenge for advertisers is how to best find potential customers in the large, but atomized, digital world. Search advertising has emerged as the main answer. Search, which did not exist a decade ago, now has about 4% of the overall ad market and accounted for 47% of the digital ad market in the second quarter of 2009.[104] In the search model, advertisers bid for certain key words such as "Aruba vacation." If they win, their ad is displayed on a Web page when search results are listed. Advertisers generally pay only if a consumer clicks on their ad.

The advantage of search is that it allows advertisers to target individual consumers who are actively looking for a certain product or service. Using data generated by searches, advertisers can further refine ad campaigns to deliver additional, relevant ads to individuals based on their previous searches. Google had 64% of the search market in August 2009, according to comScore,[105] but faces new challenges after a July 2009 announcement by Microsoft and Yahoo that they have formed a partnership on Internet search, under which Yahoo will use Microsoft's Bing search engine.[106]

As search has become more prominent, it has spawned a cottage industry of analysts and media buyers who help businesses navigate the online auction system.[107] One strategy, search optimization, describes the practice of companies configuring their websites to have the attributes search engines are programmed to seek, giving them a better chance of appearing in an organic list of search results. To accomplish this, consulting firms try to figure out the algorithms large search firms use in their auctions.[108]

Ad Networks

Companies also are using smaller ad networks or ad brokers to place their advertisements across the Web and digital platforms. Some established companies say such tactics affect prices for all ad-dependent companies because ad networks buy up blocks of residual or less attractive ads and release them on the market at fire-sale prices. The Online Publishers Association, a coalition of media and entertainment companies with an digital presence such as the *Wall Street Journal*, *New York Times* and *ESPN.com*, in August released a study arguing that ads sold via brokers were less effective than ads sold directly on their websites—for which they can charge higher prices.[109] But many prominent media companies that use ad networks to sell as least part of their own inventory that they cannot sell directly. Ad networks are also an important tool for small, mom and pop-type Web ventures to sell ads.

Behavioral Advertising

As they browse the web, blog, join social networks and play online games, consumers are providing advertisers with reams of data. Advertisers and marketing firms can generate still more information when consumers sign up for email promotions or buy products online. Behavioral advertising firm Tacoda (purchased in 2007 by America On Line) "has more than 4,500 sites, collects more than 135 million individual behaviors 50 times each month and has segmented the online audience into behavioral buckets," according to a report by Booz & Co., for a coalition of advertising organizations.[110]

Most online activity is monitored via cookies, small text files that can store data, which are placed on that user's computer when he or she visits a website. The information can be used to create behavioral advertising—targeted ads based on individual information. Behavioral advertising was estimated at $775 million in 2008 and is expected reach to $4.4 billion by 2012.[111]

A coalition of consumer groups has called for limits on the practice.[112] Congress and federal regulators are considering whether such tactics raise privacy concerns. The Progress and Freedom Foundation says tough Internet privacy standards could impede the growth of behavioral advertising and hurt media companies, for example.[113] Newspaper chain McClatchy Co. announced in its second quarter 2009 earnings report that it had increased online ad rates by using behavioral targeting.[114]

AD PLATFORMS

Another difference in the digital world, as opposed to traditional media, is that consumers are creating much of the content, through social networks, blogs or filming and posting homemade videos on sites like YouTube. Some experts say consumers are exercising more control over what they see, watch or hear. They can time television programs with digital recording devices, and fast forward through ads. Some ads are repressed by pop-up blockers or spam filters.

There is debate about whether advertisers are at disadvantage in the emerging digital world. In a widely discussed essay this spring Eric Clemons, professor of operations and information management at the University of Pennsylvania's Wharton School of Business, argued that consumers are in control in the digital sphere and will not accept unwanted or unneeded advertising. "The internet is not replacing advertising but shattering it, and all the king's horses, all the king's men, and all the creative talent of Madison Avenue cannot put it together again," Clemons wrote.[115]

Others say the concerns are overstated. While the change initially may be jarring, the Web opens myriad possibilities, including the ability to carry on a dialogue with consumers. "Old structures and ways of working persist, but are fundamentally challenged by newer, more dynamic more innovative alternatives. Numerous developments have brought the industry to this transition point. Consumers have more control and choice. Their media usage has fragmented. Many more advertising platforms exist. And marketers are insisting on greater precision in … targeting and accounting for their ad spend," according to a *Digital Darwinism* report by the IAB.[116]

Table 3. Projected Growth in U.S. Interactive Ad Revenues, 2009-2014
Dollar amounts in millions

	2009	2010	2011	2012	2013	2014	CAGR[a]
Mobile Marketing	$391	$561	$748	$950	$1,131	$1,274	27%
Social Media	$716	$935	$1,217	$1,649	$2,254	$3,113	34%
Email Marketing	$1,248	$1,355	$1,504	$1,676	$1,867	$2,081	11%
Display Advertising	$7,829	$8,395	$9,846	$11,732	$14,339	$16,900	17%
Search Marketing	$15,393	$17,765	$20,763	$24,299	$27,786	$31,588	15%
Total	$25,577	$29,012	$34,077	$40,306	$47,378	$54,956	17%
Percent of Total Ad Spending	12%	13%	15%	17%	19%	21%	

Source: Forrester Research Interactive Models 4/09 and 10/08 (US only)
a. Compound Annual Growth Rate.

Advertisers are going after digital consumers where they live: online. Among the emerging platforms:

- **Mobile**—Use of touchscreen phones, such as the IPhone, as well as other advanced mobile phones, is expanding rapidly. U.S. touchscreen phone use alone grew 159% from August 2008 to August 2009 to 23.8 million units.[117] Other mobile options include handheld reader devices. Research firm eMarketer expects U.S. mobile ad spending to rise from $648 million in 2008 to more than $3 billion by 2013.[118] Text messages are the main form of advertising on mobile phones, but that is expected to change as technology advances. One emerging example is "quick response" codes— a type of bar code placed on advertisements, department store displays, restaurant menus and other material that can be scanned with a cell phone or other mobile device. Consumers can use the codes to download coupons, offers, ads or other information related to a specific product.[119] Such codes are already being used with airline tickets, for example. iPhone-type applications are growing, including those produced by companies as marketing and sales tools. More than 2 billion iPhone applications had been downloaded as of September 2009, according to Apple.[120]
- **Social networks**—Social arenas include sites or networks such as Facebook and MySpace. Two-thirds of Internet consumers worldwide visit a social network or blogging site, and the segment accounts for nearly 10% of all time spent on the Internet—making it the fourth most popular Internet activity.[121] Some big companies have developed successful Facebook pages with more than a million fans. But advertisers have yet to really crack the market. Paid advertising on social networks is expected to decline by 3% in 2009 partly due to the recession. Ad spending at such sites is forecast to rise from $1.1 billion in 2009 to $1.4 billion by 2011.[122] Other forecasts peg spending on social networks somewhat higher. On social networks "members have a greater sense of 'ownership' around the personal content they

provide and are less inclined to accept advertising around it. A well-used analogy is that advertising on a social network is like gate-crashing a party," according to Nielsen.[123]

- **Gaming**—About two-thirds of American households have at least one family member who plays video or online games, according to the Entertainment Software Association, 40% of them women.[124] Advertisers are trying to reach these consumers by running ads before games on online sites or embedding their ads into the games—such as on billboards that line the roads in car racing games. The Lifetime Channel, a cable television channel with programming aimed at women, has a website with applications including games. Called "Games Women Play" the selections include "Create a Mall" and "Fashion Solitaire."[125]

- **Website Marketing**—Businesses are building in-house promotion and marketing capabilities. Typical of the emphasis on consumer interaction, Kraft Foods provides weekly recipes via email, runs a website that offers promotions to win free prizes or donate to needy families, online videos from guest bloggers and links to YouTube, and chat boards where consumers can swap recipes and talk about issues like kids and cooking or entertaining.[126] Kraft has Internet games for children based on products such as its Nabisco brand Corn Nuts cereal.

- **Video**—More than a third of Internet users recently watched a TV show or movie online, compared to 16% who did so in 2007. In addition, 62% of adult Internet users said they recently watched a video on a site like YouTube or Google Video.[127] Advertisers initially struggled to figure out how to sell ads against consumer-generated content, but have recently made inroads. Google has reached a deal with Time Warner to display content from cable stations CNN and TNT.[128]

YouTube is experimenting with running ads on popular videos, with the creators' consent. Another advertising strategy associated with video is viral ads—videos and other promotions that gain an audience through online word of mouth. *Advertising Age* magazine runs a monthly list of the top 10 viral ads.[129]

ADVERTISING REGULATION

Given the persuasive power of the ad industry, Congress and the courts have regulated advertising to protect consumers and ensure fair competition. U.S. laws govern, among other things, alcohol advertising, tobacco advertising, advertising by mail, advertising by telephone and commercial email or spam.[130]

In addition to Congress, the advertising industry is monitored by a variety of federal agencies.

- The Food and Drug Administration is charged with ensuring that certain product claims are truthful and detail the possible side effects of major drugs. The agency enforces the Federal Food, Drug and Cosmetic Act, looks at food package labeling and health claims.

- The Federal Trade Commission (FTC) is the main regulator of products sold in interstate commerce, and is charged with protecting consumers from claims that are misleading or unfair. The FTC is currently looking at issues including Internet privacy, as businesses and marketers develop sophisticated tools for tracking consumer information.
- The Federal Communications Commission (FCC) is an independent agency that regulates radio, television, telephone, satellite and cable television and the Internet. The FCC is looking at the growing use of product placement, or embedded advertising, in programming and is taking a new look at children and the digital media landscape.[131]

Self Regulation

The advertising industry has its own, parallel regulatory structure. The National Advertising Review Council (Council) was formed in 1971 as alliance by the Association of National Advertisers, the American Association of Advertising Agencies, the American Advertising Federation and the Council of Better Business Bureaus. The Council seeks to ensure that adverting is factual and accurate through a compliance system that includes recommendations for corrective actions and an internal appeals process.[132]

The Council also sets policies for the National Advertising Division (NAD) of the Council of Better Business Bureaus and the Children's Advertising Review Union (CARU). The bodies look into specific complaints regarding possibly inaccurate product claims, and more general questions about whether certain advertising is appropriate, particularly for children.[133] The Council is overseeing an initiative, for example, to promote healthier food and beverage choices in advertising aimed at children, an initiative on electronic advertising, and a set of principles for online behavioral advertising.

The Interactive Advertising Bureau (IAB), founded in 1996, has been developing rules of the road for emerging online businesses and advertisers. The organization is a coalition of more than 375 media and technology companies that sell nearly 90% of all U.S. online advertising. The IAB includes such firms as Google, Disney, The New York Times, Yahoo, and Microsoft.

One of the IAB's self-described goals is to fend off intrusive legislation. In that vein, it worked with other advertising organizations to craft voluntary guidelines for behavioral advertising, which were released in the summer of 2009.[134] The IAB has also set guidelines for advertising in social media like Facebook and on mobile platforms, such as cell phones, I-phones and hand-held readers. It has tried to standardize online advertising, issuing definitions for terms like "click" and "impression" as well as ad sizes and use of techniques such as pop-up ads.[135]

Pending Regulation and Oversight

Regulators and lawmakers are trying to keep up with an emerging world in which "mommy bloggers" move merchandise, children are exposed to "gamevertising" designed to sell breakfast cereal, and corporations are nesting in social networks. Add to that the rise of embedded advertising—Coca Cola paying to have American Idol judges drink its products on stage[136] and companies striking deals to have their products written into scripts for television sitcoms, for example—and some critics worry that advertising is becoming both more pervasive and more difficult to distinguish from other content. Consumer groups argue that greater scrutiny is needed to prevent abuse.

"In 50 years, we've gone from loosely regulated advertising based on the art of persuasion, to more regulated, perfectly legal and often spectacular ads based on the art of engagement, to anything goes," author and former advertising executive James Othmer recently wrote in the *Washington Post*. "As a result, it is increasingly difficult to determine what is authentic."[137]

The changing market structure and tactics have prompted scrutiny from consumer groups, lawmakers and regulators.[138] In a reflection of the industry outlook *Advertising Age* magazine in a recent article tallied up pending legislative and regulatory proposals and declared that the advertising and marketing sector had become "an unpopular and easy target ripe for regulation."[139]

On the legislative front, Representative Boucher, chairman of the House Energy and Commerce subcommittee on Communications, Technology, and the Internet, has announced plans to introduce legislation setting tighter standards for online privacy.[140] "Because consumers need an assured level of control over the collection, use and sharing of information about them, a statute providing those assurances is now called for," Boucher wrote in a recent op-ed in *The Hill* newspaper.[141] The legislation comes amid signs of consumer concern about behavioral advertising, including a recent study by the University of Pennsylvania and University of California, Berkeley that said two-thirds of Americans object to online tracking by advertisers.[142]

Senator Al Franken has introduced S. 1763 to repeal tax exemptions for pharmaceutical advertising to consumers and marketing to health care providers.[143] The move comes as companies are looking to sell pharmaceutical products in new venues, such as mobile phone applications.[144]

On the regulatory front, the FDA plans November hearings on the rise of pharmaceutical advertising on the Internet, including in social networks.[145] The FTC on October 5, 2009 issued updated guidelines for testimonials and endorsements, updating a policy altered in 1980. As part of the change, the FTC said that bloggers who make a product endorsement must disclose any material connections with the seller of the product or service.[146] The online advertising industry in an October 15, 2009 letter to the FTC asked that the guidance be rescinded, saying it would "unfairly and unconstitutionally impose penalties on online media for practices in which offline media have engaged for decades."[147]

The FDA in the spring of 2009 warned 14 large pharmaceutical firms that their Internet search ads were misleading because they did not include required information about potential risks of the products. The FDA now plans hearings on drug marketing online, including in social networks.[148] In addition, the FTC plans a December forum on the financial viability of media in the Internet age.[149]

The advertising industry is trying to ward off new regulation, saying it has moved aggressively with self regulation, including its recent guidelines on behavioral advertising. A group of the nation's largest online advertising firms formed the Network Advertising Initiative to argue against heavy regulation. The IAB also commissioned a study on the economic impacts of the Internet to underscore the case that digital commerce is vital to the nation's overall well-being.[150]

Whatever the outcome of the current initiatives, dramatic changes in the delivery of news, entertainment, and advertising are likely to continue, creating complex questions for lawmakers and regulators regarding consumer privacy, competition, and free speech. Media and cultural critic Marshall McLuhan in the 1960s argued that each new medium has its own intrinsic effect, changing the nature of society and commerce. Four decades later, technological advances are forcing media companies and advertisers to refine and reshape their messages to reach consumers in new venues, from mobile phones to handheld readers to online gaming networks. The developing forms of communication are, in turn, influencing the content of advertising as companies attempt to become part of the conversation on social networks or part of the landscape by embedding products in news and entertainment programming. Consumers must figure out how to determine the value and veracity of advertising and media, as regulators determine how to craft a workable oversight system that stretches beyond advertising on traditional media, to the rapidly expanding digital world.

End Notes

[1] CRS Report RL32177, *Federal Advertising Law: An Overview*, by Henry Cohen.
[2] Federal Trade Commission, "FTC Publishes Final Guides Governing Endorsements, Testimonials," press release, October 5, 2009. http://www.ftc.gov/opa/2009/10/endortest.shtm.
[3] Food and Drug Administration, "Promotion of Food and Drug Administration-Regulated Medical Products Using the Internet and Social Media Tools; Notice of Public Hearing," Federal Register, September 21, 2009. http://edocket.access.gpo.gov/2009/E9-22618.htm.
[4] Federal Communications Commission, "FCC Releases Notice of Inquiry on Serving and Protecting Children and Empowering Parents in an Evolving Media Landscape," press release, October 23, 2009. http://hraunfoss.fcc.gov/ edocs_public/attachmatch/DOC-294197A1.pdf.
[5] Office of Senator Al Franken, "Franken Introduces Bill to End Tax Breaks for Drug Company Advertising," press release, October 8, 2009. http://franken.senate.gov/press/?page=release&release_item= Franken_Introduces _Bill_to_End_Tax_Breaks_for_Druge_Company_Advertising.
[6] Clifford, Stephanie, "Two-Thirds of Americans Object to Online Tracking," *New York Times*, September 29, 2009. http://www.nytimes.com/2009/09/30/business/media/30adco.html?ref=business.
[7] Joint Economic Committee, "The Future of Newspapers: The Impact on the Economy and Democracy," hearing, September 24, 2009.
[8] Nielsen Company, "U.S. Ad Spending Fell 15.4% in the First Half, Nielsen Reports," press release, September 1, 2009. http://en-us.nielsen.com/main/news/news_releases/2009/september/us_ad_spending_fell.
[9] *Advertising Age*, "Spending in midst of 3-year drop, first since Depression; Measured media began to fall in March 2008. Advertising is slumping in key areas, including retail, auto and telecom," December 29, 2008.
[10] Ibid.
[11] Wieser, Brian, *MAGNA Media Advertising Forecast*, MAGNA, July 13, 2009. http://www.mediabrandsww.com/ Attachments/NewsPress/MAGNA%20Media%20Forecast%20July%202009.pdf.
[12] Bureau of Labor Statistics data for advertising and related services, NAICS Code 5418.
[13] Paper Cuts. http://graphicdesignr.net/papercuts/.
[14] Pricewaterhouse Coopers and Interactive Advertising Bureau, *IAB Advertising Revenue Report, 2008 Full Year Results*, March 2009, p. 6. http://www.iab.net/media/file/IAB_PwC_2008_full_year.pdf.
[15] VanBoskirk, Shar, "Interactive Marketing Nears $55 Billion; Advertising Overall Declines," Forrester Research, July 7, 2009. http://blogs.forrester.com/marketing/2009/07/interactive-marketing-nears-55-billion-advertising-overall-declines.html.
[16] Vollmer, Christopher, *Digital Darwinism*, a joint report by Booz & Company, Association of National Advertisers, Interactive Advertising Bureau, and American Association of Advertising Agencies, July 9, 2009, p. 4. http://www.booz.com/global/home/what_we_think/reports_and_white_papers/ic-display/46079566
[17] eMarketer, "Monetizing Mobile Ads," August 4, 2009. http://www.emarketer.com/Article.aspx?R=1007209

[18] Vollmer, Christopher, *Digital Darwinism*, a joint report by Booz & Company, Association of National Advertisers, Interactive Advertising Bureau, and American Association of Advertising Agencies, July 9, 2009, p. 10. http://www.booz.com/global/home/what_we_think/reports_and_white_papers/ic-display/46079

[19] IBIS*World, Advertising Agencies in the US: 54181*, April 14, 2009, p. 32; Fine, Jon, "Marketing's Drift Away from the Media," *Business Week*, August 6, 2009. http://www.businessweek.com/magazine/content/09_33/b4143064876775.htm.

[20] Interactive Advertising Bureau, *IAB Internet Advertising Revenue Report*, 2009 Second Quarter and First Six Month Results, October 2009, p. 7. http://www.iab.net/media/file/IAB-Ad-Revenue-Six-month-2009.pdf.

[21] Ibid.

[22] Newton, Tyler, *Traditional Media: Down But Not Out*, Catalyst Investors, July 7, 2009, p. 4. http://www.catalystinvestors.com/files/pdf/Catalyst-Traditional_Media_Down_but_Not_Out_7-7-09.pdf.

[23] Berman, Saul, Bill Battino, and Karen Feldman, *Beyond Advertising, Choosing a strategic path to the digital consumer*, IBM Global Services, February 2009, p. 1. http://www-05.ibm.com/de/media/downloads/beyond-advertising-qr.pdf.

[24] Wiener, Bryan, *2009 Social Marketing Playbook*, 360i , June 9, 2009. http://blog.360i.com/social-media/playbook

[25] *Advertising Age*, "The Advertising Century, Advertising History Timeline," 1999. http://adage. com/century/timeline/ index.html.

[26] Arens, William F., David H. Schaefer, and Michael Weigold, *Essentials of Contemporary Advertising*, Second Edition, McGraw-Hill Irwin, 2008, p. 34.

[27] Ibid.

[28] CRS Report RL34101, *Does Price Transparency Improve Market Efficiency? Implications of Empirical Evidence in Other Markets for the Health Sector*, by D. Andrew Austin and Jane G. Gravelle.

[29] Edelman, Benjamin, *Towards a Bill of Rights for Online Advertisers*, September 21, 2009. http://www.benedelman.org/advertisersrights/.

[30] Nayaradou, Maximilien, *Advertising and Economic Growth*, The University of Paris Dauphine (doctoral thesis partly funded by French Advertisers' Association), June 2006.

[31] Morrison, Dianne See, "Consumer Groups Target Mobile Advertising; FTC Complaint Alleges Deceptive Practices," *mocoNews.net*, January 13, 2009. http://moconews.net/article/419-consumer-groups-hit-out-at-mobile-advertising-ftc-complaint-alleges-unf/.

[32] Standard & Poor's Industry Surveys, *Publishing & Advertising*, August 21, 2008, p. 9.

[33] CRS Report R40700, *The U.S. Newspaper Industry in Transition*, by Suzanne M. Kirchhoff.

[34] Arens, William F., David H. Schaefer and Michael Weigold, *Essentials of Contermporary Advertising*, Second Edition, McGraw-Hill Irwin, 2009, p. 27; Nayaradou, Maximilien, *Advertising and Economic Growth*, The University of Paris Dauphine (doctoral thesis partly funded by French Advertisers' Association), June 2006.

[35] http://purplemotes.net/2008/09/14/us-advertising-expenditure-data/; U.S. Census Bureau's *Historical Statistics of the United States, Colonial Times to 1970*. http://www2.census.gov/prod2/statcomp/documents/CT1970p2-07.pdf.

[36] Arens, William F., David H. Schaefer and Michael Weigold, *Essentials of Contemporary Advertising*, Second Edition, McGraw-Hill Irwin, 2009, p. 6.

[37] Elliott, Stuart, "Madison Avenue's Chief Seer," *New York Times*, March 22, 2009. http://www.nytimes.com/2009/03/ 23/business/media/23adcol.html.

[38] Magna, "Magna Media Advertising Forecast: New 2010 Figures Reflect Improving Economic Conditions," press release, October 13, 2009.

[39] Mandese, Joe "The Case of the Missing Billions: Interpublic Giveth, But Mostly It Taketh Away," *MediaPost News*, July 14, 2009. http://www.mediapost.com/publications/?fa=Articles.showArticle&art_aid=109734

[40] Census Department, *Annual and Quarterly Services*. http://www.census.gov/services/index.html

[41] Some other forecasts call for Internet advertising to rise in 2009 overall including eMarketer which projects a 4.5% increase in online spending in 2009 from 2008.

[42] Nielsen Company, "U.S. Ad Spending Fell 15.4% in the First Half, Nielsen Reports," press release, September 1, 2009.

[43] Wilkerson, David B., "U.S. Advertising Spending Seen Plunging 13% in 2009, "*MarketWatch*, March 12, 2009. http://www.marketwatch.com/story/us-advertising-revenue-plunge-13-2009

[44] MAGNA, "MAGNA Media Advertising Forecast: New 2010 Figures Reflect Improving Economic Conditions," press release, October 13, 2009.

[45] Johnson, Bradley, "Spending fell (only) 2.7% in '08. The real issue: '09," *Advertising Age*, June 22, 2009. p. 1

[46] Arens, William F., David H. Schaefer, Michael Weigold, *Essentials of Contemporary Advertising*, McGraw-Hill Irwin, Second Edition, p. 13.

[47] Holland, Donald R. "Volney B. Palmer: The Nation's First Advertising Agency Man," *The Pennsylvania Magazine of History and Biography*, Vol. 98, No. 3 (July 1974), pp. 353-381. http://www.jstor.org/stable/20090872.

[48] Simpson, Joanne Cavanaugh, "It's All in the Upbringing," *Johns Hopkins Magazine*, April 2000. http://www.jhu.edu/~jhumag/0400web/35.html.

[49] *Advertising Age*, "The Advertising Century," Advertising History Timeline, 1999. http://adage.com/ century/ timeline/ index.html.

[50] Mashon, Michael, *Sponsor*, The Museum of Broadcast Communications. http://www.museum.tv/archives/etv/S/ htmlS/sponsor/sponsor.htm; The Original Old Time Radio (OTR) WWW Pages "The Highest Rated Programs During Radio's Golden Age, 1930-31 Season." http://www.old-time.com/ratings/by%20 season/1930s/19301931eve.html.

[51] Arens, William F., David H. Schaefer, Michael Weigold, *Essentials of Contemporary Advertising*, McGraw-Hill Irwin, Second Edition, p. 16.

[52] *Time*, "Builders & Titans, Leo Burnett," December 7, 1998. http://www.time.com/time/time100/builder/profile/ burnett.html.

[53] *Advertising Age*, "The Advertising Century, Top 100 Advertising Campaigns," 1999. http://adage.com/century/ campaigns.html.

[54] Arens, William F., David H. Schaefer, and Michael Weigold, *Essentials of Contemporary Advertising*, McGraw-Hill Irwin, Second Edition, p. 13.

[55] Ibid, p. 16.

[56] Borrell Associates/Clickable, *Economics of Search Marketing*, June 2009. http://www.borrellassociates.com/ component/content/article/76-economics-of-search-marketing-addressing-the-challenges-of-a-scalable-local-advertising-model.

[57] Morrison, Maureen, "Verizon Tops AT&T as Most-Advertised Brand," *Advertising Age*, June 22, 2009. http://adage.com/datacenter/article?article_id=137407.

[58] Ibid.

[59] CRS Report R40590, *Direct-to-Consumer Advertising of Prescription Drugs*, by Susan Thaul.

[60] *Advertising Age*, "Agency Report 2008," May 5, 2008.

[61] Silk, Alvin J. and Charles King, III, *Concentration Levels in the U.S. Advertising and Marketing Services Industry: Myth vs. Reality*, Harvard Business School Working Paper 09-044, September 24, 2008, p. 6. http://www.hbs.edu/ research/pdf/09-044.pdf.

[62] Peters, James and William H. Donald, *Industry Surveys, Advertising*, Standard & Poor's, August 9, 2007.

[63] Bureau of Labor Statistics, U.S. Department of Labor, *Advertising and Public Relations Services*. http://www.bls.gov/oco/cg/cgs030.htm.

[64] Landry, Edward, Carolyn Ude and Christopher Vollmer, *HD Marketing 2010: Sharpening the Conversation*, Booz & Co. with the Association of National Advertisers, Interactive Advertising Bureau and American Association of Advertising Agencies, 2009, p. 6. http://www.boozallen.com/media/file/ HD_Marketing_2010.pdf.

[65] Standard & Poor's Industry Survey, *Publishing & Advertising*, August 21, 2008, p. 16.

[66] Department of Labor employment data.

[67] U.S. Census, *Advertising and Related Services: 2002*, Table 1. http://www.census.gov/prod/ec02/ec0254i08t.pdf Economic consulting firm IHS Global Insight, in studies for the advertising industry, has estimated U.S. advertising employment at about a million people including in-house staff at large corporations involved in marketing and advertising.

[68] IBIS*World, Advertising Agencies in the US*, April 14, 2009, p. 19.

[69] Arzaghi, Mohammad, Ernst R. Berndt, James C. Davis, and Alvin J. Silk, *Economic Factors Underlying the Unbundling of Advertising Agency Services*, National Bureau of Economic Research, September 2008, p. 3. http://ideas.repec.org/p/nbr/nberwo/14345.html.

[70] Ibid.

[71] *Associated Press*, "Status of Newspaper Publishers that filed Ch. 11," September 14, 2009. http://www.google. com/ hostednews/ap/article/ALeqM5glKJRt4h5si3xUGoATac4MLbNAqgD9AN9E083.

[72] Clifford, Stephanie, "Conde Nast Closes Gourmet and 3 Other Magazines," *New York Times*, October 5, 2009. http://www.nytimes.com/2009/10/06/business/media/06gourmet.html.

[73] Borrell, Gordon, "The Rumors of Newspapers' Death," *Borrell Associates*, August 6, 2009. http://www. borrellassociates.com/wordpress/2009/08/06/the-rumors-of-newspapers-death/.

[74] Mutter, Alan, "How to sell news on the web: A checklist," *Reflections of a Newsosaur*, October 5, 2009. http://newsosaur.blogspot.com/2009/10/how-to-sell-news-on-web-checklist.html.

[75] *MediaPost News*, "CPM Prices Falling Precipitously," January 26, 2009. http://www.mediapost.com/ publications/? fa=Articles.showArticle&art_aid=99087.

[76] Farhi, Paul, "Build that Pay Wall High," *American Journalism Review*, August/September 2009. http://www.ajr.org/ Article.asp?id=4800.

[77] Kaplan, David, "Yahoo Newspaper Consortium Adds Five Members," *PaidContent*, June 16, 2009. http://paidcontent.org/article/419-yahoo-newspaper-consortium-adds-five-members/.

[78] Perez-Pena, Richard, "Newsday Plans to Charge for Online News," *New York Times*, October 22, 2009. http://www.nytimes.com/2009/10/23/business/media/23newsday.html.

[79] Maxwell, Kenneth, "News Corp Sees Advertising Markets Improving," *Dow Jones Newswires*, October 5, 2009. http://online.wsj.com/article/BT-CO-20091005-709507.html.

[80] Gannett Company, "Gannett Co. Inc. Reports Third Quarter Results," press release, October 19, 2009. http://www.gannett.com/news/pressrelease/2009/3Q09.pdf.

[81] Newspaper Association of America, *Advertising Expenditures*. http://www.naa.org/Trendsand Numbers/Advertising-Expenditures.aspx.

[82] Newspaper Association of America, *Quarterly Advertising Expenditures*, August 9, 2009. http://www.naa.org/TrendsandNumbers/Advertising-Expenditures.aspx.

[83] Ibid.

[84] Wolf, Gary, "Why Craigslist is Such a Mess," *Wired*, August 24, 2009. http://www.wired.com/entertainment/theweb/ magazine/17-09/ff_craigslist.

[85] Borrell, Gordon, "The Rumors of Newspapers' Death," *Borrell Associates,* August 6, 2009. http://www.borrellassociates.com/wordpress/2009/08/06/the-rumors-of-newspapers-death/.

[86] Magazine Publishers of America, "PIB: Recession Continues to Impact Magazine Advertising in the First Half," press release, July 10, 2009. http://www.magazine.org/advertising/revenue/by_ad_category/2009Q2.aspx.

[87] Clifford, Stephanie, "Conde Nast to Close Gourmet, Cookie and Modern Bride," *New York Times*, October 3, 2009. http://mediadecoder.blogs.nytimes.com/2009/10/05/conde-nast-to-close-gourmet-magazine/?hp.

[88] Mandese, Joe, "Online Ad Spending Rises at Double Digit Rates, Gains Share Vs. All Other Media," *Online Media Daily*, July 6, 2009. http://www.mediapost.com/ publications/?fa=Articles. showArticle&art_aid=109200.

[89] Radio Advertising Bureau, "Radio Continues to Mine New Advertisers," press release, August 21, 2009. http://www.rab.com/dailypress/RevenueReportQ2_2009.pdf.

[90] Ibid.

[91] Picard, Robert, "Radio Stations Face Significant Strategic Challenges," September 3, 2009. http://themediabusiness.blogspot.com/feeds/posts/default.

[92] Television Bureau of Advertising, "Total Broadcast Television Revenues Were Down 12.8% in Second Quarter," press release, August 28, 2009. http://www.tvb.org/nav/build_frameset.aspx.

[93] Chmielewski, Dawn C. and Meg James, "Will Hulu make you pay to watch?," *Los Angeles Times*, October 5, 2009. http://www.latimes.com/business/la-fi-ct-hulu5-2009oct05,0,980649.story.

[94] IAB, "Internet Ad Revenues at $10.9 Billion for First Half of 2009," press release, October 5, 2009

[95] Edelman, Benjamin, *Towards a Bill of Rights for Online Advertisers*, September 21, 2009. http://www.benedelman. org/advertisersrights/.

[96] Ibid.

[97] Martin, Ashley, *Nolej Studios: Growing a Creativity-Based Business*, Tuck School of Business at Dartmouth University, Case #6-0028, May 5, 2008.

[98] Interactive Advertising Bureau, *IAB Internet Advertising Revenue Report*, March 2009, p. 8. http://www.iab.net/media/file/IAB_PwC_2008_full_year.pdf .

[99] comScore, "comScore and Starcom USA Release Updated 'Natural Born Clickers' Study Showing 50 Percent Drop in Number of U.S. Internet Users Who Click on Display Ads," press release, October 1, 2009. comScore also has 1 million consumer panelists abroad.

[100] Ibid.

[101] Sullivan, Laurie, "Study: Half of Ad Impressions, 95% Of Clicks Fraudulent," *MediaPost News*, September 17, 2009. http://www.mediapost.com/publications/?fa=Articles.showArticle&art_aid=113734.

[102] Hamp, Andrew, "Media Companies Roll Out Efforts to Improve Audience Measurement," *Advertising Age*, August 26, 2009.

[103] eMarketer, "How Much Time People Really Spend with Ads," August 24, 2009. http://www.emarketer.com/Article.aspx?R=1007241.

[104] PricewaterHouse Coopers and Interactive Advertising Bureau, *IAB Advertising Revenue Report, 2009 Second Quarter and First Six Months Results*, October 2009, p.2. http://www.iab.net/media/file/IAB-Ad-Revenue-Six-month-2009.pdf.

[105] comScore, "comScore releases August 2009 U.S. Search Engine Ratings," press release, September 22, 2009. http://www.comscore.com/Press_Events/Press_Releases/2009/9/comScore_Releases_August_2009_U.S._Search_Engine_Rankings.

[106] *Associated Press,* "Microsoft, Yahoo Announce Search Deal," July 29, 2009. http://www.msnbc.msn.com/id/32193887/ns/business-us_business/.

[107] Levy, Steven, "Secret of Googlenomics: Data-Filled Recipe Brews Profitability," *Wired*, May 22, 2009. http://www.wired.com/culture/culturereviews/magazine/17-06/nep_googlenomics?currentPage=all.

[108] Interview with Keystroke Marketing, a Pennsylvania Internet marketing firm. September, 2009.

[109] Online Publishers Association, "OPA Members' High-Quality Content Environments Raise Awareness, Message Association, Brand Favorability and Purchase Intent More than Portals and Ad Networks," press release, August 13, 2009. http://www.online-publishers.org/newsletter.php?newsType=pr&newsId=545.

[110] Landry, Edward, Carol Ude, and Christopher Vollmer, *HD Marketing 2010: Sharpening the Conversation*, Booz& Co., Association of National Advertisers, Interactive Advertising Bureau and the American Association of Advertising Agencies, 2009, p. 7.

[111] Hallerman, David, "Behavioral Targeting: Marketing Trends," eMarketer, June 2008 http://www.emarketer.com/Reports/All/Emarketer_2000487.aspx.

[112] Eggerton, John, "Consumer Groups Want Constraints on Online Behavioral Advertising," *Broadcasting & Cable*, September 1, 2009. http://www.broadcastingcable.com/article/339171-Consumer_Groups_Want_Constraints_on_Online_Behavioral_Advertising.php.

[113] Szoka, Berin and Mark Adams, *The Benefits of Online Advertising & Costs of Privacy Regulation*, Progress and Freedom Foundation Working Paper, July 10, 2009.

[114] McClatchy Company Second Quarter 2009 Earnings Call Transcript, July 21, 2009. http://74.125.95.132/search?q=cache:jvOwJ2PrGhcJ:www.bnet.com/2462-14052_23-323057.html+mcclatchy+co+second+quarter+earnings+report+2009+behavioral+advertising&cd=2&hl=en&ct=clnk&gl=us.

[115] Clemons, Eric, "Why Advertising is Failing on the Internet," *TechCrunch*, March 22, 2009. http://www.techcrunch.com/2009/03/22/why-advertising-is-failing-on-the-internet/.

[116] Vollmer, Christopher, *Digital Darwinism*, a joint report by Booz & Company, Association of National Advertisers, Interactive Advertising Bureau, and American Association of Advertising Agencies, July 9, 2009, p. 4 . http://www.booz.com/global/home/what_we_think/reports_and_white_papers/ic-display/46079566.

[117] comScore, "Touchscreen Mobile Phone Adoption Grows at Blistering Pace in U.S. During Past Year," press release, November 3, 2009. http://www.comscore.com/Press_Events/Press_Releases/2009/11/Touchscreen_Mobile_Phone_Adoption_Grows_at_Blistering_Pace_in_U.S._During_Past_Year.

[118] eMarketer, *Mobile Advertising and Usage*, April 2009. http://mobimatter.files.wordpress.com/2009/05/emarketer_mobile_advertising_and_usage.pdf.

[119] Federal Trade Commission Staff Report, *Beyond Voice, Mapping the Mobile Marketplace*, April 2009, p. 24. http://www.adlawbyrequest.com/uploads/file/2009_04%20FTC%20Report%20-%20Mobile%20Marketplace.pdf.

[120] Apple Inc., "Apple's App Store Downloads Top Two Billion," press release, September 28, 2009. http://www.apple.com/pr/library/2009/09/28appstore.html.

[121] Nielsen Company, *Global Faces and Networked Places*, March 2009, p 1. http://blog.nielsen.com/nielsenwire/wp-content/uploads/2009/03/nielsen_globalfaces_mar09.pdf.

[122] eMarketer , "Social Network Ad Spending: A Brighter Outlook Next Year," July 2009.

[123] Nielsen Company, *Global Faces and Networked Places*, March 2009, p 5. http://blog.nielsen.com/nielsenwire/wp-content/uploads/2009/03/nielsen_globalfaces_mar09.pdf.

[124] Chang, Rita, "Game Advertising Goes Mainstream," *Advertising Age*, July 13, 2009; Entertainment Software Association, "Industry Facts." http://www.theesa.com/facts/index.asp.

[125] http://www.mylifetime.com/games/download/fashion-solitaire.aspx.

[126] http://www.Kraftfoods.com.

[127] Madden, Mary, *The Audience for Online Video Shoots Up*, Pew Internet and American Life Project, July 2009. http://www.pewinternet.org/~/media//Files/Reports/2009/The-Audience-for-Online-Video-Sharing-Sites-Shoots-Up.pdf.

[128] Helft, Miguel, "YouTube in a Deal to Show Clips from CNN and TNT," *New York Times*, August 19, 2009.

[129] http://adage.com/rss-feed?section_id=674.

[130] CRS Report RL32177, *Federal Advertising Law: An Overview*, by Henry Cohen. For more information on Supreme Court regulation of commercial speech, see CRS Report 95-815, *Freedom of Speech and Press: Exceptions to the First Amendment*, by Henry Cohen.

[131] Federal Communications Commission, "FCC Releases Notice of Inquiry on Serving and Protecting Children and Empowering Parents In and Evolving Media Landscape," press release, October 23, 2009. http://hraunfoss.fcc.gov/ edocs_public/attachmatch/DOC-294197A1.pdf.

[132] National Advertising Review Council. The Direct Marketing Association, Electronic Retailing Association and Interactive Advertising Bureau also joined in 2008. http://www.narcpartners.org/about/partners.aspx.

[133] Ibid.

[134] Interactive Advertising Bureau, "Key Trade Groups Release Comprehensive Privacy Principles for Use and Collection of Behavioral Data in Online Advertising," press release, July 2, 2009. http://www.iab.net/about_the_iab/ recent_press_releases/press_release_archive/press_release/pr-070209.

[135] Interactive Advertising Bureau. http://www.iab.net/about_the_iab.

[136] Barker, Andrew, "Advertisers Starting to Embrace DVR," *Variety*, March 27, 2009. http://www.variety.com/article/ VR1118001776.html?categoryid=3579&cs=1.

[137] Othmer, James, "Skip Past the Ads But You're Still Being Sold," *Washington Post*, August 16, 2009. http://www.washingtonpost.com/wp-dyn/content/article/2009/08/14/AR2009081401629.html.

[138] Chester, Jeff, Executive Director, Center for Digital Democracy, "Testimony on Behavioral Advertising: Industry Practices and Consumers' Expectations," House Committee on Energy and Commerce,

Subcommittee on Commerce, Trade and Consumer Protection and the Subcommittee on Communications, Technology, and the Internet, June 18, 2009. http://www.democraticmedia.org/doc/cdd-testimony-20090618.

[139] Ives, Nat and Rich Thomaselli, "Marketing Takes a Beating in the Beltway," *Advertising Age,* July 27, 2009.

[140] Clifford, Stephanie, "Two-Thirds of Americans Object to Online Tracking," *New York Times*, September 29, 2009. http://www.nytimes.com/2009/09/30/business/media/30adco.html?ref=business.

[141] Boucher, Rick, "Behavioral Ads: The need for privacy protection," *The Hill*, September 24, 2009. http://thehill.com/   special-reports/technology-september-2009/60253-behavioral-ads-the-need-for-privacy-protection#.

[142] Turow, Joseph, Jennifer King, Chris Jay Hoofnagle, Amy Bleakley, and Michael Hennessey, *Americans Reject Tailored Advertising and Three Activities that Enable It*. SSRN: http://ssrn.com/abstract=1478214.

[143] Sen. Al Franken, "Franken Introduces Bill to EndTax Breaks for Drug Company Advertising," press release, October 8, 2009. http://franken.senate.gov/press/?page=release&release_item= Franken_Introduces_Bill_to_ End_Tax_Breaks_for_Druge_Company_Advertising.

[144] Thomaselli, Rich, "Need to Check Your Cholesterol? There will be an App for That?" *Advertising Age*, June 1, 2009.

[145] Food and Drug Administration Docket FDA-2009-N-0441, "Promotion of Food and Drug Administration-Regulated Medical Products using the Internet and Social Media Tools; Notice of Public Hearing," *Federal Register*, September 21, 2009. http://edocket.access.gpo.gov/2009/E9-22618.htm.

[146] Federal Trade Commission, 16 C.F.R. Part 255, *Guides Concerning the Use of Endorsements and Testimonials in Advertising*. http://www.ftc.gov/os/2008/11/P034520endorsementguides.pdf.

[147] Interactive Advertising Bureau, "IAB Calls on FTC to Rescind Blogger Rules; Questions Constitutionality," press release, October 15, 2009. http://www.iab.net/about_the_iab/recent_press _releases/press_release_ archive/ press_release/pr-101509?o12499=.

[148] Food and Drug Administration, "Promotion of Food and Drug Administration-Regulated Medical Products Using the Internet and Social Media Tools; Notice of Public Hearing," *Federal Register* notice, September 21, 2009. http://edocket.access.gpo.gov/2009/E9-22618.htm.

[149] Federal Trade Commission, "Extra! Extra! FTC Announces Revised Schedule for Workshop: From Town Criers to Bloggers; How Will Journalism Survive the Internet Age," press release. http://www.ftc.gov/opa/2009/08/ news2009.shtm.

[150] Hamilton Consultants, John Deighton, and John Quelch, Harvard Business School, *Economic Value of the Advertising-Supported Internet Ecosystem*, Interactive Advertising Bureau, June 10, 2009. http://www.iab.net/media/ file/Economic-Value-Report.pdf.

In: Advertising: Developments and Issues in the Digital Age   ISBN: 978-1-61761-783-6
Editor: William L. Poulsen   © 2011 Nova Science Publishers, Inc.

Chapter 2

PRIVACY LAW AND ONLINE ADVERTISING

Kathleen Ann Ruane

SUMMARY

To produce revenue, websites have placed advertisements on their sites. Advertisers will pay a premium for greater assurance that the advertisement they are purchasing will be seen by users that are most likely to be interested in the product or service offered. As a result, technology has been developed which enables online advertisements to be targeted directly at individual users based on their web surfing activity. This practice is widely known as "behavioral" or "e-havioral" advertising.

This individual behavioral targeting has raised a number of privacy concerns. For instance, questions have been asked whether personally identifiable information is being collected; how the information collected is being protected; and whether current laws are being violated if data are being collected without the consent of the parties involved. It is often unclear whether current laws, such as the Electronic Communications Privacy Act and the Communications Act, apply to online advertising providers that are collecting data through click tracking, capturing search terms, and other methods. However, it is likely that in many cases these laws could be held to apply to such activities and that these methods of data collection would be forbidden unless consent is obtained from one of the parties to the communication. This chapter will examine the application of these statutes to online behavioral advertising in more detail.

There are no current federal regulations specific to online behavioral advertising. The FTC maintains that self-regulation is preferable to agency regulations, because the state of the industry is fluid and complex. To aid the industry in self-regulation of online behavioral advertising, in 2009, the FTC released a set of self-regulatory principles for the use of web sites and behavioral advertisers. The principles set forth guidance for the industry regarding the information that may be collected online and how companies should notify their customers about the collection. The FTC also applauded the efforts of industry groups to develop more detailed guidance on the issue. Organizations such as the Network Advertising Initiative, Interactive Advertising Bureau, and Privacy Group Coalition have created policies, similar to the FTC's recent release, which many online advertising providers have pledged to follow that represent industry best practices for protecting the privacy of web users.

For more information about the online advertising industry, see CRS Report R40908, *Advertising Industry in the Digital Age*, by Suzanne M. Kirchhoff.

INTRODUCTION AND TECHNICAL BACKGROUND

Many website operators produce income by selling advertising space on their sites. Advertisers will pay a premium for ads that are more likely to reach their target demographic. In other media, such as broadcasting, advertisers engage in targeting by purchasing advertising time during programs that those who buy their products are most likely to watch. The Internet presented new challenges and opportunities for advertisers to reach their target audiences. Technology has been developed that allows advertisers to target advertising to individual web users. This is seen as an advantage for advertisers, because, rather than aiming their ads at groups of people who visit a particular site, their ads are aimed at the individual user. This maximizes the odds that the user who sees the ad will be interested in the product or service it touts. Targeting advertising to individuals involves gathering information about that individual's web surfing habits. The collection of this information has raised concerns among some over the privacy of web activity, particularly if the data collected are personally identifiable. Some have alleged that online advertisers are violating privacy laws by collecting these data.

In online advertising's simplest form, a commercial website rents out "space" on its site to another website which places a hot link banner advertisement in that space.[1] The banner ad, when clicked, sends the user directly to the advertiser's website. In this scenario, no matter who visits a particular website, that user will see the same advertisement, regardless of whether he/she may be interested in that product or service. However, many advertisers will pay a premium for the increased likelihood that users viewing their advertisement would be interested in the product or service offered. As a result, technology has developed to more accurately target online ads to the desired audience.

Online advertising providers, such as DoubleClick and NebuAd, have developed the ability to target ads to individual Internet users who would be most interested in seeing those ads. These techniques are known generally as "behaviorally targeted advertising." Behaviorally targeted advertising delivers ads that are geared toward specific Internet users by tracking certain, though not necessarily all, web activity of each user and inferring each user's interests based on that activity. Most online advertising providers monitor individual Internet users by placing a "persistent cookie" on that user's computer. "Cookies" are small text files that can store information. "Persistent cookies" reside on a hard drive indefinitely, unlike most "cookies" which expire when a browser window is closed. Generally, online advertisers give the "cookies" they place on user computers a unique alphanumeric code that identifies that user to the advertising company purportedly without revealing any personally identifiable information. "Cookies" may be placed on an individual's computer when an individual visits a website affiliated with the online advertisement supplier; however, the exact moment of "cookie" placement may be different when the relevant advertising partnership is between a user's Internet Service Provider (ISP) and an online advertising provider.

Once the cookie is in place, it gathers certain information related to that user's online activity on a continuous basis and relays that information to the online advertising provider. The advertising provider assembles that data into an individual profile that is then used to target advertising to that user's interests. This process is ongoing, but, in general, the user may opt out of continued monitoring at any point, assuming they are aware that it is occurring. In most types of behaviorally targeted advertising technology, the advertising firm gathers information about user activities on websites that are affiliated with the advertising firm. The behavioral advertiser DoubleClick, for instance, operates on this model. Information on individual users is transmitted to DoubleClick by DoubleClick's clients. In a newly emerging behavioral advertising model, the advertising provider is attempting to partner with the users' ISP. This partnership will presumably grant the advertising provider access to all web activity in which an ISP's subscribers engage. Both of these types of potential partnerships raise a number of questions regarding potential violations of existing privacy protections in federal law.

ELECTRONIC COMMUNICATIONS PRIVACY ACT

Concerns have been raised that online advertising providers, websites, and ISPs that agree to collect certain data generated by Internet traffic to behaviorally target advertising may be violating the Electronic Communications Privacy Act (ECPA)100 Stat. 1848, 18 U.S.C. 2510-2521.[2] ECPA is an amendment to Title III of the Omnibus Crime Control and Safe Streets Act of 1968, 87 Stat. 197, 18 U.S.C. 2510-2520 (1970 ed.), which prohibits the interception of electronic communications unless an exception to the general prohibition applies.[3] ECPA also prohibits electronic communications service providers from intentionally divulging information while in transit to third parties, unless an exception applies. This section will discuss the potential application of ECPA to online advertising providers and the potential application of ECPA to ISPs.

The Online Advertising Provider

The first question that must be addressed is whether ECPA applies to the activities of online advertising providers. Online advertising providers are acquiring information such as the fact that a user clicked on a particular link (an action which is the equivalent of asking the site providing the link to send the user information), and they are acquiring that information while the communication is in transit.[4] Furthermore, these advertisers may acquire information, such as words entered into a search engine or answers to online forms, while it is in transit.[5] Under ECPA, it is illegal, with certain enumerated exceptions, for any person to "intentionally intercept, endeavor to intercept, or procure any other person to intercept or endeavor to intercept, any wire, oral or electronic communication."[6] It is important to lay out the statutory definitions of each of the key terms in order to assess whether the ECPA prohibition and/or any of its exceptions applies to activities conducted by online behavioral advertisers.

- "Intercept" means the aural or other acquisition of the contents of any wire, electronic, or oral communication through the use of any electronic, mechanical, or other device.[7]
- "Contents" when used with respect to any wire, oral, or electronic communication includes any information concerning the substance, purport, or meaning of that communication.[8]
- "Electronic Communication" means any transfer of signs, signals, writing, images, sounds, data, or intelligence of any nature transmitted in whole or in part by a wire, radio, electromagnetic, photoelectronic, or photo optical system that affects interstate or foreign commerce.[9]

Because the advertisers record that a particular user requested information from a website by clicking on a particular link or sent information to a website via a search entry or other method, the advertisers appear to be "intercepting" the "contents" of those "electronic communications." Therefore, the interceptions are likely covered by ECPA.[10]

Merely determining that this type of data acquisition by online advertisers is an interception for the purposes of ECPA does not end the analysis. ECPA excepts certain communication interceptions from its prohibition. The exception to ECPA that would most likely apply to these types of interceptions is the exception that allows for interception of communications with the consent of one of the parties.[11] The question of when and how consent to the interception may be given is addressed below.

The Internet Service Provider

The second question to be addressed is whether ECPA applies to ISP providers that would allow online advertising providers to gather data from traffic over the ISP's network. ECPA prohibits any person or entity providing an electronic communications service from intentionally divulging the "contents of any communications ... while in transmission on that service to any person or entity other than an addressee or intended recipient of such communications or an agent of such addressee or intended recipient."[12] This section seems to apply to ISPs that would agree to allow online advertising providers to acquire portions of the web traffic of ISP customers, because the ISP would be allowing the advertising providers to acquire the contents of communications while they are in transmission and neither the advertising provider nor the ISP would, in most cases, be the addressee or intended recipient of the communications.

Again, determining that the data collection is likely covered by ECPA does not end the analysis. An ECPA exception may apply. ISPs are allowed to divulge the contents of communications while in transit if the divulgence is part of "any activity which is a necessary incident to the rendition of [that service] or to the protection of the rights or property of the provider of that service."[13] It does not seem likely that this exception applies to ISPs when contracting with online advertising providers. Though the service for which they contract may help keep the websites of the advertising provider's clients free to the public by producing advertising revenue, the interception is not necessary to maintain an ISP's proper function or solvency and, therefore, likely is not necessary to the rendition of Internet access service.[14] ISPs also are allowed to divulge the contents of a communication in transit "with the lawful consent of the originator or any addressee or intended recipient of such communication."[15] If the ISPs obtain the consent of their customers to intercept some of their online activities, this exception to ECPA would seem to apply. Again, the questions of how and when consent may be obtained and what constitutes "lawful consent" arise and are addressed in the following section.

The Consent Exception to ECPA

As noted above, interception of electronic communications is not prohibited by ECPA if one of the parties to the communications has consented to the interception. Consent is not defined by ECPA; nor do precise instructions of how and when consent may be obtained under ECPA appear in regulation. Therefore, it has been left largely to the courts to determine when consent to intercept a communication otherwise covered by ECPA's prohibitions has been granted.[16] There have been few cases dealing with ECPA's application to online advertising providers and none examining ECPA's application to agreements between ISP providers and online advertising providers. As a result, many open-ended questions exist regarding how to obtain adequate consent. This section first will examine whether the consent exception to ECPA applies to data collection agreements between online advertising providers and website operators. It will then examine whether and how the consent exception applies to data collection agreements between ISPs and online advertising providers.

Data Collection Agreements between Website Operators and Online Advertising Providers

Agreements for online advertising providers to monitor certain web traffic may be between the online advertising provider and the website operators seeking to have ads placed on their sites. The advertising providers receive information about user activity on participating websites and aggregate that data to better target ads. In litigation against the online advertising provider DoubleClick for violations of ECPA, the court examined whether websites were "users" of electronic communications services under ECPA.[17] ECPA defines a "user" as "any person or entity who (A) uses an electronic communication service; and (B) is duly authorized by the provider of such service to engage in such use."[18] The court reasoned that websites are "users" (and, therefore, "parties to the communications" at issue) because they actively respond to requests they receive over electronic communications services by deciding whether to send the requested document, breaking the document down into TCP/IP protocol, and sending the packets over the Internet.[19] Because websites are "users" of electronic communications, the court found that websites are also "parties to the communications" in dispute; therefore, website owners have the ability to consent to a communication's interception.[20]

The court also held that the website operators had consented, by virtue of their contract with DoubleClick, to allow the company to intercept certain traffic on their websites in order to target advertising to website visitors.[21] Consent for private interceptions of electronic communications cannot be granted if the purpose of the interception is the commission of criminal or tortious conduct.[22] The court noted that the focus of the determination of criminal or tortious purpose under ECPA is "not upon whether the interception itself violated another law; it is upon whether the purpose for the interception—its intended use—was criminal or tortious."[23] Applying that standard, the court found that the plaintiffs had not alleged that DoubleClick's primary motivation for intercepting communications was to injure plaintiffs tortiously. In the court's view, even if DoubleClick's actions ultimately proved tortious or criminal, there was no evidence that DoubleClick was motivated by tortious intent. As a result, the court found that the consent exception to ECPA was satisfied.[24]

In a similar suit against online advertising provider Pharmatrak, the court outlined limitations to the consent exception regarding these types of agreements. In that case, Pharmatrak had contracted with certain drug companies to provide advertising on their websites. Included in the agreement was permission for the advertising provider to record certain web traffic that did not include personally identifiable information.[25] Perhaps inadvertently, the online advertising provider did collect a small amount of personally identifiable information though it had pledged not to do so. The advertiser argued that consent had been granted for such interception. The court disagreed. According to the court, it is for the party granting consent to define its scope, and the parties in this case had not consented to the collection of personally identifiable information.[26] In collecting personally identifiable information by intercepting data without the consent of one of the parties, the online advertiser potentially had violated ECPA, but may have lacked the requisite intent to be found liable under the statute.[27] The appeals court directed the trial court to conduct further investigation into the matter.

Given the conclusions in the above cases, it appears that online advertising providers, like DoubleClick, that partner to collect data from individual websites generally are not violating ECPA, because the websites are "parties to the communication" with the ability to consent to interception. Based on these cases, the advertising providers will not be seen as running afoul of ECPA so long as the data the advertising providers collect do not fall outside the scope of the data the advertising providers' clients have agreed to disclose.

Data Collection Agreements between ISPs and Online Advertising Providers

On the other hand, when the partnership is between the ISP and the online advertising provider, neither of the parties to the agreement to intercept web traffic is a party to the communications that are being intercepted. Therefore, it would appear that consent for the interceptions must be obtained from individual customers of the ISPs. The questions, in these circumstances, are whether consent must be "affirmative," or if it can be "implied," and if consent must be "affirmative" what process must be used to obtain such consent from individual users.

"Affirmative" or "Implied" Consent

Consent to interceptions has been implied by the surrounding circumstances of communications. While consent may be implied, it may not be "casually inferred."[28] It seems unlikely, as a result, that merely by using an ISP's service, a customer of that service has implied her consent to the interception of her electronic communications by online advertising providers. If consent likely may not be implied simply from use of an ISP's service, then a form of affirmative consent from the ISP's customer would be necessary.

"Opt-in" v. "Opt-out" Consent

In other statutes requiring consent for certain types of disclosure, regulatory regimes have developed to define when and how affirmative consent should be obtained.[29] A similar debate is occurring now involving how ISPs should obtain consent from their customers to share data about their online activities with online advertising providers. The debate centers around whether ISPs and advertisers must obtain "opt-in" consent or if they may continue to obtain "opt-out" consent for these interceptions.

"Opt-in" consent is obtained when a party to the communication is notified that his or her ISP has agreed to allow an online advertiser to track that person's online activity in order to better target advertising to that person. The advertiser, however, may not begin to track that individual's web activity until the individual responds to the notification granting permission for such activity.[30] If the individual never responds, interception can never begin. "Opt-out" consent, by contrast, is obtained when a party to the communication is notified that his or her ISP has agreed to allow an online advertiser to track that person's online activity and the advertising provider will begin such tracking *unless* the individual notifies the ISP or the advertiser that he or she does not grant permission for such activity.[31] If the individual never responds, interception will begin. Currently, it appears that companies such as NebuAd are obtaining or planning to obtain "opt-out" consent for the information gathering they engage in with ISPs.[32] The present question is whether "opt-out" consent is sufficient to satisfy the ECPA consent requirement. This question has yet to be addressed by a federal court or clarified by legislation or regulation. However, as discussed below, if Section 631 of the Communications Act applies to this type of data collection, "opt-in" consent may already be required for cable companies acting as ISPs (though this may not be required of telco companies such as Verizon or AT&T that operate as ISPs).

SECTION 631 OF THE COMMUNICATIONS ACT

It is also possible that privacy provisions of the Communications Act apply to agreements between cable operators acting as ISPs and online advertising providers.[33] Section 631 of the Communications Act provides basic privacy protections for personally identifiable information gathered by cable operators.[34] Specifically, cable operators must provide notice to subscribers, informing them of the types of personally identifiable information the cable operator collects, how it is disclosed, how long it is kept, etc.[35] Cable operators are prohibited from collecting personally identifiable information over the cable system without a subscriber's prior written or electronic consent.[36] Cable operators are also forbidden to disclose personally identifiable information without prior written or electronic consent of subscribers and must take action to prevent unauthorized access to personally identifiable information by anyone other than the subscriber or cable operator.[37] NebuAd has argued that Section 631 does not apply to the activities of cable operators when cable operators are acting as cable modem service providers.[38]

Section 631 governs the protection of information about subscribers to "any cable service or other service" provided by a cable operator. "Other service" is defined as "any wire or radio communications service provided using any of the facilities of a cable operator that are used in the provision of cable service."[39] In its order classifying cable modem services as "information services," the FCC stated the belief that "cable modem service would be included in the category of 'other service' for the purposes of section 631."[40] Furthermore, in 1992, Congress added the term "other services" to Section 631 as part of the Cable Television and Consumer Protection and Competition Act.[41] The House Conference Report on the law clarified that provisions redefining the term "other services" were included in order "to ensure that new communications services provided by cable operators are covered by the privacy protections" of Section 631.[42]

Section 631 is judicially enforced, however, and it is for the courts to interpret the scope of its application absent more specific guidance from Congress.[43] It is unclear whether all of the provisions of Section 631 encompass Internet services. "Other services" have been interpreted by at least one district court to encompass Internet services.[44] On the other hand, in 2006, the Sixth Circuit Court of Appeals found that the plain language of Section 631(b) precluded its application to broadband Internet service.[45] Section 631(b) prohibits cable operators from using their cable systems to collect personally identifiable information without the consent of subscribers.[46] The court based its decision that Internet services were not covered by this prohibition on its interpretation of the definition of "cable systems."[47] The court found that the systems that deliver Internet services are not the systems that Section 631(b) addresses, and therefore, cable operators were not prohibited by Section 631(b) from collecting personally identifiable information over systems that delivered Internet access services. The Supreme Court has yet to rule on this issue.

Even if Section 631(b) does not prevent cable operators from collecting personally identifiable information over broadband Internet services, Section 631(c) may prohibit the disclosure of such information to third parties regardless of whether the information was collected over the cable system.[48] Section 631(c) of the Communications Act states that "a cable operator shall not disclose personally identifiable information concerning any subscriber without the prior written or electronic consent of the subscriber concerned and shall take such actions as are necessary to prevent unauthorized access to such information by a person other than the subscriber or cable operator."[49] If a cable operator, as an ISP, agrees to allow an online advertising provider to inspect traffic over its cable system and to acquire some of that information, it seems that the cable operator/ISP is disclosing information to the online advertising provider. Such disclosure would apparently be a violation of the Communications Act if (1) the information disclosed is personally identifiable information and (2) the cable operator/ISP is disclosing it without the prior written or electronic consent of the subscribers to whom the information pertains.

Whether online advertising providers are gathering personally identifiable information in order to provide their services is a matter of much debate. Section 631 does not define what personally identifiable information is; it defines what personally identifiable information is not. According to 631, Personally Identifiable Information (PII) does not include "any record of aggregate data which does not identify particular persons."[50] Online advertising providers claim that they do not collect any personally identifiable information.[51] Public interest groups and other commentators disagree, citing scenarios in which data which was not supposed to contain personally identifiable information was used to identify individuals.[52] Because

Section 631 is judicially enforced, it is likely that whether online advertisers are acquiring personally identifiable information as opposed to aggregate data that do not identify particular persons will be a determination made by a federal trial court. To date, there have been no cases addressing this question.

Assuming even that online advertising providers are gathering personally identifiable information, cable operators are allowed to disclose personally identifiable information as long as they obtain the prior written or electronic consent of the relevant subscribers, essentially an "opt-in" standard.[53] In the event that online advertising companies are determined to be gathering personally identifiable information and that Section 631(c) applies to cable operators in their provision of cable modem services, cable operators would be required to obtain consent for such disclosure under an "opt-in" regime.

FEDERAL TRADE COMMISSION ONLINE ADVERTISING SELF-REGULATORY PRINCIPLES

In February of 2009, the FTC released a new set of Self Regulatory Principles for Online Behavioral Advertising.[54] These principles represent the most recent step in the FTC's ongoing examination of behavioral advertising practices, which began with the release of proposed self-regulatory principles for public comment in December of 2007.[55] Among other things, the finalized principles clarified the types of advertising to which they should be applied and discussed what types of Non-PII should be included when notifying a consumer about what types of data the site or advertiser is collecting about him/her. A brief sketch of the principles follows.[56]

- The FTC's principles cover only online behavioral advertising. Online behavioral advertising means "the tracking of a consumer's online activities *over time*." The principles make clear that so-called "first party" advertising (where no information is shared with a third party) and contextual advertising (where the ad is based on a single page visit or search) are not covered by the principles.
- According to the principles, websites engaged in online behavioral advertising should provide clear notification to consumers regarding the types of data being collected on the site and why, as well as the opportunity for consumers to choose whether their data may be collected for such purposes.
- Companies collecting the data should provide reasonable security for the data. The security measures should be concomitant with the sensitivity of the data (the more sensitive the data, the more protected it should be). The data should be retained only so long as necessary to fulfill a legitimate business purpose or as required by law.
- Companies must keep the promises they make to their customers. If the company decides to use *previously* collected data for purposes that differ materially from the uses the company described to the customer at the time data collection began, the company should obtain the affirmative express consent of affected customers.
- Companies should collect sensitive data (e.g., social security number, medical information, financial account information, etc.) for behavioral advertising only after obtaining affirmative express consent from the consumer.

The FTC noted that the release of these principles is a step in the ongoing process of evaluating the online behavioral advertising industry. The principles do not absolve the companies of their responsibilities under other governing laws (i.e., Section 5 of the Federal Trade Commission Act). the FTC pledged to continue to monitor online behavioral advertising issues and its affect on consumer privacy.

INDUSTRY SELF-REGULATORY PRINCIPLES

The principles announced by the FTC were intended to aid self-regulatory organizations in designing privacy, data gathering, and consent guidelines for their members. There are at least three separate industry guidelines for online behavioral advertising, each of which takes a different approach to complying with the FTC's self-regulatory principles. The Interactive Advertising Bureau (IAB) has published their "Self-Regulatory Program for Online Behavioral Advertising" with which their member organizations must comply.[57] The Network Advertising Initiative (NAI) has released its "Self-Regulatory Code of Conduct."[58] And a collection of ten advocacy organizations, known collectively as the Privacy Group Coalition, has recommended that regulation be built around a framework of Fair Information Practices (FIPs).[59]

Each of these sets of guidelines and principles share broad similarities, but have many important differences as well. For instance, they disagree on the definition of online behavioral advertising.[60] The definition of such advertising is broader under the IAB's guidelines than the NAI's Guidelines. Consequently, the IAB's requirements apply to a broader range of ad-delivery techniques than the NAI's. There are also differences among the levels of protection accorded to different types of data. Sensitive Data, for example, receives the highest level of protection from each regulatory framework. However, no single regulatory framework defines sensitive data in the same way.[61] There are also differences in enforcement mechanisms, notification and consent practices, data retention policies, etc.

Currently, if a consumer wishes to opt-out of online behavioral advertising data collection practices or even to find out what sites are collecting their data and how, the consumer must first figure out which companies are collecting their data and then determine to which industry self-regulatory organization the companies belong. If they belong to differing industry organizations, then different rules may apply to the same data sets that are being collected. As noted above, different definitions may apply to similar or identical terms, different methods of rescinding consent for the collection of data may also be applied depending upon the self-regulatory organization, and different methods of enforcement for companies that fail to comply with the agreed upon principles may apply as well.

In December of 2009, the Center for Democracy and Technology (CDT) issued a report entitled Online Behavioral Advertising: Industry's Current Self-Regulatory Framework is Necessary, But Still Insufficient on its Own to Protect Consumers.[62] The report analyzes the current self-regulatory framework and provides recommendations for strengthening consumer protection in this rapidly growing industry. Among their recommendations to the self-regulatory organizations themselves, CDT calls upon Congress to enact a comprehensive privacy bill and to grant the FTC broader rulemaking authority to regulate in this space.

End Notes

[1] For a basic description of the technology involved in delivering behaviorally targeted advertising, please see the following source material: In re DoubleClick, Inc. Privacy Litigation, 154 F.Supp. 2d 497 (S.D.N.Y. 2001), In re Pharmatrak Privacy Litigation, 329 F.3d 9 (1st Cir. 2003), and Paul Lansing and Mark Halter, *Internet Advertising and Right to Privacy Issues*, 80 U. Det. Mercy L. Rev. 181 (2003). *See also,* Testimony of Mr. Robert R. Dykes, CEO of NebuAd Inc., *Privacy Implications of Online Advertising: Hearing Before the S. Comm. On Commerce, Science, and Transportation*, 110th Cong. (2008)(hereinafter NebuAd Testimony), available at http://commerce.senate.gov/public/_files/RobertDykesNebuAdOnlinePrivacyTestimony.pdf.

[2] Testimony of Ms. Leslie Harris, CEO of the Center for Democracy and Technology, *Privacy Implications of Online Advertising: Hearing Before the S. Comm. On Commerce, Science, and Transportation*, 110th Cong. (2008)(hereinafter CDT Testimony), available at http://commerce.senate.gov/public/_files/Leslie HarrisCDTOnlinePrivacyTestimony.pdf.

[3] For a more detailed discussion of the history of ECPA, see CRS Report 98-326, *Privacy: An Overview of Federal Statutes Governing Wiretapping and Electronic Eavesdropping*, by Gina Stevens and Charles Doyle.

[4] *See e.g.,* NebuAd Testimony at 3-4.

[5] *See id.;* In re DoubleClick, Inc. Privacy Litigation, 154 F.Supp. 2d 497 (S.D.N.Y. 2001).

[6] 18 U.S.C. §2511(1)(a).

[7] 18 U.S.C. §2510(4).

[8] 18 U.S.C. §2510(8).

[9] 18 U.S.C. §2510(12).

[10] It is worth noting that there has yet to be a court case to decide definitively that ECPA applies to this type of data collection. In the cases cited here, the online advertising providers made their cases by assuming, but not conceding, that ECPA applied to the data collection. *See* In re Pharmatrk, Inc. Privacy Litigations, 329 F.3d 9 (1st Cir. 2003); In re DoubleClick, Inc. Privacy Litigation, 154 F.Supp. 2d 497 (S.D.N.Y. 2001).

[11] "It shall not be unlawful under this chapter for a person not acting under color of law to intercept a wire, oral, or electronic communication where such person is a party to the communication or where one of the parties to the communications has given prior consent to such interception unless such communication is intercepted for the purpose of committing any criminal or tortious act in violation of the Constitution or laws of the United States or any State." 18 U.S.C. §2511(2)(d).

[12] 18 U.S.C. §2511(3)(a). It is worth noting that this section does not require that the divulgence of information while it is in transit by an electronic communications service be an "interception" in order for it to be prohibited. Data acquisition can only be categorized as an "interception" for the purposes of ECPA "through the use of any electronic, mechanical, or other device." 18 U.S.C. §2510(4). The statute makes clear that "electronic, mechanical, or other device" does not mean the equipment or facilities of a wire or electronic communications service that are used in the ordinary course of the provider's business. 18 U.S.C. 2510(5). Therefore, it is possible that when an ISP allows a third party to collect data that is in transit over its network the ISP may not be "intercepting" that data as the term "intercept" is defined by ECPA. Nonetheless, "intentionally divulging the contents of any communication while in transmission" over an ISP's network is prohibited by 18 U.S.C. §2511(3)(a), unless it meets one of the exceptions outlined in 18 U.S.C. § 2511(3)(b).

[13] 18 U.S.C. §2511(2)(a)(i).

[14] *See, e.g.,* U.S. Census 2006 Annual Survey (Information Sector), *Internet Service Providers—Estimated Sources of Revenue and Expenses for Employer Firms: 2004 Through 2006* at 32, Table 3.4.1 (April 15, 2006) (indicating that internet access service are responsible for the greatest percentage of revenue earned by ISPs) available at http://www.census.gov/svsd/www/services/sas/sas_data/51/2006_NAICS51.pdf; Comcast Corporation, Quarterly Report (Form 10-Q) (June 30, 2008) (reporting that 95% of Comcast Corporation's consolidated revenue is derived from its cable operations, which includes the provision of high-speed internet services) available at http://sec.gov/ Archives/edgar/data/1166691/000119312508161385/d10q.htm.

[15] 18 U.S.C. 2511(3)(b)(ii).

[16] *See e.g.,* United States v. Friedman, 300 F.3d 111, 122-23 (2d Cir. 2002)(inmate use of prison phone);United States v. Faulkner, 439 F.3d 1221, 1224 (10th Cir. 2006)(same); United States v. Hammond, 286 F.3d 189, 192 (4th Cir. 2002) (same); *United States v. Footman*, 215 F.3d 145, 154-55 (1st Cir. 2000) (same); Griggs-Ryan v. Smith, 904 F.2d 112, 116-17 (1st Cir. 1990) (use of landlady's phone); United States v. Rivera, 292 F. Supp. 2d 838, 843-45 (E.D. Va. 2003)(inmate use of prison phone monitored by private contractors). For a discussion of the consent exception to the Wiretap Act as it is applied in other contexts, see, CRS Report 98-326, *Privacy: An Overview of Federal Statutes Governing Wiretapping and Electronic Eavesdropping*, by Gina Stevens and Charles Doyle.

[17] In re DoubleClick, Inc. Privacy Litigation, 154 F.Supp. 2d 497 (S.D.N.Y. 2001).

[18] 18 U.S.C. §2510(13).

[19] In re DoubleClick, Inc. Privacy Litigation, 154 F.Supp. 2d at 508-09.

[20] *Id.* at 514.

[21] *Id.* at 509-513.

[22] 18 U.S.C. §2511(2)(d).

[23] In re DoubleClick, Inc. Privacy Litigation, 154 F.Supp. 2d at 516 (quoting Sussman v. ABC, 196 F.3d 1200, 1202 (9th Cir. 1999)).

[24] *Id.* at 518-19.

[25] In re Pharmatrk, Inc. Privacy Litigations, 329 F.3d 9 (1st Cir. 2003).

[26] *Id.* at 20.

[27] *Id.* at 23.

[28] Williams v. Poulos, 11 F.3d 271, 281 (1st Cir. 1993)(finding that defendant corporation violated the Wiretap Act, because it did not have implied consent or a business necessity to place wiretaps).

[29] *See e.g., In the Matter of Implementation of the Telecommunications Act of 1996; Telecommunications Carriers; Use of Customer Proprietary Network Information and Other Customer Information; IP-Enabled Services,* 22 FCC Rcd 6927 (2007)(outlining under what circumstances voice service providers must obtain "opt-in" v. "opt-out" consent in order to disclose Customer Proprietary Network Information(CPNI)). For a discussion of the FCC's CPNI disclosure regulations, see CRS Report RL34409, *Selected Laws Governing the Disclosure of Customer Phone Records by Telecommunications Carriers,* by Kathleen Ann Ruane.

[30] *See* The Network Advertising Initiative's Self-Regulatory Code of Conduct for Online Behavioral Advertising, Draft: For Public Comment, available at http://networkadvertising.org/networks/ NAI_Principles_2008_Draft _for_Public.pdf (last visited July 28, 2008). *See also,* 47 C.F.R. §2003(k)(defining "opt-in" approval in the CPNI context).

[31] *See* The Network Advertising Initiative's Self-Regulatory Code of Conduct for Online Behavioral Advertising, Draft: For Public Comment, available at http://networkadvertising.org/networks/ NAI_Principles_2008 _Draft_for_Public.pdf (last visited July 28, 2008). *See also,* 47 C.F.R. §2003(l)(defining "opt-out" approval in the CPNI context).

[32] NebuAd Testimony at 4.

[33] Testimony of Ms. Leslie Harris, CEO of the Center for Democracy and Technology, *Privacy Implications of Online Advertising: Hearing Before the S. Comm. On Commerce, Science, and Transportation,* 110th Cong. (2008).

[34] Codified at 47 U.S.C. §551. It is important to note that those providing DSL Internet service over phone lines, such as Verizon or AT&T, would not be subject to the provisions of Section 631, because they are not cable operators. Testimony of Ms. Gigi B. Sohn, President, Public Knowledge, *Broadband Providers and Consumer Privacy: Hearing Before the S. Comm. On Commerce, Science, and Transportation,* 110th Cong. (2008)(hereinafter Public Knowledge Testimony), available at http://commerce.senate.gov/ public/_files/SohnTestimony.pdf.

[35] 47 U.S.C. §551(a).

[36] 47 U.S.C. §551(b).

[37] 47 U.S.C. §551(c).

[38] Memorandum from NebuAd, Inc., Legal and Policy Issues Supporting NebuAd's Services at 6.

[39] 47 U.S.C. Sec. §551(a)(2)(B).

[40] *In the Matter of Inquiry Concerning High-Speed Access to the Internet Over Cable and Other Facilities; Internet Over Cable Declaratory Ruling; Appropriate Regulatory Treatment for Broadband Access to the Internet Over Cable Facilities,* 17 FCC Rcd at 4854, ¶ 112.

[41] Cable Television and Consumer Protection and Competition Act, P.L. 102-385.

[42] H.Rept. 102-862.

[43] *See* 47 U.S.C. 551(f).

[44] *See* Application of the United States of America for an Order Pursuant to 18 U.S.C. Sec. 2703(D), 157 F. Supp. 2d 286, 291 (SDNY 2001)(finding that the notice requirement for the disclosure of personally identifiable information under 47 U.S.C. §551 included Internet services, except under 47 U.S.C. §551(h), which was exempt specifically from the broad definition of "other services").

[45] Klimas v. Comcast Cable, Inc., 465 F.3d 271, 276 (6th Cir. 2006).

[46] 47 U.S.C. §551(b)(1).

[47] *Klimas,* 465 F.3d at 276.

[48] 47 U.S.C. §551(c)(1).

[49] 47 U.S.C. §551(c)(1). Cable operators, however, may collect such information without consent for the purposes of obtaining information necessary to provide cable services or other services provided to the subscriber or to detect unauthorized reception of cable communications. Cable operators may disclose personally identifiable information without consent when it is necessary to render cable services or other services provided by the cable operator to the subscriber, pursuant to a valid court order, and in other limited circumstances. 47 U.S.C. 551 (c)(2). These exemptions do not appear to apply in this case.

[50] 47 U.S.C. §551(a)(2)(A).

[51] *See, e.g.,* NebuAd Testimony.

[52] *See, e.g.,* CDT Testimony.

[53] 47 U.S.C. §551(c).

[54] FTC Staff, *Self-Regulatory Principles for Online Behavioral Advertising* (Feb. 12, 2009), *available at* http://www.ftc.gov/os/2009/02/P085400behavadreport.pdf.

[55] FTC Staff, *Online Behavioral Advertising: Moving the Discussion Forward to Possible Self-Regulatory Principles* (Dec. 20, 2007), *available at* http://www.ftc.gov/os/2007/12/P859900stmt.pdf.

[56] FTC Staff, *Self-Regulatory Principles for Online Behavioral Advertising*, at 46-47 (Feb. 12, 2009), *available at* http://www.ftc.gov/os/2009/02/P085400behavadreport.pdf.

[57] Interactive Advertising Bureau, Self-Regulatory Program for Online Behavioral Advertising, July, 2009, available at http://www.iab.net/media/file/ven-principles-07-01-09.pdf. (hereinafter IAB Guidelines)

[58] Network Advertising Initiative, Self-Regulatory Code of Conduct (2008), available at http://www. networkadvertising.org/networks/2008%20NAI%20Principles_final%20for%20Website.pdf. (hereinafter NAI Guidelines).

[59] Privacy Group Coalition, Online Behavioral Tracking and Targeting, Legislative Primer, September 2009, available at http://www.uspirg.org/uploads/nE/27/nE27slalKXMxhjOdnoYLEA/Online-Privacy—Legislative-Primer.pdf.

[60] NAI defines Third-Party Online Behavioral advertising as "any process used whereby data are collected across multiple web domains owned or operated by different entities to categorize likely consumer interest segments for use in advertising online." NAI Guidelines, *supra* note 58. IAB defines online behavioral advertising more broadly as "the collection of data from a particular computer or device regarding web-viewing behaviors over time and across non-affiliate web sites for the purpose of using such data to predict user preferences or interests to deliver advertising to that computer or device based on the preferences or interests inferred from such web viewing behaviors. Online Behavioral Advertising does not include the activities of First Parties, Ad Delivery or Ad-Reporting, or contextual advertising (i.e. advertising based upon the content of a web page being visited, a consumer's current visit to a web page, or a search query). IAB Guidelines, *supra* note 57.

[61] IAB defines sensitive data as "financial account numbers, Social Security numbers, pharmaceutical prescriptions, or medical records about a specific individual." IAB Guidelines, *supra* note 57. NAI defines sensitive data more broadly as "Social Security numbers or other government identifiers, insurance plan numbers, financial account numbers, information that describes the precise real time geographic location of an individual derived through location based services such as through GPS enabled services, and precise information about past, present, or potential future health or medical conditions or treatments, including genetic, genomic, and family medical history." NAI Guidelines, *supra* note 58.

[62] Center for Democracy and Technology, Online Behavioral Advertising: Industry's Current Self-Regulatory Framework is Necessary, But Still Insufficient on its Own to Protect Consumers, December 2009, available at http://www.cdt.org/files/pdfs/CDT%20Online%20Behavioral%20Advertising%20Report.pdf.

In: Advertising: Developments and Issues in the Digital Age   ISBN: 978-1-61761-783-6
Editor: William L. Poulsen   © 2011 Nova Science Publishers, Inc.

Chapter 3

DIRECT-TO-CONSUMER ADVERTISING OF PRESCRIPTION DRUGS

Susan Thaul

SUMMARY

A phenomenon that has become more and more important over the last decade, direct-to-consumer (DTC) advertising has grown from about $800 million in 1996 to over $4.7 billion in 2007. Its supporters point to more informed consumers who then visit their doctors and become more involved in their own treatment, leading to better and earlier diagnosis of undertreated illnesses. The critics believe that industry's presentation of the balance of drug benefit and risk information may encourage the inappropriate use of advertised products and lead to higher than necessary spending. In addition to concerns with accuracy and balance, health professionals point out that DTC ads rarely mention alternative treatments, such as other or generic medications or non-drug interventions.

In 1962, Congress gave the Food and Drug Administration (FDA) certain authorities to regulate prescription drug advertising. Except in extreme circumstances, the law does not allow FDA to require pre-release review of ads. Regulations—written at a time when most ads were printed in medical journals for a physician audience—require that all drug ads disclose all of a drug's known risks.

However, as drug makers considered moving into broadcast advertising and wanted to get their messages to consumers, they noted, without explicit guidance from FDA, the difficulty in including all risks in the format of a 30-second commercial. FDA issued guidance in 1999 stipulating that broadcast ads had to include the advertised product's most important risks in the audio portion of the advertisement and should give sources where more complete risk information about a drug would be available.

FDA reviews ads once they are launched, and its enforcement options are notice-of-violation and warning letters, criminal prosecution (through the Department of Justice), civil monetary penalties, product seizures, and withdrawal of approval for sale. Despite these activities, Members of Congress and the public ask what FDA could do differently in light of the safety problems involving some heavily advertised medications.

Congress could consider a variety of options to allay concerns about DTC drug advertising. It could encourage FDA to expand activities allowed under current legislative authority, including provisions in P.L. 110-85 (the FDA Amendments Act of 2007): FDA could increase post- publication review of ads, expand its role in consumer education, and increase its enforcement activities. Other possible options would require Congress to grant new authority so that FDA could require pre-release review and approval; require changes to ads; use stronger enforcement tools; require data collection; require public posting of risk information; prohibit DTC ads when a drug is first approved; and set limits on the timing and placement of ads. Congress could go beyond FDA to encourage other industry-independent entities to provide public education or set standards; it could also use tax and other financial incentives to make DTC advertising less profitable to industry.

INTRODUCTION

In 2007, pharmaceutical companies spent $4.774 billion on DTC advertising. It was the first year such spending had declined, but it was still six times as much as the industry had spent in 1996.[1] DTC advertising of prescription drugs attracted enough congressional attention to warrant at least six bills in the 110th Congress as well as concerns from members in the 111th . Beyond the sheer size of this marketing operation, what are the issues that concern Members? What actions do critics propose—and supporters of DTC ads oppose? Is there common ground between both groups?

There is a spectrum of opinion about DTC ads.

Proponents of DTC advertising say the ads:

- educate consumers about medical conditions;
- alert them to treatments that exist;
- fairly present risks as well as benefits;
- detail non-drug approaches to improve health;
- remind and motivate consumers to comply better with drug therapy regimes; and
- help to de-stigmatize conditions.

Critics of DTC advertising say the ads:

- minimize the risks of some medications while promoting their benefits;
- lure patients into expensive drugs when cheaper ones work as well, thus increasing healthcare costs;
- persuade patients to ignore other medications with fewer side effects and more established safety track records;
- provide information that would be more credible coming from non-industry sources; and
- are susceptible to marketing needs that interfere with objective presentations.

Not all of these views necessarily conflict. It is possible to educate about medical conditions *and* omit information about alternate therapies, for example. As Congress considers arguments for and against DTC advertising of prescription drugs, context becomes important. All pharmaceuticals carry some risks. Human drugs, by their definition, are substances intended to affect the structure or function of the body.[2] Consumers can take too much—or too little. They can take drugs that interact with each other in ways not yet understood.

Researchers do not know all risks at the time FDA first approves a drug for marketing. In fact, one effect of the 2005 controversy over Vioxx was that it heightened public awareness of how incomplete the data really are before tens of thousands of consumers use a drug in real-life conditions, which include use beyond the carefully controlled limits of clinical trials. Scientists then attributed approximately 100,000 excess heart attacks and sudden cardiac deaths to an unanticipated cardiovascular side effect of that heavily advertised blockbuster drug and others in its class (COX-2 inhibitors developed to treat pain without the associated stomach side effects common to other nonsteroidal anti-inflammatory drugs) before they were withdrawn from the market.[3]

While critics and supporters of DTC ads sharply disagree on many things, people all along the spectrum often seem united in their belief that DTC ads should meet four criteria. They must be:

- *Accessible.* We want consumers to have *access* to *information* that could—along with the treating physician—help them make the healthcare decisions they face. To do so, the information must be *understandable*, *accurate* (true), *balanced*, and *up-to-date*.
- *Understandable.* Although researchers—whether in academia, government, or industry—disagree about what it is that viewers need to learn from advertisements (drug, brand, disease recognition; risks; benefits; indication), they agree ads should present the information so that average Americans can understand it.
- *Accurate* **and** *up-to-date*. There is little disagreement about whether DTC ads should be accurate and up-to-date. There is, however, disagreement about exactly what those terms mean. When should ads change to include postmarket findings? When risks or benefits vary by age or disease stage and other treatments, how much of these details should the ads present?
- *Balanced.* Most players in the debate acknowledge the need for some discussion of the balance between risks and benefits of a drug. They often disagree over the breadth of comparisons (for example, whether to consider other drugs or other treatments or cost) or methods to use.

Appearing on TV and radio, and in popular magazines and pop-up windows on the Internet, DTC ads are an anomaly when it comes to federal regulation. The Federal Trade Commission (FTC) regulates most advertising in the United States. In 1962, however, Congress assigned the regulation of prescription drug advertising to the Food and Drug Administration (FDA). In doing so, though, it did not give the agency enforcement authority similar to that granted to the FTC. According to some critics of DTC ads, this has prevented effective oversight, and created a phenomenon more misleading than educational. To other critics, however, FDA's organizational structure, reliance on industry fees, and inadequate appropriations are more important factors in what they see as the agency's less than rigorous enforcement of law and regulation.

Nevertheless, support for some form of DTC ads from industry and consumers is strong: industry wants to increase sales,[4] and consumers want to actively participate in decisions about their own health. That, combined with advances in information technology and possible relevance to constitutional protections of free speech, makes an outright ban on DTC ads unlikely.

The concerns about DTC ads already expressed by Members of the 111th Congress are similar to those that have surfaced in the past. Interest in the 109th Congress was sparked by some Members who had seen its growth and noted controversies over heavily advertised drugs such as Vioxx. Senate and House committees in the 110th Congress considered drug safety bills that included restrictions on DTC advertising. The Food and Drug Administration Amendments Act of 2007 (FDAAA, P.L. 110-85) included some of those provisions, such as new industry fees for the advisory review of DTC television ads; expanded authority of the Secretary of Health and Human Services (HHS) to require certain disclosures and statements; and civil monetary penalties for false or misleading ads. So far, Members of the 111th Congress have indicated interest in DTC advertising in the context of drug safety, tax treatment of advertising expenses, risk communication, and general FDA-activity authority and oversight, sometimes in the context of broader discussions of health care costs and reform.

This chapter examines these and other issues. It (1) describes the current status of DTC drug advertising; (2) analyzes issues surrounding it; and (3) discusses potential options for Congress. Specifically,

Part I–Current Picture

- describes the types, history, and extent of direct-to-consumer drug advertising in the United States;
- reviews the authority Congress has given FDA to regulate DTC advertising and how FDA has used that authority; and
- describes voluntary guidelines of some interested groups.

Part II–Issues

- explores what manufacturers, clinicians, and consumers want the ads to achieve;
- examines how DTC ads affect consumers, clinicians, and drug manufacturers; and
- discusses the major issues now debated by proponents and opponents of DTC drug advertising.

Part III–Potential Options

- discusses potential oversight and legislative options for Congress; and
- concludes by relating DTC drug advertising to some of the larger issues affecting U.S. health care: cost, access, safety, among others.

CURRENT PICTURE OF DTC ADVERTISING

Defining DTC Advertising

The World Health Organization defines "drug promotion" as "all informational and persuasive activities by manufacturers, the effect of which is to induce the prescription, supply, purchase and/or use of medicinal drugs."[5] Richard G. Frank, Harvard Medical School professor of health economics, describes DTC advertising more specifically as "[A]ny promotional effort by a pharmaceutical company to present prescription drug information to the general public in the lay media."[6]

Although the Federal Food, Drug, and Cosmetic Act (FFDCA) regulates prescription drug "advertising," Congress did not define the term in the law.[7] In its regulations, however, FDA has listed examples: "advertisements in published journals, magazines, other periodicals, and newspapers, and advertisements broadcast through media such as radio, television, and telephone communication systems."[8] Academic experts in prescription drug law have noted that "FDA generally interprets [prescription drug advertising] to encompass information, other than labeling, that promotes a drug product and is sponsored by a manufacturer."[9]

DTC print advertising appears in magazines, newspapers, non-medical journals, pharmacy brochures, and direct-mail letters; companies also run DTC ads on television, radio, videos, billboards, and Internet Web sites. The ads usually fall into one of three categories.

- *Help-seeking ads* discuss a particular disease or health condition, advise the consumer to "see your doctor," but do not mention the product's name. They are directed towards consumers, make no health claims, and mention no specific drug.
- *Reminder ads* call attention to the product's name but make no reference to the health condition it treats. They make no health claims and FDA does not require that they contain full risk information. Although reminder ads may acquaint consumers with brand names of products, they are directed primarily towards doctors and health care professionals who are more likely than consumers to know about the product and its use.
- *Product-claim ads*—the type of most concern to FDA—include a product's name and a therapeutic claim for it. The regulations require that therapeutic claims not be false or misleading and that the ad present full risk information.

FDA's regulatory oversight is minimal for the first two, reflecting its statutory authority.[10] The third commands most of its attention and resources. DTC advertising is only one of the pharmaceutical industry's tools to influence prescription drug sales. Companies also promote drugs to physicians. They use direct advertising, such as ads in medical journals; reminders, such as logo-embossed pads and pens; and less well-defined tools, such as industry-funded seminars, residency training support, drug samples, and visits by "detailers," drug company representatives who visit doctors' offices with drug samples and educational materials. Although not a focus of this chapter, industry promotion to physicians appears to influence prescribing patterns.[11]

Table 1. Total U.S. Promotional Spending on Prescription Drugs, 1996-2007 (dollars in millions)

Type of promotion	1996	1997	1998	1999	2000	2001	2002	2003	2004	2005	2006	2007
Direct to consumers	791	1,069	1,317	1,848	2,467	2,679	2,638	3,235	4,024	4,237	4,811	4,774
Direct to office-based physicians and hospital-based physicians and pharmacists[a]	3,010	3,364	4,057	4,320	4,803	5,491	6,200	6,938	7,336	6,777	6,741	6,262
Journal ads	459	510	498	470	484	425	437	448	499	429	464	417
Subtotal	4,260	4,943	5,872	6,638	7,754	8,595	9,275	10,621	11,859	11,443	12,016	11,453
Retail value of samples	4,904	6,047	6,602	7,230	7,954	10,464	11,909	13,531	15,866	[b]	[b]	[b]
Total	9,164	10,990	12,474	13,868	15,708	19,059	21,184	24,152	27,725			

Source: Data from "Total U.S. Promotional Spend by Type, 2003," "Total U.S. Professional Spend by Type," and "Total U.S. Value of Free Product Samples," IMS Health, Integrated Promotional Services[TM] and CMR, June 2004; "Total U.S. Promotional Spend by Type, 2005," "Total U.S. Professional Promotional Spend by Type, 2005," and "Total U.S. Value of Free Product Samples, 2004"; and "Total U.S. Promotional Spend by Type, 2007," at http://www.imshealth.com.

a. For 2003-2005, IMS Health presented a combined figure for office-based physicians and hospital-based physicians and directors of pharmacies.

b. IMS Health has not provided the retail value of samples for years after 2004; this also affects the total

Spending on DTC Advertising

The pharmaceutical industry increased its DTC spending by 536% from 1996 to 2007.[12] To put this growth in perspective, the Consumer Price Index (all items) (which approximates the change in real dollars of the cost of placing advertising spots increased 24% during the same time period.[13] The increase in DTC advertising spending was more than 22 times higher than the CPI.

The top row in Table 1 shows pharmaceutical industry spending on DTC advertising for the last 10 years; the other rows show pharmaceutical industry spending for other categories of prescription drug promotion and advertising. Using data from IMS Health, a for-profit source for "pharmaceutical market intelligence,"[14] Table 1 also includes spending directed to professional promotion (to physician offices, hospital-based physicians and pharmacists, and medical journals), and the reported retail value of product samples given to office-based physicians. In 2007, according to IMS data, drug companies spent 41.7% of their reported promotional spending on DTC advertising ($4.774 billion out of $11.453 billion).[15]

Manufacturers actually may spend more than that on promoting prescription drugs to consumers. Some analysts may use data that Table 1 does not include, such as industry expenses for new ways to reach consumers. An online news reporter wrote, in May 2006, that "Coupons, money- back guarantees, rebates and other supermarket-friendly promotions offering '10 percent off,' 'free-trial offers' or 'buy six prescriptions, get one free' are now standard marketing tools for many top-selling prescription drugs."[16]

As in the past, television and magazines continue to be the major media targets for DTC advertising. In 2007, they accounted for over 90% of spending.[17] Table 2 shows drug industry spending on DTC ads by placement.[18] For the past decade, media analysts have predicted large increases in Internet ad spending.[19] In 2007, however, Internet ads represented about 3% of DTC drug ad spending, indicating the anticipated growth has not yet occurred.[20]

As drug companies expand their use of social marketing techniques, the traditional definition of DTC advertising may evolve.[21] The published data do not include other areas in which some observers suggest industry may be promoting its products. For example, product placement: "the insertion of a product or service into a script or scene of a TV show or movie, usually for a price negotiated with the network, producer, or scriptwriter."[22] This marketing tool is used to promote cars and computers, but its use for pharmaceutical products has not been confirmed. One researcher, having shown an increase in prescription drug mentions on TV shows, notes a "regulatory void" that FDA and the Federal Communications Commission (FCC) have yet to address.[23]

Chronological History of FDA's Authority to Regulate DTC Advertising

The Federal Food, Drug, and Cosmetic Act (FFDCA) sets forth the statutory requirements that pharmaceuticals must meet before they can be approved for marketing in the United States.[24] The initial 1938 law (P.L. 75-717), in addressing FDA's regulatory authority over *labeling*, prohibited statements to the effect of "This drug is FDA-approved" in any labeling or advertising material.[25] Otherwise, until the 1962 Kefauver-Harris amendments to the FFDCA (P.L. 87-781), statutory authority for regulating any *advertising*—including that for prescription and non-prescription drugs—lay with the Federal Trade Commission (FTC).[26]

In 1962, Congress added Section 502(n) to the FFDCA to give the FDA the authority to regulate not only labeling, but also prescription drug advertising, including DTC advertisements, and other descriptive printed matter.[27] At the time, advertising was primarily printed material directed towards physicians. However, Congress prohibited ("except in extraordinary circumstances") FDA from issuing any regulations that would require *prior approval* of the content of any advertisement.

Initial Regulations (1969)

After passage of the 1962 FFDCA amendments, FDA needed to promulgate regulations and to provide guidelines to an industry producing what were now called "prescription" drugs.[28] In 1969, therefore, it issued final regulations governing drug advertising.[29] Under them, advertisements had to have four basic attributes:

(1) they could not be false or misleading;
(2) they had to present a fair balance of information about the drug's risks and benefits;
(3) they had to contain facts relevant to the product's advertised uses; and
(4) in general, the advertisement's "brief summary" of the drug had to include every risk listed in the product's approved labeling.

The regulations required that companies submit promotional materials to FDA at the same time they make them available to the public.[30] The promotion within these materials had to be supported by scientific evidence and be consistent with FDA-approved product labeling.[31] The ads could be the approved labeling or other promotional materials, but could not recommend or suggest any use of a drug that was not listed in the approved drug's labeling.

When FDA wrote the 1969 regulations, industry advertised its drugs to physicians through print ads in medical journals. Complying with the regulations was relatively straightforward. In 1981, when companies wanted to direct ads to consumers, FDA, after a two-year moratorium on DTC ads, announced that the current regulations were sufficient to protect the consumer. If a product- claim *print* advertisement mentioned the name of the prescription drug and its intended medical indications, it had to include *all* the information about side effects, contraindications, and precautions from the product's approved labeling.[32]

Table 2. DTC Spending on Product Ads, by Medium (dollars in millions)

Medium	2006		2007	
Television	2,667	56.3%	2,870	58.5%
Magazine	1,689	35.6%	1,768	36.1%
Newspaper	152	3.2%	75	1.5%
Radio	55	1.2%	30	0.6%
Internet	163	3.4%	155	3.2%
Outdoor	11	0.2%	4	<0.1%
Total	**9**	**100%**	**4**	**100%**

Source: TNS Media Intelligence, in *Medical Marketing & Media*, vol. 43, no. 6, June 2008, p. 53.

It remained unclear, however, how TV and radio ads could comply with the regulations. Conveying all of a product's risk information in print advertising may be cumbersome but it is not difficult. However, the drug industry asserted,[33] including all details in a 30-second broadcast ad is cumbersome, expensive, and unlikely to be possible. FDA had not issued any interpretation of how broadcast advertisements could fulfill that requirement, so, until 1997, the industry assumed that FDA expected broadcast DTC advertising to meet the same requirements as ads in print.[34]

Guidance for Broadcast Ads (1999)

In August 1997, FDA issued draft guidance on how pharmaceutical companies could fulfill the existing regulatory requirements for advertising drugs on radio and television. It published the final guidance, without major change, two years later.[35] The agency explained that the 1969 regulations had always allowed broadcast advertisements to either include all the drug's risks or ensure that consumers would have easy access to the full prescribing information within FDA- approved labeling. The guidance made clear that DTC broadcast advertisements had to include what FDA called the "major statement"—the product's most important risks. This had to be in the audio portion of the advertisement, and could be in the video portion as well.[36] In addition, the advertisement had to describe how the consumer could obtain the full package labeling.

With the 1999 guidance—which is still in effect now—FDA attempted to ensure that consumers with different information-seeking needs and abilities have adequate access to the product labeling. As part of that attempt, the guidance presented "one acceptable approach" to the required broad dissemination of this information: that ads include an Internet site and a toll-free telephone number where listeners could get that information; a reminder that one's doctor may have more information and a list of other print sources with large circulations.[37]

Draft Guidance for Print Ads (2004)

By 2004, after an enormous increase in DTC ads, FDA moved to change its policy on those appearing in print. It was concerned that the long and technical risk descriptions in ads were hard for consumers to understand. FDA requires that any prescription drug advertisement contain "information in brief summary relating to the side effects, contraindications, and effectiveness" of the drug.[38] The information on the risks of the product (known as the brief summary) must disclose all the risk-related information in the drug's package labeling. Consequently, ads in print often include the entire section of the approved professional labeling with its side-effects and warnings.

Therefore, in January 2004, FDA issued three draft guidances: *Brief Summary: Disclosing Risk Information in Consumer-Directed Print Advertisements* (referred to as Brief Summary Guidance below), *"Help-Seeking" and Other Disease Awareness Communications by or on Behalf of Drug and Device Firms* (referred to as Disease Awareness Guidance below), and a third on medical device advertising (which will not be discussed here).

FDA had long required that drug firms disseminate truthful, non-misleading, and scientifically accurate information. FDA now tried, with each of these three guidances, to improve required formats so consumers and health care practitioners could understand and use the information. Now, in 2009, while FDA still describes these documents as draft guidances, they represent current FDA practice.

Brief Summary Guidance

This 2004 draft guidance indicated that, to be in compliance with the statutory brief summary requirement, the following must be printed: all contraindications; all warnings; the major precautions, including any that describe serious adverse drug experiences or steps to be taken to avoid such experiences; and the three to five most common nonserious adverse reactions most likely to affect the patient's quality of life or compliance with drug therapy. The draft guidance then offered manufacturers three options (other than printing the entire professional labeling) for presenting that information to satisfy the brief summary requirement for DTC print ads.[39]

The first option would be to reprint the FDA-approved *patient* labeling in full.[40] For the second option, the manufacturer could print a portion of the patient labeling, including the risk information but omitting, for example, directions for use. The third option would allow printing the "highlights" section of the professional labeling, a format FDA had proposed earlier.[41] But because this highlights section would be written for medical professionals, FDA recommended that it be rewritten so consumers could understand it. The agency also asked drug firms to consider the costs and benefits of each of these options and decide for themselves which option is best.

Supporters of the draft guidance say that shorter ads would mean that industry will spend less and consumers will understand more. Critics argue that this approach may be appropriate for only a small subset of products. They also argue that FDA should develop guidelines requiring risk disclosures that patients can use in discussions with health professionals.[42]

Because the Federal Trade Commission (FTC) regulates most advertising in the United States, FDA asked it to review the three January 2004 draft guidance documents. FTC staff agreed that presenting risk information in more accessible language would be better than reprinting the brief summary. The FTC report recommended, however, that FDA conduct consumer research to "determine ... the most effective means of providing drug risk information in DTC print ads."[43] They suggested assessing the various ways to present risk information, the influence on industry's advertising incentives, and other costs and benefits of the proposed and other formats.

Disease-Awareness Guidance

The agency clarifies in this guidance when it does and does not have jurisdiction over help- seeking ads, which encourage consumers to seek treatment for a medical condition.[44] The draft "Disease Awareness Guidance"[45] provides recommendations on how to make these ads perceptually distinctive from product advertising.[46]

FDA Amendments Act of 2007

Congress addressed DTC advertising more than once in its wide-ranging FDAAA. The issue fit within provisions for funding, drug safety, labeling, and enforcement.[47]

New Fees for the Advisory Review of Advertisements

The law authorized the assessment and collection of fees relating to advisory review of certain drug advertisements. Manufacturer requests for pre-dissemination review of direct-to-consumer (DTC) television drug advertisements would be voluntary, and FDA responses would be advisory. Only manufacturers that request such reviews would be assessed the new fees, which would include an advisory review fee and an operating reserve fee. The law authorized $6.25 million in revenue for each of FY2008 through FY2012, adjusted for inflation and workload. It also set a date by which the Secretary would have to had collected at least $11.25 million in advisory review fees and operating reserve fees combined or else the DTC television advertisement advisory review user fee program could not begin.

FDA announced in January 2008 that it would not begin the DTC television advertisement advisory review fee program. FDAAA authorized FDA to collect and spend user fee funds for the advisory review of DTC television advertisement only if the fees have been appropriated. The Consolidated Appropriations Act, 2008 (P.L. 110-161) did not appropriate user fee funds for that program (*Federal Register*, vol. 73, no. 11, January 16, 2008, p. 2924).

Review before Dissemination

FDAAA authorized the Secretary to require a pre-review (at least 45 days before dissemination) of any television advertisement for a drug. Based on this review, the Secretary may recommend changes that are necessary to protect the consumer, or that are consistent with prescribing information for the product under review; and, if appropriate, statements to include in advertisements to address the specific efficacy of the drug as it relates to specific population groups, including elderly populations, children, and racial and ethnic minorities. The Secretary may, in formulating recommendations, take into consideration the impact of the advertised drug on elderly populations, children, and racially and ethnically diverse communities. Although the amended law described the process for the Secretary to make recommendations, it did not authorize the Secretary to make or direct changes in any material submitted pursuant to this subsection. [Note that this provision addresses the law's earlier prohibition of FDA's requiring *pre*-publication review and approval of an ad. The law continues to require the manufacturer to submit the ad to FDA upon its release.]

Disclosure Requirements

The Secretary may require inclusion of a disclosure in an advertisement if the Secretary determines that the advertisement would be false or misleading without a specific disclosure about a serious risk listed in the labeling of the drug involved.

The Secretary may require, for not more than two years from approval, the advertisement o include a specific disclosure of the approval date if the Secretary determines that the advertisement would otherwise be false or misleading.

Presentation of Side Effects and Contraindications

In a television or radio direct-to-consumer (DTC) advertisement of a drug that states the name of the drug and its conditions of use, the major statement relating to side effects and contraindications must be presented in a clear, conspicuous, and neutral manner. The Secretary must establish standards, by regulation, for determining whether a major statement meets those criteria.

Civil Penalties

FDAAA established civil penalties for the sponsor of a drug or biologic who disseminates a DTC advertisement that is false or misleading. It authorized a civil monetary penalty not to exceed $250,000 for the first violation in any three-year period, and not to exceed $500,000 for each subsequent violation in any three-year period. No other civil monetary penalties in this act shall apply to a violation regarding DTC advertising. Repeated dissemination of the same or similar advertisement prior to the receipt of a written notice shall be considered one violation. After such notification, all violations under this paragraph occurring in a single day shall be considered one violation. The law directed how to consider publications published less frequently than daily, and specifies procedures, after the provision of written notice and opportunity for a hearing, regarding reviews, subpoenas, modifications, and judicial review. Civil penalties may not be assessed if the sponsor had submitted an advertisement for pre-review and incorporated each comment received from the Secretary. If an applicant fails to pay an assessed civil penalty, the Attorney General may recover that amount plus interest.

Study on Risk Communication in DTC Advertising

The Secretary must, with the advice of the Advisory Committee on Risk Communication and within two years of enactment, report to the Congress on DTC advertising and its ability to communicate to subsets of the general population. The Advisory Committee on Risk Communication must study DTC advertising as it relates to increased access to health information and decreased health disparities for these populations, and make recommendations in a report that the Secretary must submit to Congress.

Study on Benefit-Risk Assessments

The Commissioner must submit to Congress, within a year of enactment, a report on how best to communicate to the public the risks and benefits of new drugs and the role of the FDAAA-required risk evaluation and mitigation strategy (REMS) in assessing such risks and benefits. As part of such study, the Commissioner shall consider the possibility of including in the labeling and any DTC advertisements of a newly approved drug or indication a unique symbol indicating the newly approved status of the drug or indication for a period after approval.

Toll-Free Number in Print Ads

Any published DTC advertisement must include the following statement printed in conspicuous text: "You are encouraged to report negative side effects of prescription drugs to the FDA. Visit www.fda.gov/medwatch, or call 1-800-FDA-1088."

The Secretary must, in consultation with the Advisory Committee on Risk Communication, study whether the statement required in published DTC advertisements is appropriate for television DTC advertisements; and report findings and determinations to Congress. If the Secretary determines that including the statement is appropriate, the Secretary must issue regulations to implement such a requirement.

FDA's Review and Enforcement Activities

In 2003, FDA received approximately 38,000 promotional items from drug companies. Of those, somewhat more than 6,000 were print or broadcast ads, and other pieces, aimed at consumers.[48] Manufacturers submit these ads to fulfill the legal requirement that they notify FDA that the ads were running. Manufacturers are not seeking approval of the content or permission to run the ads. It is up to FDA to decide whether the agency should review an ad to see whether it contained false or misleading information—or left out information the law required.

If FDA believes an ad is problematic, it can respond with increasingly severe steps. While the passage of FDAAA in 2007 authorized additional tools (described earlier in this chapter), FDA continues to respond through its traditional steps: an untitled letter, a warning letter, and an injunction.

Letters. FDA can send two types of letters to inform the company that the advertisement violates the FFDCA. The first step is a Notice of Violation, which the agency calls an "untitled letter." Often, the letter states that the ad is misleading because it overstates or guarantees the product's effectiveness, expands the population approved for treatment, or minimizes risk. FDA has the authority to use a second and stronger option. The "warning letter" orders advertisers to respond by a specific deadline. If they don't FDA can take a third step.

Injunction. If warning letters don't succeed, FDA can work with the Department of Justice to seek injunctions against companies. These present companies with a number of possibilities: criminal prosecution, FDA seizure of drugs intentionally misbranded or misleadingly advertised, or the withdrawal of FDA approval for the drug. Very few such cases have actually come to court. In 1995, though, a prominent company pleaded guilty to having promoted its acne treatment drug for use in treating sun-wrinkled or "photoaged" skin. The company paid a $5 million fine and $2.5 million for the costs of the investigation.

FDA believes that the threat of such action makes the warning letter a powerful tool in its regulatory arsenal.

How often does FDA take any of these actions? In 2008, the agency sent 21 letters—10 warning and 11 untitled—concerning promotional labeling, broadcast ads, or print ads that did not comply with regulations.[49]

What kinds of corrections does FDA usually demand? It asks companies to stop running the offending ad. It also may ask them to disseminate corrective information to segments of the audience such as physicians, pharmacists, and patients. At times, FDA directs the companies to run ads in the same media to correct the misleading impressions left earlier.

Courts that have examined FDA's authority to regulate DTC advertisements, have ruled that the agency should not impose unnecessary restrictions on "commercial speech."[50] One unfavorable court decision[51] on such regulation led the agency to question whether it continues to have enough authority to do so. In reaction, FDA published in the Federal Register in May 2002 a notice requesting comment on "commercial speech" issues under the First Amendment.[52] The notice solicited public comments about FDA's legal basis for its regulations, guidances, policies, and practices to ensure the agency continues to comply with the law. Comments have come in over the years but FDA has not yet responded.

The Government Accountability Office (GAO) November 2006 report on DTC drug advertising, noting that FDA reviews only some of the ads, pointed to FDA's "lack of documented criteria for identifying and prioritizing DTC materials for review." Nor does FDA, wrote GAO, track what ads are received or which are reviewed.[53] GAO had made similar comments in a 2002 report.[54] Both reports discussed the amount of time FDA takes to issue regulatory letters, a period during which consumers are exposed to false or misleading information. That length of time increased between the two reports, which the GAO attributes to a 2002 FDA policy that requires the Office of the Chief Counsel to review all draft regulatory letters.

FDA has the statutory authority to impose requirements on the content of advertisements to ensure that ads provide accurate and balanced information. Although FDA officials say the agency does not keep track of the number of ads it receives and reviews, it does not review all DTC ads. In its proposal for a new user fee program to fund its review of DTC television advertising (enacted in FDAAA), FDA proposed a FY2008 performance goal that indicated the agency's current limited resources. Based on an estimated 225 ads (both original and resubmissions), FDA proposed to review 50% of the original submissions within 45 days.

The 111th Congress will likely assess how FDA—with its FDAAA-enhanced authority and possible new directions from a new administration—proceeds.

So far this section has reviewed steps in the formal procedure granted FDA by statute. There is an important informal practice, however, that influences ads aimed at consumers: *prior review*.

Although the law prohibits FDA from requiring prior approval of ads, it does allow FDA to review draft materials that manufacturers voluntarily submit for comment. Drug manufacturers do that to avoid the expense of pulling an already launched ad campaign. In 2007, the agency issued 520 advisory letters to companies regarding their proposed promotional pieces, including items intended for both consumers and clinicians.[55]

These voluntary submissions give FDA an opportunity to object to ads that either omit or minimize risks, promote unapproved uses of the drug or make unsubstantiated claims about how effective and safe the drugs are or how effective the advertised drugs are relative to competitive products.[56]

Funding

Within FDA's Center for Drug Evaluation and Research (CDER), the Division of Drug Marketing, Advertising, and Communications (DDMAC) handles the bulk of review and enforcement activities regarding drug promotion.[57] According to FDA's Office of Budget and Program Analysis, the DDMAC's total budget for FY2008 was over $9 million, of which 63% was for the review of DTC advertisements. This reflects about a $6 million increase in direct appropriations for DTC advertising review that Congress also included in the Omnibus Appropriations Act for FY2009 (P.L. 11 1-8).[58]

One source of funds for regulating DTC advertising could be fees collected under the Prescription Drug User Fee Act (PDUFA).[59] PDUFA's initial authorization in 1992 and its 1997 reauthorization (PDUFA II) restricted FDA's use of user fees to new drug reviews. The Public Health Security and Bioterrorism Preparedness and Response Act of 2002 (P.L. 107-188), which included the PDUFA III authorization, expanded that authority to drug safety activities. It also *authorized* added funds for the DDMAC: an increase of $2.5 million for FY2003, $4 million for FY2004, $5.5 million for FY2005, $7.5 million for FY2006, and $7.5 million for FY2007. The funds were to be used to hire additional staff to monitor broadcast and Internet ads more vigilantly to ensure that the messages conveyed do not mislead consumers. Although the authorization reflected Congress' general concern over drug safety, Congress did not appropriate those sums.

In the reauthorization process for PDUFA III, FDA committed to doubling (to almost 100) the number of staff assigned to monitor the side effects of drugs already on the market and to increase the agency's efforts to provide consumers with the latest information about newly approved drugs.[60]

Critics contend that the reliance on PDUFA funding for employees has created a "cozy relationship" between the agency and drugmakers that has led to less scrutiny of ads and other activities. Agency officials and industry spokesmen say that the user fee funding has not led to a lessening of agency objectivity.[61]

PDUFA IV, part of FDAAA of 2007, authorized $6.25 million per year in new user fees to help fund the review of the DTC television ads that manufacturers ask FDA to review before their public release. FDA noted that this would more than double the entire DDMAC budget and increase sevenfold the amount spent on review of DTC ads. The fees would fund an additional 27 full-time equivalent (FTE) reviewers; currently, there are about 8 FTEs who review broadcast ads.[62] Rather than allow the collection of this new user fee, the appropriators increased the direct appropriations for DTC advertising review, as noted above.

Voluntary Guidelines from Other Interested Parties

To continue the status quo leaves the United States as one of only two countries that allow DTC prescription drug advertising.[63] The federal government, though, is not the only organization trying to create ethical standards for DTC ads. The American Medical Association (AMA) adopted changes in its policy statement on DTC advertising at its annual convention in June 2006.[64] The Pharmaceutical Research and Manufacturers of America (PhRMA) issued a set of 15 DTC advertising guidelines, effective January 2006, as part of a plan that included a new Office of Accountability, an Independent Review Panel, and reports to the public. In a December 2008 revision (effective March 2, 2009), PhRMA added items reflecting the AMA position on physician participation in ads and actors portraying physicians.[65]

ISSUES

Most of the controversy over DTC advertising revolves around five questions:

- Does DTC advertising create an adequately informed consumer?
- Does DTC advertising increase communication between doctor and patient?
- Does DTC advertising lead to better diagnosis, treatment, or disease management?
- Does drug use influenced by DTC advertising harm patients?
- Does DTC advertising affect consumer spending?

These questions are addressed below.

Does DTC Advertising Create an Adequately Informed Consumer?

There is little dispute that DTC advertising informs consumers; however, the extent to which consumers are adequately informed is less clear. In general, ads describe real conditions, list documented symptoms, and contain or refer to pages of labeling information carefully reviewed for accuracy by the FDA.

DTC ads reach many people, as well. In a 2002 FDA national telephone survey, most patients (81%) were aware of DTC ads and knew that the ads contained both benefit and risk information.[66] A 2003-2004 telephone survey by *Prevention* magazine focused on ads for eleven prescription drugs. It found that 96% of its 1,502 interviewees had seen an ad for at least one of the drugs.[67]

But if one defines "informed consumers" as those who not only read or hear an ad, but also understand it—and understand the limitations of what the ad includes—then the picture is less clear.

The question that concerns critics of DTC ads is really whether consumers are *adequately* informed. Are the ads accurate enough? Are they complete enough? Do they balance the discussion of risks and benefits in a way that reflects the research? Can consumers understand them?

To look closely at those questions is to see several important issues. First, most people do not read the entire ad. After seeing a DTC print ad, only 10% of respondents to the FDA survey said they read the entire "brief summary"—the detailed material dealing with risks and benefits.[68]

Second, not all consumers understand the DTC ads they do read or hear. Half of all American adults read at or below an eighth grade reading level.[69] What does this mean when it comes to health literacy and behavior? The most often-quoted survey on this issue is still a 1995 Emory University study of patients seeking care at two urban, public hospitals. One telling finding: 42% could not understand the sentence, "Do not take on an empty stomach."[70]

That many consumers cannot understand the technical language in DTC ads does not necessarily implicate the pharmaceutical industry. Researchers on "health literacy" now see the effects of reading levels on how Americans seek care, follow treatment and medication instructions, and use Internet health material. Compounding these difficulties is an artifact of the historical development of DTC drug advertising. In the 1960s, when Congress added the advertising section to the FFDCA and FDA promulgated the related regulations, almost all drug ads were print ads aimed at doctors.[71] The requirement that those print ads contain the FDA-approved labeling language ensured that physician-readers would have all the information about a drug's risks and benefits. The requirement continues today. Thus, even now the labeling language that appears in many ads is more complicated than what a consumer at an average reading level could understand.[72]

In addition to what consumers do or understand, there is a third issue contributing to whether they are adequately informed. Information may be understandable but not be wholly accurate or balanced. One 2000 study found that less than a third of DTC ads acknowledge competing treatments, and only 9% contain estimates of how often drugs are effective.[73]

In 2000, questions about the information conveyed in advertising led the American Medical Association (AMA) Council on Ethical and Judicial Affairs to review studies of ad content accuracy, arguments for and against DTC advertisements, and physician attitudes.[74] The Council found, for example, that 44% of promotional material to physicians "would lead to improper prescribing," and recommended that physicians "assess and enhance the patient's understanding of what the treatment entails ... resist commercially induced pressure to prescribe such drugs when not indicated ... deny requests for inappropriate prescriptions ... educate patients ... [and] remain vigilant to ensure that DTC advertising does not promote expectations."

Language and persuasion experts agree that one way of persuading audiences is to use the well- respected expert. But what if pharmaceutical ads present an actor who plays an expert in a show, or celebrities Americans admire—and therefore trust—with no expertise at all? Recently such ads have starred well-known performers speaking of their own conditions (Dorothy Hamill, Robert Dole), popular actors (Mandy Patinkin), or real physicians who are not experts in the condition they endorse (Robert Jarvik). Other celebrities (Terry Bradshaw) appear on talk shows, speaking about their own medical difficulties and treatment without acknowledging that a drug company pays them for that exposure.

Concerned that these activities could mislead the public, the American Medical Association issued guidelines in 2006 urging advertisers to, first, not cast actors as physicians in DTC drug ads, and, second, if they do, to include a prominent disclaimer. The AMA guidelines also urged its members to avoid appearing in DTC promotions.[75]

The 2006 AMA trustees' committee report on DTC ads asked "Is DTC educational?" It reported that survey data indicate most doctors would not agree and that their "views are supported by a growing body of scientific research that suggests DTC is not as educational as its proponents would like it to be believed."[76]

A recent study of what information people would like to see in drug advertisements indicated that consumers wanted additional—and quantitative—information about side effects. The author notes that these preferences go beyond what FDA now requires; he concludes by recommending that FDA make specific changes to its regulations.[77]

But DTC ads do not have to meet all the claims of their boosters to be educational. "The good news," says health economist Frank, referring to ads about depression, "is that many people now come in [for treatment] who have serious problems, who otherwise might not."[78] Billy Tauzin, president and CEO of the Pharmaceutical Research and Manufacturers of America (PhRMA), an association representing U.S. research-based pharmaceutical and biotechnology companies, refers to DTC advertising as "a powerful tool for reaching and educating millions of people,"[79] and gives examples of people learning from ads about diseases and treatments.

In addition to citing evidence of the important and positive effects of DTC promotion, Tauzin spoke of ongoing challenges that other industry leaders acknowledge, referring to DTC advertising as "a lightening-rod in the health care debate." Introducing PhRMA's *Guidelines on Direct-to-Consumer Advertising*, Tauzin acknowledged responsibilities that go beyond legal compliance with FDA regulations.[80]

Do DTC ads adequately inform consumers? The cautious tone of the AMA statement, as well as the questions that both critics and supporters raise about understandability, completeness, and accuracy, suggest that consumers could still use more—or different—information than they get.

Does DTC Advertising Increase Useful Communication between Doctor and Patient?

According to surveys of patients and clinicians, DTC ads do increase discussions. Those surveys, however, indicate mixed views of whether that communication is useful. The FDA patient survey reported that DTC ads prompted 43% of respondents to look for more information about a drug or medical condition, with almost 89% of those individuals seeking the information from their physicians (i.e., about 38% of all surveyed).[81] Similarly, 32% of respondents to the *Prevention* survey reported discussing an advertised drug with their physicians.

In April 2006, *PLoS* (Public Library of Science) *Medicine* ran seven essays on "disease mongering," which the lead article defined as "... the selling of sickness that widens the boundaries of illness and grows the markets for those who sell and deliver treatments."[82] The next month, a *Washington Post* article—with the headline "Marketing the Illness and the Cure? Drug Ads May Sell People on the Idea That They Are Sick"—used "restless legs syndrome" to point out the inexact line between attempts to diagnose and treat the small number of people with a serious "bona fide condition," and industry and media actions that take "something that is within normal bounds and label[ing] it a disease needing pharmaceutical treatment."[83]

In a 2002 survey, FDA asked office-based physicians how DTC advertising influenced their practices and their relationships with patients. The respondents reported mixed opinions, saying that DTC ads increased patients' awareness of possible treatments (72%), but lead patients to overestimate the drugs' efficacy (75%). Among the primary care physicians, 38% responded that the overall influence on their patients and practices of DTC ads was somewhat or very negative; 27% of the specialists responded similarly.[84]

Does DTC Advertising Lead to Better Diagnosis, Treatment, or Disease Management?

The 2002 FDA survey found that DTC ads *can* improve patient compliance with physician advice, particularly if physicians remind patients to take the medication as prescribed.[85] At least as of 2000, the authors noted that there is "little research on the clinical consequences" of DTC advertising.[86] To examine this would involve measurement of compliance, outcomes, and other issues.

The industry argues, and some consumers report, that DTC ads encourage patients to seek medical advice for conditions that sometimes go untreated. IMS Health cites urinary incontinence and erectile dysfunction as examples of underdiagnosed and undertreated conditions for which some consumers would not seek medical attention or would be reluctant to discuss with a clinician. The information and tone in DTC ads could precipitate a visit to a doctor.[87]

There is some quantitative evidence supporting the view that DTC ads influence at least some diagnoses and treatment decisions. A group of Harvard and Harris poll researchers asked consumers and physicians how DTC ads affected their encounters. Among consumers who had seen a DTC advertisement, 35% had discussed advertised drugs with their doctors, one-fifth discussed a new concern, one-third discussed a possible change in treatment, and one-quarter were given new diagnoses. The authors discussed the benefits of these diagnoses, 41% of which were for what they called "high priority" conditions.[88]

Despite those figures, the Harvard/Harris survey drew a response from another Harvard health researcher, Jerry Avorn, who criticized the study's industry funding and its conclusion that the "practice [of DTC advertising] is benign."[89] Avorn wrote that the group's data showed, "those heavily influenced by (DTC ads) were no more likely to have new conditions diagnosed or confirmed and were much less likely to have laboratory studies ordered or lifestyle changes recommended."

The Harvard/Harris group sounded a cautionary note, however, when it reported on its interviews with physicians. It found that when patients requested a drug they had seen advertised, doctors would prescribe the drug 39% of the time. But this didn't mean the doctors believed this was the best medical—or economic—option. Over half of the time, the physicians felt that another drug would be equally as effective. Almost 6% of the time that they prescribed a requested advertised drug, physicians felt another drug or type of treatment would have been better for the patient.[90]

Does Drug Use Influenced by DTC Advertising Harm Patients?

Little statistical evidence exists on the scope of harm potentially resulting from DTC ads. Many researchers, though, point to *ways* such adverse effects occur. Sometimes a harmful reaction to a drug occurs in such a small proportion of the people taking it, that the association cannot be identified until after extensive use. Once on the market, a heavily advertised drug can reach millions of people before researchers uncover the potential risk.[91] This was the case not only with Vioxx but also with the heartburn medicine Propulcid following reports of heart rhythm abnormalities and deaths, and the statin Baycol following reports of muscular weakness.[92]

DTC ads potentially put a second group of people at risk: those with characteristics or conditions for which the drug has not been carefully researched. With very few exceptions, once a drug is approved, a physician can prescribe that drug for any purpose.[93] Many of these people will have personal and disease characteristics different from those in the initial clinical trials. A drug approved for use in adults may be prescribed to children. A drug approved for one disease may be prescribed to treat another. Safety and effectiveness for these uses, not having been examined by FDA, are not indicated on the FDA-approved product labeling—hence, the term *off-label* uses.

Off-label use is not necessarily bad; in fact, it can be very good medicine. However, no one, including physicians, yet fully understands the effects of new drugs on unresearched groups or conditions. Even a careful reader of a DTC ad will not learn about the potential risks of off-label use.

Health experts mention indirect damage from what DTC ads might lead people *not* to do. They describe four possibilities.

First, patients might insist on a drug that treats symptoms they have seen described in an ad for one disease, when they have a different disease causing the same symptoms. One researcher cites hypothyroidism and depression as two diseases sometimes confused, but with very different treatments.[94] Although the key error here would be the physician's failure to adequately work-up the patient, a contributing factor could be the persuasive power of DTC ads.

Second, people who have managed a small health problem with over-the-counter medications or lifestyle actions (such as diet or exercise) may now press physicians to provide prescription drugs. FDA's director of the Center for Drug Evaluation and Research, Janet Woodcock, has called this kind of indirect effect the "medicalizing of health," saying that some believe, due to DTC advertising, that "all aches should be treated with some pill."[95]

Third, a person may insist on an advertised drug rather than a more appropriate one. A favorite example of DTC critics: taking Claritin, which at the FDA-approved dose worked only 11% better than a placebo, instead of medicine that relieves allergy symptoms more effectively. "The great majority of DTC drugs," argues Marcia Angell, former Journal of the American Medical Association editor, "are for very expensive me-too drugs that require a lot of pushing because there is not good reason to think they are any better than drugs already on the market."

Finally, there is a fourth indirect effect that deserves a section of its own—the effect of DTC advertising on spending.

Does DTC Advertising Affect Consumer Spending?

It seems likely that DTC advertising does influence consumer behavior, although it is difficult to obtain precise information on how DTC ads affect consumer drug purchasing. However, in 2004, IMS Management Consulting studied 49 advertised drugs for the advertising's return on investment (ROI). For 90% of the drugs, the study showed a positive ROI; that is, more was gained than was spent on advertising. One brand showed a return of $6.50 per advertising dollar invested.[96] A Kaiser Family Foundation study of 1996-1999 data found that a dollar spent on DTC advertising yielded an additional $4.20 in sales.[97]

Although some had posited that by allowing competition via advertising, prices to consumers would be lower,[98] the consensus of economists seems to be that recent growth in DTC advertising has persuaded consumers to substitute new, more expensive drugs for older, lower-priced ones.[99] Although some suggest that advertising costs are passed on to consumers as higher prices, the data on how pharmaceutical companies set prices are proprietary.

Both price and quantity affect total spending. Overall spending reflects more than the price of a specific drug. Increases in drug spending also include significantly greater number of prescriptions being written for an aging population, new standards of medical practice encouraging greater use of drugs, and treatment of previously untreated patients.[100] To assess whether a particular spending level or trend is appropriate would involve more than just examining the amount consumers spend on one advertised drug.

DTC advertising supporters sometimes argue that DTC ads increase spending on drugs but reduce health care spending in other areas. Studies sponsored by both industry and academic researchers suggest that this can sometimes be the case.[101] For example, one National Institutes of Health study found that clot-busting drugs used to treat stroke patients save, on average, $4,300 a year per patient by reducing the need for hospitalization, rehabilitation, and nursing-home care.[102] Others who study the cost-effectiveness of pharmaceuticals, though, say it "depends critically on the context in which the drug is used and the intervention to which it is being compared."[103]

DISCUSSION AND POSSIBLE LEGISLATIVE OPTIONS

The expectations consumers bring to DTC ads may lead them to inaccurate conclusions. A 1999 study found that 43% of the public believed that only "completely safe" drugs could be advertised and half believed that such ads had been submitted to FDA for approval.[104] Neither belief is correct. Many FDA-approved drugs carry risks for certain consumers and may be harmful if used inappropriately by anyone. DTC ads do not have the imprimatur of the agency.

Nevertheless, both industry and consumers strongly support some form of DTC ads. Industry wants to increase sales,[105] and consumers want to actively participate in decisions about their own health. That, combined with advances in information technology and possible relevance to constitutional protections of free speech, makes an outright ban on DTC ads unlikely.[106]

However, Members of the 111th Congress have indicated interest in DTC advertising in the context of drug safety, tax treatment of advertising expenses, risk communication, and general FDA-activity authority and oversight, sometimes in the context of broader discussions of health care costs and reform. Legislators with concerns about DTC advertising still have a range of options to address those concerns. Some would require new statutory authority and some FDA could institute with its current authority.

Activities for Which FDA Already Has Authority

Congress could urge FDA to act more aggressively in its review of ad content, consumer education, and enforcement. FDAAA explicitly directed FDA to increase its dissemination of drug safety and effectiveness information to the public. The law specified, for example, clinical trial results, reviews of approved new drug applications, labeling decisions, adverse event analyses, risk evaluation and mitigation strategy (REMS) decisions. It also required FDA to study how to communicate risk and benefit information to the public.

Increase Post-Publication Review

Although the law explicitly prohibits FDA from requiring pre-publication review and approval of an ad, it does require the manufacturer to submit the ad to FDA upon its release. In congressional testimony and budget justification documents, FDA indicates that it reviews less than half of those within 45 days. That delay in identifying possible inaccurate or imbalanced presentation of risk and benefit information could put the public at risk. FDA could:

- Do a more complete and timely post-publication review of all DTC ads. Set goals; estimate needed resources to do so.

- Track the ensuing recommendations and industry response. With documented counts of numbers of violations; requests for change; and speed, completeness, cooperation (not just the letter of the law); FDA could assess what it could do better under current law and what changes in law it might need to do better.

Expand Industry-Independent Consumer Education

Critics who question the educational component of DTC advertisement have suggested alternatives to consumers' relying on the benefit and risk information gained through submitted DTC ads.[107] FDA or other industry-independent sources could then counter any misinformation or omissions contained in DTC advertising. FDAAA provisions[108] might boost the likelihood of some of the experts' suggestions:

- Rather than leave dissemination of information about new medications to DTC advertisers, FDA could mount public information campaigns itself or encourage or fund others to do so.[109]
- Coordinate consumer information dissemination and research with other federal agencies, such as the Centers for Medicare and Medicaid Services (CMS) and the Agency for Healthcare Research and Quality (AHRQ).
- Create greater access to post-marketing surveillance or clinical trial data.
- Make information available to the public through the Internet, and, possibly, through local pharmacies.[110]
- Clarify to the public the extent of its control over ad content. Surveys indicate that many consumers believe, wrongly, that FDA approves all ads and that some consumers believe, wrongly, that FDA allows ads for only "completely safe" drugs or that these drugs have been shown to be "better" than other drugs.
- Sponsor public education campaigns. In these, FDA could explain the risks and benefits of various types of classes of drugs, the role of promotional materials, and the need for patients to talk to their physicians.
- Study consumer reaction to ads. FDA could increase its study of consumer understanding of risk and benefit information presented by ads or whether the information (such as Patient Medication Guides) about the risks and benefits received by the patient with each new prescription is used. Nonetheless, the agency cannot guarantee how patients will use the added information.[111]
- Create drug information to counter any "biased" or "unbalanced" pictures the manufacturers present in DTC ads. FDA could also use that information to provide patients with medication guides outlining the risks of particular drugs. The FDA advisory committees that met in February 2005 to assess the safety of Vioxx and other COX-2 inhibitors considered these options.[112]

Establish a Commission to Recommend DTC Advertising Standards

If Congress encouraged it to do so, FDA might establish an advisory panel under the Federal Advisory Committee Act which could either itself recommend standards for prescription drug ads,[113] or encourage the drug industry to develop a new set of standards for self-regulation.[114] Some in the drug industry believe that the formation of another advisory panel is unnecessary, and that the industry itself is able to voluntarily adopt its own standards to ensure that ads are reliable, understandable, and trustworthy.[115]

Increase FDA's Enforcement Activity

Until the expanded authority from FDAAA, when FDA saw objectionable things in an ad, it could send what is called an "untitled letter" explaining its objections, refer the matter to the Department of Justice, seize the product as misbranded, or revoke product approval. Even in the small percentage of ads FDA reviews, it rarely takes any of these steps. Congress could encourage FDA to take such steps more often, use the new FDAAA-authorized tools, and even set target goals for increased enforcement activity.

Activities Requiring New Legislation

There are some options Congress might consider for which FDA does not have authority. The most extreme would be a total ban on DTC drug advertising. Aside from that, Congress could opt to not intervene at this time or it could act to increase FDA's authority and ability to take strong, but less absolute, action.

Give FDA Additional Resources

FDA current authority covers more consumer education and DTC advertising enforcement activities than most observers think the agency has the resources to fulfill. To increase the funds available to FDA, Congress could, as examples:

- Amend the user fee statute. As first enacted, the prescription drug user fee statute applied to new product review only. When reauthorizing it in 2002, the Congress expanded FDA's authority to use the collected fees to include limited parts of postmarket surveillance.
- Require industry to bear the cost, through user fees, of direct-to-consumer advertising oversight.[116]
- Create an industry-financed fund to allow an independent entity to perform a range of activities. Examples given include development of ads, Internet and other public information activities, comparative assessment research, and research into what makes ads effective.[117]
- Provide appropriations that more closely match the task.

Ban DTC Advertising

The most extreme approach would be for Congress to ban DTC advertising, although opponents of this approach have raised constitutional issues.[118] Many members of the federal drug advisory panel that considered the COX-2 inhibitors recommended banning DTC ads for these drugs; some recommending a ban on all DTC advertising. Two of six DTC advertising resolutions presented at the 2005 American Medical Association annual meeting proposed a total ban.[119]

A group of 39 organizations, including the American Medical Student Association, Commercial Alert, Florida Alliance for Retired Americans, Gray Panthers, National

Women's Health Network, and Physicians for a National Health Program, began in 2006 to circulate a draft Public Health Protection Act that would ban DTC advertising and serves as an example of what some consumers would like to see. The draft bill presents a set of provisions that would go into effect if the courts were to find that a ban is unconstitutional. These include additional warnings to inform consumers that this drug was approved based on testing of only a few thousand people and that it may be dangerous to your health in ways that this limited research has not yet revealed; a statement that FDA does not certify that this drug is more effective, safer or cheaper than other drugs in its class; changes to the tax code to make DTC advertising expenses not deductible and to add a windfall profits tax to fund NIH-controlled comparative effectiveness studies and their dissemination.[120]

Require Pre-Release Review and Approval

Congress could mandate that FDA review and approve all or a subset of DTC ads prior to their release to the public. The federal advisory meeting mentioned above suggested one possible first step: categorize ads by their potential to create harm. For example, FDA might institute a more rigorous review for extremely popular drugs posing a large opportunity for harm were information to be misleading. FDAAA authorized the Secretary to require review of a television advertisement before its dissemination; the law specifically prohibits the Secretary from requiring changes, allowing only recommendations about changes to the planned ad.

Authorize FDA to Require Changes to Advertising and Labeling Material

Until FDAAA, FDA had approval control over every detail of labeling at the time of a drug's approval, but could not require changes to labeling based on information (about either risk or benefit) that it learns afterward. FDAAA expanded the Secretary's authority to require labeling changes.[121] Because advertising content is limited by law to FDA-approved labeling information, Congress might review FDA's implementation of the FDAAA provisions and then assess the need for more explicit authority regarding changes to advertisements.

Increase Compliance and Enforcement Tools

- Authorize FDA to impose punitive sanctions against companies that violate the law. As FDA begins to implement its FDAAA-provided authority to impose civil monetary penalties for false or misleading advertisements, Congress could assess whether the authorized penalty levels are sufficient to encourage company compliance.

Require Data Collection on All New Drugs Having DTC Ads

Right now, FDA requires drug companies to report quarterly (and annually after three years) about potential problems with a drug and within 15 days of learning of a serious and unexpected adverse event.[122] In response to questioning at Congressional hearings, FDA scientists noted that a signal of a true adverse event can be lost in the enormous amount of material the companies submit.[123]

- Congress could direct FDA to identify a better procedure for industry to flag important safety data and authorize the agency to require companies to comply.

Currently, FDA is not generally authorized to require studies designed to aggressively follow patients (and their diagnoses, pharmaceutical and other medical treatments, and outcomes). Congress, with FDAAA, increased FDA authority to require postmarket studies in certain circumstances. As FDA proceeds with implementation, Congress could assess whether to amend the law with additional or revised authority to:

- Change post-market study requirements to include mandatory reevaluation.
- Strengthen risk evaluation and mitigation strategy (REMS) options or implementation.
- Require commitments to specific postmarket surveillance and studies for initial approval.
- Require commitments to comparative effectiveness trials for initial approval.
- Require commitments to study likely users not considered in preapproval trials.
- Require postmarket studies of situations that had not been anticipated at the time of approval

Prohibit DTC Ads When a Drug Is First Approved

Ray Woosley, president of the Critical Path Institute, testified to the Senate Committee on Health, Education, Labor, and Pensions that a new drug's benefit-risk ratio should be better understood before millions of people are put at risk. He suggested that the agency require data collection on all new drugs that advertise to consumers.[124] At the same hearing, former FDA official William Schultz suggested that "[o]ne possibility is to ban consumer advertising for a period of time (one or two years) after a drug has been approved, as additional data are collected on the drug's safety. Another alternative is to require more explicit and more prominent disclosures [in the ads] about the safety of prescription drugs. In the case of new drugs, manufacturers could be required to include a standard disclosure about the inherent risks of new drugs."[125] FDAAA gave the Secretary the authority to require, for not more than two years from approval, that an advertisement include a specific disclosure of the approval date if the Secretary determines that the advertisement would otherwise be false or misleading.

Set Limits on Timing and Placement of Ads

Some suggest that the agency could also limit the number, type, or content of ads for a particular drug, or the places where the ad was aired, or when the ads could be seen.

- Restrict ads with adult themes to programming aimed at adult audiences. There are those who see a danger to the public, not just in the ad itself but when and where it is placed.

Make DTC Advertising Less Profitable to Industry

There are those who feel DTC ads are not in the public interest and favor banning DTC ads, but see such restrictions as politically or constitutionally unfeasible. They have proposed changes to the Internal Revenue Code and the Social Security Act (SSA) that would decrease the incentive of drug companies to advertise. Three such proposals:

- Prohibit a tax deduction for any amount paid or incurred by the manufacturer for DTC advertising.
- Deny tax deductions for drug ad expenses for manufacturers who do not participate in negotiated rebate and discount agreements with the federal government for residents not otherwise eligible for reduced price prescription drugs.
- Attach requirements to Medicare or Medicaid participation. Because a manufacturer's price is lowered by the rebates and discounts it negotiates with state governments, pharmacies, and others, some have proposed changing the SSA to reflect in those rebates the amount a manufacturer spends on advertising.

CONCLUSION

In his book *Protecting America's Health: The FDA, Business, and One Hundred Years of Regulation*, Philip Hilts describes the early days of patent medicines as "one of the first fully national markets that used nationwide marketing."[126] DTC advertising is not new, and the government's role—to protect the public's health—has not changed. But, as biologic, chemical, and manufacturing knowledge has increased, so too have societal medical and social standards. Current law gives government responsibility for assuring that drugs are safe and effective, yet many now ask increasingly complex questions: Just *how* safe and *how* effective do we want these drugs to be? How much information does the consumer or the doctor need?

Should they rely completely on the government's assessment of the balance of known risks and expected benefits? Is it possible to satisfy the expectation that we summarize what some scientists study for decades in a 60-second television commercial clearly enough for the general U.S. public [127]—to understand?

Finally, we can analyze DTC advertising while paying attention to its role as part of a larger picture. DTC advertising—and the issues it raises of accuracy and balance of safety and effectiveness information—is one piece of the healthcare picture. Widening the focus one step brings us to advertising and other promotion to healthcare providers and the issue of the continuing education of doctors. Other safety and effectiveness issues include drug approval; comparative effectiveness research (among drugs and between drugs and other kinds of treatment); and consideration of off-label prescribing and changing patterns of use. Even broader concerns involve drug research and development and incentives toward the development of drugs that address major public health conditions (measured by number of people affected and seriousness of the disease); risk communication; and access to medical care, including drugs.

End Notes

[1] "Total U.S. Promotional Spend by Type, 2007," IMS Health, 2007 U.S. Sales and Prescription Information, May 14, 2008, at http://www.imshealth.com. Although IMS Health has not yet released its 2008 data, news reports indicated that DTC drug advertising spending declined again in 2008 (Rich Thomaselli, "DTC Spending Falls for Second Consecutive Year: Recession, Regulation and Fewer Blockbusters Mean Less Ads," *Advertising Age*, November 12, 2008).

[2] 21 USC 353(b)(1).

[3] Testimony of David J. Graham, MD, MPH, to the Senate Committee on Finance hearing "FDA, Merck and Vioxx: Putting Patient Safety First?" November 18, 2004, at http://finance.senate.gov/hearings/testimony/2004test/ 111804dgtest.pdf; and Alex Berenson, "Plaintiffs Find Payday Elusive in Vioxx Cases," *New York Times*, August 21, 2007.

[4] Drug companies rely on DTC advertising to stimulate demand and to increase sales for the products (Testimony of Gregory J. Glover, representing the Pharmaceutical Research and Manufacturers of America before the U.S. Congress, Senate Committee on Commerce, Science, and Transportation, Subcommittee on Consumer Affairs, Foreign Commerce, and Tourism, *Prescription Drug Issues*, hearings, 107th Cong., 1st sess., July 24, 2001, hereinafter cited as Glover testimony).

[5] Pauline Norris, Andrew Herzheimer, Joel Lexchin, and Peter Mansfield, *Drug promotion: what we know, what we have yet to learn*, World Health Organization and Health Action Int'l., 2005, p. 3, at http://www.who.int/medicines/ areas/rational_use/drugPromodhai.pdf.

[6] Michael S. Wilkes, Robert A. Bell, and Richard L. Kravitz, "Direct to Consumer Prescription Drug Advertising: Trends, Impact, and Implications," *Health Affairs*, March/April 2000. The authors attribute the definition to R.G. Frank et al., *Prescription Drug Policy Issues In California*, a report prepared for the California HealthCare Foundation, April 1999.

[7] The Federal Food, Drug, and Cosmetic Act (21 U.S.C. Sec. 301 et seq.) is the primary source of FDA's authority to regulate drugs.

[8] 21 CFR 202.1(l)(1).

[9] Francis B. Palumbo and C. Daniel Mullins, "The Development of Direct-to-Consumer Prescription Drug Advertising Regulation," *Food and Drug Law Journal*, vol. 57, no. 3, 2002.

[10] FDA, at http://www.fda.gov/cder/handbook/adverdef.htm.

[11] Most doctors deny that these items improperly influence them (see, for example, Frederick S. Sierles, "Clinical Case: The gift-giving influence," *Virtual Mentor: Ethics Journal of the American Medical Association*, vol. 9, no. 6, June 2006, pp. 372-376, at http://www.ama-assn.org/ama/pub/category/16252.html; and Ashley Wazana, "Physicians and the Pharmaceutical Industry: Is a Gift Ever Just a Gift?" *Journal of the American Medical Association*, vol. 283, no. 3, January 19, 2000, pp. 373-380).

Those who disagree point to social science research that finds that even small gifts create an often unconscious "impulse to reciprocate" (TA Brennan, DJ Rothman, L Blank, D Blumenthal, SC Chimonas, JJ Cohen, J Goldman, JP Kassirer, H Kimball, J Naughton, Neil Smelser, "Health Industry Practices That Create Conflicts of Interest: A Policy Proposal for Academic Medical Centers," *Journal of the American Medical Association*, vol. 295, no. 4, January 25, 2006, pp. 429-433).

IMS, conducting a test for an advertising agency, sent e-mail product reminders to one group of doctors and none to a control group. Those sent the e-mails wrote 11.2% more new prescriptions for those brands than did the others (IMS Health, "The E-Detail: How Well Does it Work? Objectively Measuring Program Impact," at http://www.imshealth.com.

[12] Data from "Total U.S. Promotional Spend by Type, 2003," "Total U.S. Professional Spend by Type," and "Total U.S. Value of Free Product Samples," IMS Health, Integrated Promotional Services™ and CMR, June 2004; and "Total U.S. Promotional Spend by Type, 2005," "Total U.S. Professional Promotional Spend by Type, 2005," and "Total U.S. Value of Free Product Samples, 2004," at http://www.imshealth.com.

[13] Bureau of Labor Statistics, Consumer Price Index (CPI-U all items), 1996-2005, Department of Labor, at http://data.bls.gov/PDQ/servlet/SurveyOutputServlet.

[14] IMS Health, "Total U.S. Promotional Spend by Type, 2003," "Total U.S. Professional Spend by Type," and "Total U.S. Value of Free Product Samples," IMS Health, Integrated Promotional Services™ and CMR, June 2004, at http://www.imshealth.com.

[15] In earlier years, IMS included the retail value of drug samples provided to health care professionals in its tables of promotional spending, although the actual cost of the samples to industry is only a small fraction of the retail price. When the total is calculated to include the retail value of samples, the DTC advertising percentage of all reported promotional spending is greatly reduced. For example, see 2004, the last year for which IMS provided the retail value of samples. Excluding samples, DTC advertising was 33.9% of the total. Including samples, DTC advertising was 14.4% of the total.

Although IMS Health has not reported drug sample values for years after 2004, other sources have described decreased numbers of samples in 2007 overall, but increases in the 10 most sampled brands (Susan Vargas, "Under pressure: promotional spending is down as companies rationalize and optimize budgets," *Pharmaceutical Executive*, vol. 28, no. 5, May 2008, p. 87).

[16] Tony Pugh, "Old-style marketing for new drugs: Coupons elicit FDA attention," MercuryNews.com, May 6, 2006.

[17] TNS Media Intelligence, in *Medical Marketing & Media*, vol. 43, no. 6, June 2008, p. 53.

[18] Data used in Tables 1 and 2 come from different sources and the total DTC expenditure figures do not match; within each table, relationships among rows should be internally valid. The industry tracks subcategories of spending as well. Television, for example, includes network television, cable television, syndicated television,

spot television, Spanish language network TV, Spanish language cable TV (*Med Ad News*, vol. 25, no. 5, May 2006).

[19] A 1999 discussion of the law related to drug advertising on the Internet noted that "market researchers predict that the Internet will become the single greatest source of health care information within the next five years" (Leah Brannon, "Regulating Drug Promotion on the Internet," *Food and Drug Law Journal*, vol. 54, no. 4, 1999, p. 599). See, also, "Healthcare Advertising Faces Upheaval With Small Share of Total Online Spend, Yet Fastest Rate of Growth, According to New Outsell Report," PharmaLive.com, April 24, 2006, athttp://www.outsellinc.com/press/ press_releases/healthcare_advertising_faces_upheaval.

[20] Susan Vargas, "Under pressure: promotional spending is down as companies rationalize and optimize budgets," *Pharmaceutical Executive*, vol. 28, no. 5, May 2008, p. 87.

[21] For example, using disease-group Web sites and other social marketing techniques "allow drug companies to reach very small niche groups, such as patients with a specific type of cancer.... " (Linda A. Johnson, "Consumer drug ads down this year, report says," *USA Today*, November 14, 2008). The Internet is one part of what some marketers call a "surround sound approach" that could include direct marketing, materials in doctors' offices, phone calls from nurse counselors, surveys, and newsletters ("United States annual pharmaceuticals direct-marketing advertising expenditures by advertising medium in dollars for 2002 to 2007, and forecast for 2008 and 2012," *Medical Marketing & Media*, vol. 43, no. 2, February 2008, p. 58). A marketer might use varied tactics in a coordinated effort to attract patients to a drug, perhaps have them switch from another brand, and then to retain the patients as customers.

[22] "Pharmaceutical product placements: the next DTC?" *Pharmaceutical Executive*, vol. 28, no. 10, October 2008, p. SS8.

[23] Ibid.

[24] For a description of the U.S. drug approval process, see CRS Report RL32797, *Drug Safety and Effectiveness: Issues and Action Options After FDA Approval*, by Susan Thaul.

[25] Section 201, FFDCA, P.L. 75-717, 1938.

[26] The two agencies acted to avoid overlap based on a 1954 "Working Agreement Between the Federal Trade Commission and the Food and Drug Administration." FDA and FTC amended the Agreement in 1968 "to provide explicit guidelines for prescription drug advertising" and again in 1971 (Francis B. Palumbo and C. Daniel Mullins, "The Development of Direct-to-Consumer Prescription Drug Advertising Regulation," *Food and Drug Law Journal*, vol. 57, no. 3, 2002).

[27] 21 USC 352(n).

[28] The 1951 Durham-Humphrey Amendment to the FFDCA defined in law for the first time a distinction between medications that required physician supervision and those that did not (Alan H. Kaplan, "Fifty Years of Drug Amendments Revisited: In Easy-to-Swallow Capsule Form," *Food and Drug Law Journal*, vol. 50, no. 5, 1995, pp. 179-196).

[29] 21 CFR 202.1.

[30] 21 CFR 314.81(b)(3)(I).

[31] FFDCA Sec. 201(m) defines labeling to include "... all labels and other written, printed, or graphic matter ... accompanying" the drug. FDA regulations (21 CFR 202.1(l)(2)) include examples of labeling, which is also known as the full prescribing information: "Brochures, booklets, mailing pieces, detailing pieces, file cards, bulletins, calendars, price lists, catalogs, house organs, letters, motion picture films, film strips, lantern slides, sound recordings, exhibits, literature, and reprints and similar pieces of printed, audio or visual matter descriptive of a drug and references published (for example, the Physician's Desk Reference) for use by medical practitioners, pharmacists, or nurses, containing drug information supplied by the manufacturer, packer, or distributor of the drug and which are disseminated by or on behalf of its manufacturer, packer, or distributor are hereby determined to be labeling as defined in section 201(m) of the FD&C Act." See FDA, "Advertising/Labeling Definitions," at http://www.fda.gov/cder/ handbook/adverdef.htm.

[32] See http://www.fda.gov/cder/guidance/index.htm.

[33] PhRMA, "Direct to Consumer Advertising," *Backgrounders and Facts*, at http://www.phrma.org/publications/ backgrounders/2000.

[34] Wayne L. Pines, "A History and Perspective on Direct-to-Consumer Promotion," *Food and Drug Law Journal*, vol. 54, no. 4, 1999, pp. 489-518.

[35] FDA, *Guidance for Industry: Consumer-Directed Broadcast Advertisements*, Division of Drug Marketing, Advertising, and Communications (DDMAC), August 1999, at http://www.fda.gov/cder/guidance /1804fnl.htm. The only significant change in the final guidance was the clarification of FDA's thinking that its guidance on broadcast DTC advertising could also be used for telephone advertisements (64 *Federal Register* 43197, August 9, 1999).

[36] Pines, 1999.

[37] FDA, *Guidance for Industry: Consumer-Directed Broadcast Advertisements*, August 1999. Also see Council on Ethical and Judicial Affairs of the American Medical Association, "Direct-to-Consumer Advertisements of Prescription Drugs," *Food and Drug Law Journal*, vol. 55, 2000, p. 120. Web-based sites, whether third-party or proprietary, usually contain a link to a site that advertises one company's product. Experts suggest that the

line between information and promotion has been blurred (Alex Frangos, "Special Report: E-Commerce; Prescription for Change," *Wall Street Journal*, April 23, 2001).

[38] FFDCA 502(n) [21 USC 352(n)].

[39] FDA, "[DRAFT] Guidance for Industry: Brief Summary: Disclosing Risk Information in Consumer-Directed Print Advertisements, Division of Drug Marketing, Advertising, and Communications," CDER, January 2004, at http://www.fda.gov/cder/guidance/5669dft.pdf.

[40] This could be the Patient Package Insert (PPI), special patient materials that FDA approves that are used to instruct patients about the safe use of the prescription product in simple, easily understood language. These materials may be given to patients by their health care provider or pharmacist and are part of FDA-regulated product labeling. They are based on the approved labeling of the drug.

[41] FDA, "[DRAFT] Guidance for Industry: Content and Format of the Adverse Reactions Section of Labeling for Human Prescription Drugs and Biologics," May 2000, at http://www.fda.gov/cder/guidance/1888dft.pdf.

[42] Rosemary C. Harold and John F. Kamp, "Grounding Regulations in Behavior Science: Strengthening FDA's Approach to DTC Risk Disclosures," *Update, Food and Drug Law, Regulation, and Education*, Issue 6, November/December 2004, pp. 8-12.

[43] FTC, "In the Matter of Request for Comments on Agency Draft Guidance Documents Regarding Consumer-Directed Promotion," Docket No. 2004D-0042. May 10, 2004, at http://www.ftc.gov/os/2004/05/040512dtcdrugscomment.pdf; and FTC, "FTC Staff Provides Comments to FDA on Direct-to-Consumer Drug and Device Ads," *FTC: For the Consumer*, May 12, 2004, at http://www.ftc.gov/opa/2004/05/dtcdrugs.htm.

[44] The FTC has jurisdiction over these types of communications and could investigate and challenge ads if they appeared to be "unfair or deceptive acts or practices" (15 U.S.C. §45, in general; 15 U.S.C. §52, specifies drugs and devices).

[45] FDA, "[Draft] Guidance for Industry: 'Help-Seeking' and Other Disease Awareness Communications by or on Behalf of Drug and Device Firms," January 2004, at http://www.fda.gov/cder/guidance/6019dft.doc.

[46] "Disease Awareness Ad Guidance Stresses Need for 'Distinct' Messages," *The Pink Sheet*, F-D-C Reports, Inc., Chevy Chase, MD, February 9, 2004, p. 6.

[47] CRS Report RL34465, *FDA Amendments Act of 2007 (P.L. 110-85)*, by Erin D. Williams and Susan Thaul.

[48] Estimate from statement of Janet Woodcock, CDER director, FDA, before the Senate Special Committee on Aging, July 22, 2003, at http://www.fda.gov/ola/2003/AdvertisingofPrescriptionDrugs0722.html.

[49] See FDA warning letters at http://www.fda.gov/cder/warn/warn2008.htm.

[50] George W. Evans and Arnold I. Friede, "The Food and Drug Administration's Regulation of Prescription Drug Manufacturer Speech: A First Amendment Analysis," *Food and Drug Law Journal*, vol. 58, no. 3, 2003, pp. 365-437.

[51] *Thompson v. Western States Medical Center*, 535 U.S. 357 (2002). In this case, the Supreme Court struck a FDA Modernization Act (FDAMA) pharmacy compounding provision. Pharmacy compounding involves a pharmacist mixing a slightly altered version of a drug for an individual, such as removing a preservative for a patient who is allergic to that preservative. The FDAMA provision said that a drug could be compounded only if the physician or pharmacist does not advertise or promote the compounding of a particular drug, class, or type of drug. The Supreme Court ruled that the provision's advertising restrictions violate the First Amendment of the Constitution. *FDA Week*, June 21, 2002.

[52] "FDA Seeks Comment on Ad Regs: Can Rx Be More Regulated Than OTCs?" *The Pink Sheet*, v. 64, no. 20, May 20, 2002, p. 14; and HHS, FDA, Request for Comment on First Amendment Issues, 67 *Federal Register* 34942, May 16, 2002. See also CRS Report 95-815, *Freedom of Speech and Press: Exceptions to the First Amendment*, by Henry Cohen.

[53] U.S. Government Accountability Office, *Prescription Drugs: Improvements Needed in FDA's Oversight of Direct-to-Consumer Advertising*, GAO-07-54, November 2006.

[54] U.S. General Accounting Office, *Prescription Drugs: FDA Oversight of Direct-to-Consumer Advertising Has Limitations*, GAO-03-177, October 2002.

[55] FDA, "CDER 2007 Update: Drug Promotion Review," July 31, 2008, at http://www.fda.gov/ cder/reports/rtn/2007/ 12_promotion_review.htm.

[56] Thomas W. Abrams, FDA Division of Drug Marketing, Advertising, and Communications, "DDMAC Update-Regulation of Prescription Drug Promotion," February 26, 2004, slide presentation at http://www.fda.gov/cder/ddmac/Presentations/DIA/DIA%20022604%20Slides.ppt.

[57] DDMAC had about 50 full-time equivalent employees in FY2008 (FDA Office of Budget and Program Analysis, telephone conversation, March 18, 2009). In 2003, about 40 people worked in DDMAC (Woodcock, July 2003 Senate testimony).

[58] The FDA Office of Budget and Program Analysis provided details of FY2008 direct appropriations for DDMAC (by telephone, March 18, 2009, in response to CRS request to the FDA Office of Legislation). In contrast, DDMAC's total budget for FY2006 was $4.26 million, of which almost 21% was for the review of DTC advertisements.

[59] For a description and analysis of PDUFA, see CRS Report RL33914, *The Prescription Drug User Fee Act (PDUFA): History, Reauthorization in 2007, and Effect on FDA*, by Susan Thaul.

[60] See CRS Report RL31453, *The Prescription Drug User Fee Act: Structure and Reauthorization Issues*, by Donna U. Vogt and Blanchard I. Randall IV.

[61] See CRS Report RL33914, *The Prescription Drug User Fee Act (PDUFA): History, Reauthorization in 2007, and Effect on FDA*, by Susan Thaul.

[62] Presentation to congressional staff by Theresa Mullin, FDA Assistant Commissioner for Planning, accompanied by Jane Axelrad and Steve Mason, January 2007.

[63] The only other country allowing DTC advertising is New Zealand. The United States and New Zealand do not have the same regulatory system. New Zealand relies on an industry-based advertising framework or code of conduct. All ads making therapeutic claims must be pre-approved by the Association of New Zealand Advertisers, Therapeutic Advertising Pre-vetting Service; also, the media, which depends on ads for revenue, is responsible for accepting only ads that have been pre-approved (Janet Hoek and Philip Gendall, "Direct-to-Consumer Advertising Down Under: An Alternative Perspective and Regulatory Framework," *Journal of Public Policy & Marketing*, vol. 21, no. 2, fall 2002, pp. 202-212). Similar to the United States, the New Zealand law requires that the advertisement contain information including active ingredients, authorized uses, appropriate precautions, contraindications and adverse reactions. New Zealand and Australia had worked to combine regulatory activities that concern prescription drugs and advertising. Their proposed model for advertising, accepted by an interim council in 2005, set forth three key principles and 11 requirements. In 2006, they issued the "Draft Australia New Zealand Therapeutic Products Regulatory Scheme (Advertising) Rule 2006" for public comment (The "Joint Regulatory Scheme for Advertising of Therapeutic Products" and other relevant documents are available at http://www.tgamedsafe.org/advert/advmodel.htm; and the 2006 rule is at http://www.anztpa.org.nz/consult/dr-advertrule.pdf). In 2007, plans for a trans-Tasmanian regulatory authority were dropped ("Postponement of the ANZTPA Establishment Project," New Zealand Medicines and Medical Devices Safety Authority, at http://www.anztpa.org.nz).

[64] The AMA website presents all of the 2006 convention recommendations marked-up to show the changes to be made to existing policy; this is available at http://www.ama-assn.org/ama1/pub/upload/mm/471/co meannotateda06.doc. The approved AMA Policy H-105.988, "Direct-to-Consumer Advertising of Prescription Drugs and Implantable Medical Devices (DTC)," is at http://www.ama-assn.org/apps/pf_new /pf_online?f_n=browse&doc=policyfiles/HnE/H-
105.988.HTM&&s_t=&st_p=&nth=1&prev_pol=policyfiles/HnE/H-
100.997.HTM&nxt_pol=policyfiles/HnE/H-105.988.HTM&.

[65] PhRMA, "PhRMA Guiding Principles: Direct to Consumer Advertisements About Prescription Medicines," revised November 2005, at http://www.phrma.org/files/2005-11-29.1194.pdf; revised December 2008, at http://www.phrma.org/files/PhRMA%20Guiding%20Principles_Dec%2008_FINAL.pdf.

[66] Kathryn J. Aikin, John L. Swasy, and Amie C. Braman, *Patient and Physician Attitudes and Behaviors Associated with DTC Promotion of Prescription Drugs: Summary of FDA Survey Research Results*, Final Report, U.S. Department of Health and Human Services, Food and Drug Administration, Center for Drug Evaluation and Research, November 19, 2004. (Hereinafter FDA–Aikin, 2004.) The survey included English-speaking adults who had visited a health care provider within the last three months for a health condition of their own. For the 1999 survey, a 65% response rate yielded 960 patients. For the 2002 survey, a 53% response rate yielded 944 people. The physician survey, which interviewed 250 primary care and 250 specialty physicians, achieved a 46% response rate from physicians chosen randomly from the American Medical Association master file.

[67] Ed Slaughter, Corporate Director, Advertising and Trends Research, Rodale Inc., 7th Annual Survey (2003-2004), "Consumer Reaction to DTC Advertising of Prescription Medicines," *Prevention Magazine*, 2004. (Hereinafter Prevention—Slaughter, 2004.)

[68] FDA–Aikin, 2004.

[69] Darrell M. West, "State and Federal E-Government in the United States, 2003," September 2003, at http://www.insidepolitics.org/egovt03us.html.

[70] M.V. Williams, P.R. Parker, D.W. Baker, N.S. Parikh, K. Pitkin, W.C. Coates and J.R. Nurss, "Inadequate functional health literacy among patients at two public hospitals," *Journal of the American Medical Association*, vol. 274, no. 21, December 6, 1995. A similar study in a Medicare managed care population found that 48% of the patients with inadequate or marginal health literacy (34% of English speakers and 54% of Spanish speakers) could not correctly interpret directions "How to take medication on an empty stomach" (Julie A. Gazmararian, David W. Baker, Mark V. Williams, Ruth M. Parker, Tracy L. Scott, Diane C. Green, S. Nichole Fehrenbach, Junling Ren, and Jeffrey P. Koplan, "Health Literacy Among Medicare Enrollees in a Managed Care Organization," *Journal of the American Medical Association*, vol. 281, no. 6, February 10, 1999, pp. 545-551).

[71] David L. Riggs, Stacy M. Holdsworth, and David R. McAvoy, "Direct-To-Consumer Advertising: Developing Evidence-Based Policy To Improve Retention And Comprehension," *Health Affairs*, Web Exclusive, April 28, 2004, pp. W4-249-252.

[72] Yet, many, but not most, consumers believe they are getting sufficient information. The *Prevention* report (Prevention—Slaughter, 2004, tables 22, 24, and 34) notes, for example, that among the 36% who read the

     "brief summary" in a print ad, 32% found it "very clear." It also found that 32% say that the DTC ad "provides enough information to decide if benefit of using advertised drugs outweighs risk."

[73] Wilkes et al., 2000.

[74] American Medical Association (AMA) Council on Ethical and Judicial Affairs, "Direct-to-Consumer Advertisements of Prescription Drugs," *Food and Drug Law Journal*, vol. 55, 2000, p. 121.

[75] Editorial, "Building a better drug ad: Direct-to-consumer marketing," *American Medical News*, July 24/31, 2006, at http://www.ama-assn.org/amednews/2006/07/24/edsa0724.htm.

[76] AMA, Report 9 of the Board of Trustees (Duane M. Cady, Chair), "Direct-to-Consumer Advertising of Prescription Drugs," for consideration at the 2006 annual meeting regarding resolutions 507, 519, 524, 532, 533, and 534 from the 2005 annual meeting, at http://www.ama-assn.org/ama1/pub/upload/mm/471/bot9A06.doc.

[77] Joel J. Davis, "Consumers' Preferences For The Communication Of Risk Information in Drug Advertising," *Health Affairs*, vol. 26, no. 3, May/June 2007, pp. 863-870.

[78] Richard Frank interview quoted in: Ashley Pettus, "Psychiatry by Prescription," *Harvard Magazine*, July-August 2006, p. 90.

[79] Billy Tauzin, "Putting Patients First to Keep Health Care in America the Best in the World," keynote address before the American Legislative Exchange Council Annual Dinner, Gaylord, Texas, October 24, 2005, at http://www.phrma.org/straight_talk_from_billy_tauzin/.

[80] Pat Kelly, "DTC Advertising's Benefits Far Outweigh Its Imperfections," *Health Affairs*, Perspectives, April 28, 2004, pp. W4-246-248; Hank McKinnell (former Chairman & CEO, Pfizer Inc.) with John Kador, *A Call to Action: Taking Back Healthcare for Future Generations*, New York: McGraw-Hill, 2005, p. 180; and Billy Tauzin, "A Research-based Pharmaceutical Sector Built to Meet The Challenges of the 21st Century," remarks before the National Venture Capital Association, San Diego, Calif., April 26, 2006, at http://www.phrma.org/straight_talk_from_billy_tauzin/.

[81] Respondents said they sought information (after seeing a DTC advertisement) from their pharmacists (51%), their physicians (89%), reference books (40%), and friends, relatives, and neighbors (38%) (FDA–Aikin, 2004).

[82] Ray Moynihan and David Henry, "The fight against disease mongering: Generating knowledge for action," *PLoS Med* 3(4):e191, April 2006.

[83] Rob Stein, "Marketing the Illness and the Cure? Drug Ads May Sell People on the Idea That They Are Sick," *Washington Post*, May 30, 2006, p. A3.

[84] FDA–Aikin, 2004.

[85] FDA–Aikin, 2004; and Testimony of Senior Assistant General Counsel Marjorie E. Powell, Pharmaceutical Research and Manufacturers of America, before the U.S. Congress, Senate Special Committee on Aging, *Direct to Consumer Advertising: What are the Consequences?*, hearings, 108th Cong., 1st sess., July 22, 2003.

[86] Wilkes et al., 2000.

[87] IMS, "DTC at the Crossroads: A 'Direct' Hit or Miss?" 2004.

[88] Joel S. Weissman, David Blumenthal, Alvin J. Silk, Kinga Zapert, Michael Newman, and Robert Leitman, "Consumers' Reports on the Health Effects of Direct-to-Consumer Drug Advertising," *Health Affairs—Web Exclusive*, February 26, 2003, pp. W3-82 to W3-95. This national telephone survey of 3,000 adults had a 53% response rate. The authors used the following "high priority" conditions: cancer, diabetes, emphysema, high cholesterol, HIV/AIDS, hypertension, ischemic heart disease, stroke, arthritis, asthma, gall bladder disease, stomach ulcer, back problems, Alzheimer's disease and other dementias, and depression and anxiety disorders.

[89] Jerry Avorn, "Advertising And Prescription Drugs: Promotion, Education, And The Public's Health," *Health Affairs*, Web Exclusive, February 26, 2003, pp. W3-104-108.

[90] Joel S. Weissman, David Blumenthal, Alvin J. Silk, Michael Newman, Kinga Zapert, Robert Leitman, and Sandra Feibelmann, "Physicians Report on Patient Encounters Involving Direct-to-Consumer Advertising," *Health Affairs*, Web Exclusive, April 28, 2004, p. W4-226. Questionnaires were sent to 1,300 physicians, of whom 53% responded.

[91] A side effect that occurs in, say, 1 out of 10,000 patients may not have been encountered in premarket trials involving 2,000 patients. It would, however, harm 100 of the first million people to take the drug after approval.

[92] FDA, "Janssen Pharmaceutica Stops Marketing Cisapride in the US," *FDA Talk Paper*, March 23, 2000, at http://www.fda.gov/bbs/topics/ANSWERS/ANS01007.html; and FDA, "Bayer Voluntarily Withdraws Baycol," *FDA Talk Paper*, August 8, 2001, at http://www.fda.gov/bbs/topics/ANSWERS/2001/ANS01095.html.

[93] Remarks by Scott Gottlieb, Deputy Commissioner for Medical and Scientific Affairs, FDA, before the American Medical Association, June 12, 2006, at http://www.fda.gov/oc/speeches/2006/ama0612.html; and statement by William B. Schultz, Deputy Commissioner for Policy, FDA, before the Committee on Labor and Human Resources, United States Senate, February 22, 1996, at http://www.fda.gov/ola/1996/s1447.html. In general, the practice of medicine (and pharmacy and other health professions) is regulated at the state level.

[94] Wilkes et al., 2000.

[95] Comments made by Janet Woodcock, then Director of the Center for Drug Evaluation and Research, at a public meeting called "Research on Consumer Directed Advertising," held by the FDA, Center for Drug Evaluation and Research, September 22-23, 2003. Wilkes et al., 2000, also refer to the "medicalization of trivial ailments," p. 121. Weissman et al., 2003, warn of the harm that follows "possibly deceptive advertising, or overuse that may result from targeting relatively healthy people or by 'medicalizing' nonmedical problems."

[96] IMS Management Consulting, "DTC at the Crossroads: A 'Direct' Hit or Miss?" *IMS Issues and Insights*, September 23, 2004, at http://www.imshealth.com.

[97] Meredith B. Rosenthal, Ernst R. Berndt, Julie M. Donohue, Arnold M. Epstein, and Richard G. Frank, "Demand Effects of Recent Changes in Prescription Drug Promotion," The Kaiser Family Foundation, June 2003, pp. 18-19.

[98] Glover testimony, 2001.

[99] Stephen Heffler, Katharine Levit, Sheila Smith, Cynthia Smith, Cathy Cowan, Helen Lazenby, and Mark Freeland, "Health Spending Growth Up In 1999; Faster Growth Expected In The Future," *Health Affairs*, vol. 20, no. 2, March/April 2001, pp. 193-202.

[100] Testimony of Paul Antony, chief medical officer, PhRMA, to the U.S. Senate Special Committee on Aging hearing on direct-to-consumer advertising, September 29, 2005, at http://www.phrma.org/publications/testimony_and_official_submissions.

[101] Frank Lichtenberg, "Benefits and Costs of Newer Drugs: An Update," *Working Paper 8996*. National Bureau of Economic Research, June 2002, at http://www.nber.org/papers/w8996.

[102] S.C. Fagan, L.B. Morgenstern, A. Petitta, R.E. Ward, B.C. Tilley, J.R. Marler, S.R. Levine, J.P. Broderick, T.G. Kwiatkowski, M. Frankel, T.G. Brott, M.D. Walker, and the NINDS rt-PA Stroke Study Group, "Cost-Effectiveness of Tissue Plasminogen Activator for Acute Ischemic Stroke," *Neurology*, vol. 50, April 1998, pp. 883-890.

[103] Peter J. Neumann, Eileen A. Sandberg, Chaim M. Bell, Patricia W. Stone, and Richard H. Chapman, "Are Pharmaceuticals Cost-Effective? A Review of the Evidence," *Health Affairs*, vol. 19, no. 2, March/April 2000, pp. 97, 99, and 104. The authors cite examples of successful interventions that produce health benefits for relatively little cost or save money for the health care system: warfarin therapy to prevent stroke in those patients with atrial fibrillation, immunosuppressive drugs for those with kidney transplants, and drug treatment for some people with depression.

[104] Wilkes et al., 2000.

[105] Drug companies rely on DTC advertising to stimulate demand and to increase sales for the products (Glover testimony, 2001, p. 5).

[106] For a related discussion, see CRS Report 95-815, *Freedom of Speech and Press: Exceptions to the First Amendment*, by Henry Cohen.

[107] "Panel Backs Interactions Database, CERTs, Adverse-Event Repository," *FDA Week*, vol. 8, no. 24, June 14, 2002, pp. 8-9; and Eric J. Topol, "Editorial: Arthritis Medicines and Cardiovascular Events—'House of Coxibs,'" *Journal of the American Medical Association*, vol. 293, no. 3, January 19, 2005, pp. 366-368.

[108] FDAAA required that the Secretary develop and maintain an Internet website with an extensive range of easily searchable drug safety information to allow patients and health care providers better access to information. The website must include links to other government sites; professional and patient labeling; FDA alerts, warning letters, guidance documents, and regulations; summaries of aggregate surveillance data; and the clinical trials registry and results data bank.

[109] In 2008, FDA launched a new Web page called "Be Smart About Prescription Drug Advertising: A Guide for Consumers" that includes a list of questions to consider when seeing a DTC advertisement (at http://www.fda.gov/cder/ ethicad/background.htm). Purporting to provide accurate science-based information, the FDA-sponsored project drew criticism from the Center for Science in the Public Interest (CSPI) and some Members of Congress because they say the nonprofit group (EthicAd) the agency contracted to develop the site has strong pharmaceutical industry ties (see "Pay No Attention to the Industry-Funded Group Behind the Website," Center for Media and Democracy, at http://www.prwatch.org/node/7765).

[110] FDA has instituted new ways to disseminate drug information to the public. WebMD, in partnership with FDA, hosts public health alerts and safety information on FDA products (at http://www.WebMD.com/FDA). Also, FDA, along with CDC, is using "social media resources," such as podcasts, YouTube video, Twitter, and blogs, to inform consumers about product recalls (HHS, "Social Media Resources Tapped to Deliver Consumers Information on Salmonella Typhimurium Outbreak, *News Release*, February 2, 2009).

[111] Complying with FDAAA requirements, FDA has met with the Advisory Committee on Risk Communication in connection with: seeking public comments regarding how DTC advertising communicates to subsets of the general population regarding increasing access to health information and decreasing health disparities (FDA, *Federal Register*, vol. 73, no. 82, April 28, 2008, pp. 22959-22960); and a study on visual distractions in broadcast ads and their relationship to whether ads meet the FDAAA requirement that side effects and contraindications be presented in a clear, conspicuous, and neutral manner (FDA, *Federal Register*, vol. 73, no. 152, August 6, 2008, pp. 45773-45776).

[112] Gardiner Harris, "F.D.A. Panel Says Pain Relievers Should Remain on Market," *New York Times*, February 18, 2005.

[113] FDA's Risk Communication Advisory Committee considers some related issues.

[114] PhRMA adopted, in April 2002, a new voluntary marketing code to govern the pharmaceutical industry's relationships with physicians and other healthcare professionals. It says that all interactions should be focused on informing healthcare professionals about products, providing scientific and educational information, and supporting medical research and education, at http://www.phrma.org/press/newsreleases//2002-04-19.390.phtml.

[115] Testimony of Michael S. Shaw, Executive Director of EthicAd, in U.S. Congress, Senate Committee on Commerce, Science, and Transportation, Subcommittee on Consumer Affairs, Foreign Commerce, and Tourism, *Direct-to-Consumer Advertising of Prescription Drugs*, hearing, 107th Cong., 1st sess., July 24, 2001.

[116] Congress authorized, in FDAAA, a new fee to cover costs of FDA advisory review of industry-proposed DTC television ads. The appropriators, however, have taken steps that prevent FDA from assessing or collecting such fees.

[117] Models could include the public-private consortia that produce public service announcements about tobacco use, drug driving, and illegal drug use.

[118] See CRS Report 95-815, *Freedom of Speech and Press: Exceptions to the First Amendment*, by Henry Cohen.

[119] At the June 2006 annual meeting, a trustees group recommended a temporary moratorium on ads for newly approved drugs rather than a total ban on DTC drug advertising (Rich Thomaselli, "AMA Gives Up Push to Ban DTC Drug Ads," *Advertising Age*, June 5, 2006; and Rich Thomaselli, "Nothing but blue skies?" *Advertising Age*, October 2, 2006).

[120] The organization Commercial Alert website posted, on May 24, 2006, the bill text, a list of sponsors, and other material at http://www.commercialalert.org/issues/health/.

[121] FDAAA authorized the Secretary, upon learning of new relevant safety information, to require a labeling change. The law also expanded the definition of misbranding to include the failure to comply with certain requirements regarding REMS, postmarket studies and clinical trials, and labeling and established civil monetary penalties for violations of those requirements.

[122] 21 CFR Sec. 310.305 Records and reports concerning adverse drug experiences on marketed prescription drugs for human use without approved new drug applications; and 21 CFR Sec. 314.80 Postmarketing reporting of adverse drug experiences.

[123] FDA's adverse event reporting system, MedWatch, is intended to identify problems encountered as drugs are used in the wider population and to relate this information back to physicians and medical care personnel. It is, however, a passive surveillance system, gathering anecdotal and often incomplete information from only those physicians and consumers who volunteer the information. It, therefore, provides a count of events but does not provide the total number of users to be able to assess impact. As such, a cluster of MedWatch-reported events serves as a red flag for the agency and at times prompts it to conduct further investigation. For a discussion of the adequacy of adverse event surveillance to protect the public, see CRS Report RL32797, *Drug Safety and Effectiveness: Issues and Action Options After FDA Approval*, by Susan Thaul.

[124] Ray Woosley, president of the Critical Path Institute at the University of Arizona, was quoted in: "Academic Hopes to Partner with FDA on Tiered Drug-Approval Plan," *Inside Health Policy*, March 3, 2005.

[125] Testimony of William B. Schultz, in U.S. Congress, Senate Committee on Health, Education, Labor and Pensions, *FDA's Drug Approval Process: Up to the Challenge?*, hearings, 109th Cong., 1st sess., March 1, 2005.

[126] Philip J. Hilts, *Protecting America's Health: The FDA, Business, and One Hundred Years of Regulation*, New York: Alfred A. Knopf, 2003, p. 23. He depicts citizens complaining in 1840 that advertisements covered every surface.

[127] The U.S. public reads, on average, at a seventh grade reading level ("Comprehension and reading level," *The Informatics Review*, e-journal of the Association of Medical Directors of Information Systems, vol. 9, no. 11, June 1, 2006, at http://www.informatics-review.com/FAQ/reading.html).

In: Advertising: Developments and Issues in the Digital Age   ISBN: 978-1-61761-783-6
Editor: William L. Poulsen   © 2011 Nova Science Publishers, Inc.

Chapter 4

FEDERAL ADVERTISING LAW: AN OVERVIEW

Henry Cohen

SUMMARY

This chapter provides a brief overview of federal law with respect to six selected advertising issues: alcohol advertising, tobacco advertising, the Federal Trade Commission Act, advertising by mail (including junk mail), advertising by telephone, and commercial e-mail (spam). There are numerous federal statutes regulating advertising that do not fit within any of these categories. As random examples, the Food, Drug, and Cosmetic Act requires disclosures in advertisements for prescription drugs; the Truth in Lending Act governs the advertising of consumer credit; and a federal criminal statute makes it illegal falsely to convey in an advertisement that a business is connected with a federal agency.

This chapter provides a brief overview of federal law with respect to six selected advertising issues: alcohol advertising, tobacco advertising, the Federal Trade Commission Act, advertising by mail, advertising by telephone, and commercial email (spam).[1] There are numerous federal statutes regulating advertising that do not fit within any of these categories. As random examples, the Food, Drug, and Cosmetic Act requires disclosures in advertisements for prescription drugs[2]; the Truth in Lending Act governs the advertising of consumer credit[3]; and a federal criminal statute makes it illegal falsely to convey in an advertisement that a business is connected with a federal agency.[4]

Alcohol Advertising

The Federal Alcohol Administration Act makes it unlawful to engage in interstate or foreign commerce in distilled spirits, wine, or malt beverages, unless such products conform to regulations of the Bureau of Alcohol, Tobacco, Firearms, and Explosives, which is in the Department of the Justice.[5] The act requires that these regulations, among other things, prohibit statements on labels and in advertisements "that are disparaging of a competitor's products or are false, misleading, obscene, or indecent."[6] A 1988 amendment to the act requires that alcoholic beverages sold or distributed in the United States, or to members of the Armed Forces outside the United States, contain a specified health warning label.[7]

In 1995, the Supreme Court held unconstitutional a provision of the act that prohibited beer labels from displaying alcohol content unless state law requires such disclosure.[8] The Court found the provision to violate the First Amendment, concluding that, although the government had a legitimate interest in curbing "strength wars" by beer brewers who might seek to compete for customers on the basis of alcohol content, the ban "cannot directly and materially advance" this "interest because of the overall irrationality of the Government's regulatory scheme."[9] This irrationality was evidenced by the fact that the ban did not apply to beer advertisements, and that the statute *required* the disclosure of alcohol content on the labels of wines and spirits.

Federal law does not prohibit the advertising of alcoholic beverages on radio or television, but, since 1936 for radio and 1948 for television, the industry voluntarily refrained from advertising hard liquor on radio or television.[10] On November 7, 1996, however, the Distilled Spirits Council of the United States said that it would lift the ban, but that it had "drawn up 26 guidelines for the industry to follow — guidelines that will avoid a younger audience but also allow this industry to compete more effectively . . . ."[11] The four major television networks announced at the time that they would not air liquor advertisements.

Next, in December, 2001, NBC announced that it would accept liquor ads, but imposed 19 rules to govern them, including limiting them to after 9 p.m E.S.T., requiring that actors in them be at least 30 years old, and requiring the liquor companies to run social-responsibility messages on subjects like designated drivers and drinking moderately. Then, in March 2002, NBC announced that it would no longer accept liquor ads. In November 2007, however, WNBC-TV in New York started to run liquor ads.[12]

Tobacco Advertising

Advertising of tobacco products is restricted by the Federal Cigarette Labeling and Advertising Act, which requires specified warning labels on all cigarette packages distributed in the United States and on all cigarette advertisements within the United States. The warnings must be rotated quarterly in accordance with Federal Trade Commission regulations. The statute also prohibits advertising of cigarettes and little cigars on any medium of electronic communications subject to the jurisdiction of the Federal Communications Commission.[13] This apparently would include radio, and broadcast, cable, and satellite television.

In 1996, the Food and Drug Administration (FDA) adopted a final rule restricting the advertising of cigarettes and smokeless tobacco products. The purpose of the final rule "is to establish restrictions on the sale, distribution, and use of cigarettes and smokeless tobacco in order to reduce the number of children and adolescents who use these products . . . ."[14] The rule did not go into effect, however, because a federal court ruled that the FDA lacked the statutory authority to restrict tobacco advertising.[15] The Supreme Court later held that the FDA lacked the statutory authority to regulate tobacco products at all.[16]

The FDA final rule would have restricted tobacco advertising in several ways, such as by banning "outdoor advertising for cigarettes and smokeless tobacco, including billboards, posters, or placards . . . within 1,000 feet of the perimeter of any public playground or playground area in a public park, . . . elementary school or secondary school," and permitting other outdoor advertising, and advertising in newspapers, magazines, and periodicals, only in "black text on a white background." It would also have prohibited any manufacturer, distributor, or retailer from sponsoring "any athletic, musical, artistic or other social or cultural event, or any entry or team in any event, in the brand name . . . , logo, motto, selling message, recognizable color or pattern of colors, or any other indicia of product identification identical or similar to, or identifiable with, those used for any brand of cigarettes or smokeless tobacco."

On November 23, 1998, attorneys general from 46 states, the District of Columbia, and the five U.S. territories signed an agreement with the major tobacco companies to settle all the lawsuits the states have brought to recover the public health costs of treating smokers. (The four other states — Mississippi, Texas, Florida, and Minnesota — had previously settled.) The settlement had to receive court approval in each state before it took effect, but it did, and it has. It limits tobacco advertising in various ways, including banning the use of cartoons, banning public transit advertising, and limiting billboard and retail-store advertising.[17]

Federal Trade Commission Act

Section 5 of the Federal Trade Commission Act is the basic federal statute prohibiting unfair or deceptive advertising. Subsection (a) of section 5 reads:

Unfair methods of competition in or affecting commerce, and unfair or deceptive acts or practices in or affecting commerce, are hereby declared unlawful.[18]

A 1980 amendment to the FTC Act provides:

The Commission shall not have any authority to promulgate any rule in the children's advertising proceeding pending on May 28, 1980, or in any substantially similar proceeding on the basis of a determination by the Commission that such advertising constitutes an unfair act or practice in or affecting commerce.[19]

The rule that this amendment foreclosed would have banned television advertising, aimed at children, of foods containing added sugar; the FTC's theory behind the rule was that, because children are unable "to understand the selling purpose of, or otherwise comprehend or evaluate, commercials," such commercials may be unfair even if literally truthful.[20] The 1980 statute allows such a rule only if it is "based upon acts or practices that are 'deceptive'"[21]; unfairness alone is not adequate.

A 1994 amendment to the FTC Act provides that an act or practice is illegal only if it "causes or is likely to cause substantial injury to consumers which is not reasonably avoidable by consumers themselves and not outweighed by countervailing benefits to consumer or to competition."[22] Section 12 of the act makes it unlawful to disseminate any false advertisement for "foods, drugs, devices, services, or cosmetics."[23] The Federal Trade Commission Act does not provide for lawsuits by individual consumers. Rather, consumers may file complaints with the Federal Trade Commission (FTC), which may take legal action when it deems it appropriate.

The Federal Trade Commission Act does not apply to banks, savings and loan institutions, Federal credit unions, common carriers (railroads and airlines), or "persons, partnerships, or corporations insofar as they are subject to the Packers and Stockyards Act of 1921 . . . ."[24] All these entities, and their advertising, are regulated by federal agencies other than the FTC.

Advertising by Mail

A federal statute provides that a person who receives in the mail "any pandering advertisement which offers for sale matter which the addressee in his sole discretion believes to be erotically arousing or sexually provocative" may request the Postal Service to issue an order directing the sender to refrain from further mailings to the addressee, and the Postal Service must do so.[25] If the Postal Service believes that a sender has violated such an order, it may request the Attorney General to apply to a federal court for an order directing compliance. This statute applies to any unwanted advertisement, regardless of content.[26]

Another section of the statute provides that any person may file with the Postal Service a statement "that he desires to receive no sexually oriented advertisements through the mails."[27] The Postal Service shall make the list available, and "[n]o person shall mail or cause to be mailed any sexually oriented advertisement to any individual whose name and address has been on the list for more than 30 days." If the Postal Service believes that any person is violating this provision, it may request the Attorney General to commence a civil action against such person in a federal district court.

Another section of the statute provides that unordered merchandise sent through the mails "may be treated as a gift by the recipient," and the sender may not bill for it.[28] Various other federal statutes prohibit mail fraud and other deceptive mailing practices.[29] In addition, the Federal Trade Commission has adopted a trade regulation rule entitled "Mail or Telephone Order Merchandise," which requires, among other things, that sellers who solicit buyers to order merchandise through the mails or by telephone ship such merchandise within the time the seller states or, if no time is stated, within 30 days after receipt of the order. Where a seller is unable to ship the merchandise within such time, it must offer the buyer the option to cancel the order and receive a prompt refund.[30]

In 1999, Congress enacted the Deceptive Mail Prevention and Enforcement Act, P.L. 106-168, which contains restrictions and requires disclosures with respect to mailed sweepstakes promotions.

Advertising by Telephone

The Telephone Consumer Protection Act of 1991 makes it illegal to, among other things, "initiate any telephone call to any residential telephone line using an artificial or prerecorded voice to deliver a message," or "use any telephone facsimile machine, computer, or other device to send an unsolicited advertisement to a telephone facsimile machine."[31] Victims of these practices may file a complaint with the Federal Communications Commission and may sue and recover actual monetary damages or $500, whichever is greater, and the court may increase the award up to three times if it finds that the defendant acted willfully or knowingly. The Junk Fax Prevention Act of 2005, P.L. 109-2 1, amended the Telephone Consumer Protection Act of 1991 to add the exception, previously promulgated by the FCC,[32] that allows senders who have an established business relationship with a recipient to send unsolicited fax advertisements to that recipient. The 2005 statute also requires senders of fax advertisements to place a clear and conspicuous notice on the first page of every fax informing the recipient of how to opt out of future faxes.[33]

The Telemarketing and Consumer Fraud and Abuse Prevention Act, enacted in 1994, required the Federal Trade Commission to "prescribe rules prohibiting deceptive telemarketing acts or practices and other abusive telemarketing acts or practices."[34] Such rules must include:

> (A) a requirement that telemarketers may not undertake a pattern of unsolicited telephone calls which the reasonable consumer would consider coercive or abusive of such consumer's right of privacy,
> (B) restrictions on the hours of the day and night when unsolicited telephone calls can be made to consumers, and
> (C) a requirement that a person engaged in telemarketing for the sale of goods or services shall promptly and clearly disclose to the person receiving the call that the purpose of the call is to sell goods or services and make such other disclosures as the Commission deems appropriate, including the nature and price of the goods and services.

The FTC's Telemarketing Sales Rule, adopted pursuant to the Telemarketing and Consumer Fraud and Abuse Prevention Act, prohibits telemarketers from, among other things, calling a person's residence, without the person's prior consent, before 8:00 a.m. or after 9:00 p.m.[35] It also prohibits initiating a call to a person who has previously stated that he or she does not wish to receive a call from the seller or charitable organization, or who has placed his or her telephone number on the "donot-call" registry maintained by the FTC.[36]

On September 23, 2003, a federal district court in Oklahoma held that the FTC does not have the authority to promulgate a national do-not-call registry, but, in response, Congress enacted a law (P.L. 108-82 (2003)) to ratify that it does.[37] On September 25, 2003, a federal district court in Colorado enjoined implementation of the do-not-call registry on the ground that it violated the First Amendment because it applied only to commercial solicitors and not to other types of speech, such as charitable or political solicitations.[38] The FTC appealed, however, and, on October 7, 2003, the court of appeals granted a stay of the lower court's order, allowing the do-not-call registry to remain in effect pending final resolution of the appeal on the merits. On February 17, 2004, the court of appeals reversed the district court's decision, finding that the do-not-call registry does not violate the First Amendment. The discrimination against commercial solicitors, the court of appeals found, was justified "based on findings that commercial telephone solicitation was significantly more problematic than charitable or political fundraising calls."[39]

The Federal Communications Commission also addresses the do-not-call issue; it requires persons who initiate a telephone solicitation to a residential phone number to institute procedures for "maintaining a list of persons who do not wish to receive telephone solicitations made by or on behalf of that person or entity."[40] The Do-NotCall Implementation Act, P.L. 108-10 (2003), requires the FCC, by September 7, 2003, to "issue a final rule it began on September 18, 2002, under the Telephone Consumer Protection Act (47 U.S.C. 227 et seq.) In issuing such rule, the Federal Communications Commission shall consult and coordinate with the Federal Trade Commission to maximize consistency with the rule promulgated by the Federal Trade Commission (16 CFR 310.4(b))."

In addition, more than 20 states have enacted statutes to establish statewide do-not-call registries.[41]

The Telephone Disclosure and Dispute Resolution Act of 1992 requires the FTC to prescribe rules "to prohibit unfair and deceptive acts and practices in any advertisement [in any medium] for pay-per-call services."[42] Such rules must require, among other things, that the person offering such services "clearly and conspicuously disclose in any advertisement the cost of the use of such telephone number," and "the odds of being able to receive [any] prize, award, service, or product [offered] at no cost or reduced cost."

Commercial E-Mail (Spam)

The CAN-SPAM Act of 2003, P.L. 108-187,[43] effective January 1, 2004, establishes civil or criminal penalties for various actions related to any "protected computer" (which as defined in section 3 of the statute effectively means any computer). These include accessing a protected computer without authorization and intentionally initiating the transmission of multiple commercial e-mails, transmitting multiple commercial e-mails with intent to deceive or mislead recipients, sending a commercial e-mail with header information that is materially false or materially misleading, sending a commercial e-mail that does not contain a functioning return e-mail address or other Internet-based mechanism that a recipient may use to request not to receive future commercial e-mails from that sender, transmitting a commercial e-mail more than 10 days after receipt of such a request, and initiating a sexually oriented commercial e-mail to a recipient who has not given prior affirmative consent to its receipt, unless the e-mail includes marks or notices prescribed by the Federal Trade Commission.

On April 19, 2004, the FTC issued a final rule implementing the CAN-SPAM Act of 2003.[44] It requires, effective May 19, 2004, that commercial electronic e-mail that includes sexually oriented material must "exclude sexually oriented material from the subject heading . . . and include in the subject heading the phrase 'SEXUALLY-EXPLICIT:' in capital letters as the first nineteen (19) characters at the beginning of the subject line." The rule also requires —

> that the content of the message that is initially viewable by the recipient when the message is opened by any recipient and absent any further actions by the recipient, include only the following information:
> (i) the phrase "SEXUALLY-EXPLICIT:" in a clear and conspicuous manner;
> (ii) clear and conspicuous identification that the message is an advertisement or a solicitation;
> (iii) clear and conspicuous notice of the opportunity of a recipient to decline to receive further commercial electronic mail messages from the sender;

(iv) a functioning return electronic mail address or other Internet-based mechanism, clearly and conspicuously displayed, that . . . a recipient may use to submit . . . a reply . . . requesting not to receive future commercial electronic mail messages from the sender . . . ."

End Notes

[1] On the issue of constitutional protection for advertising, see CRS Report 95-815 A, *Freedom of Speech and Press: Exceptions to the First Amendment*, by Henry Cohen.

[2] 21 U.S.C. § 352.

[3] 15 U.S.C. §§ 1661-1665b.

[4] 18 U.S.C. § 709.

[5] The Homeland Security Act of 2002, P.L. 107-296, § 1111, added the word "Explosives" to the name of the Bureau, and transferred it from the Department of the Treasury.

[6] 27 U.S.C. § 205(e)(4), (f)(4). The Federal Trade Commission can also regulate alcoholic beverage advertising and labeling under its general power to regulate unfair or deceptive commercial practices; see page 3, below.

[7] 27 U.S.C. § 215.

[8] Rubin v. Coors Brewing Co., 514 U.S. 476 (1995) (striking down 27 U.S.C. § 205(e)(2)). In *44 Liquormart, Inc. v. Rhode Island*, 517 U.S. 484 (1996), the Supreme Court held to violate the First Amendment a state statute that prohibited disclosure of retail prices in advertisements for alcoholic beverages.

[9] *Id*. at 1592.

[10] See CRS Report RL3 1239, *Prohibiting Television Advertising of Alcoholic Beverages: A Constitutional Analysis*, by Henry Cohen.

[11] *Washington Post*, November 8, 1996.

[12] *New York Times*, November 30, 2007.

[13] 15 U.S.C. §§ 1331-1341. In addition, 15 U.S.C. § 4402 requires warning labels on smokeless tobacco product packages and advertisements (other than outdoor billboard advertising), and prohibits advertising smokeless tobacco on any medium of electronic communications subject to the jurisdiction of the Federal Communications Commission. No similar law applies to cigars.

[14] 61 Fed. Reg. 44615 (1996).

[15] Coyne Beahm, Inc. v. United States, 958 F. Supp. 1060 (M.D. N.C. 1997), *rev'd on other grounds*, 153 F.3d 155 (4th Cir. 1998), *aff'd sub nom.*, Food and Drug Administration v. Brown & Williamson Tobacco Corp., 529 U.S. 120 (2000).

[16] *Id*.

[17] For additional information, see CRS Report RL30058, *Tobacco Master Settlement Agreement (1998): Overview, Implementation by States, and Congressional Issues*, by C. Stephen Redhead. See also [http://tobaccofreekids.org/research/factsheets/pdf/0057.pdf].

[18] 15 U.S.C. § 45(a).

[19] 15 U.S.C. § 57a(h).

[20] 43 Fed. Reg. 17967, 17969 (1978).

[21] H. Conf. Rep. 96-917, 96th Cong., 2d Sess. (1980) at 31; *reprinted at* 1980 U.S.C.C.A.N. 1148.

[22] 15 U.S.C. § 45(n).

[23] 15 U.S.C. § 52.

[24] 15 U.S.C. § 45(a)(2).

[25] 39 U.S.C. § 3008.

[26] Rowan v. Post Office Department, 397 U.S. 728, 738 (1970) ("We . . . categorically reject the argument that a vendor has a right under the Constitution or otherwise to send unwanted material into the home of another.")

[27] 39 U.S.C. § 3010.

[28] 39 U.S.C. § 3009.

[29] E.g., 18 U.S.C. §§ 1341, 1342, 39 U.S.C. §§ 3001 *et seq*.

[30] 16 C.F.R. Part 435.

[31] 47 U.S.C. § 227. Federal courts of appeals have held that this statute does not violate the First Amendment. Destination Ventures v. Federal Communications Commission, 46 F.3d 54 (9th Cir. 1995) (unsolicited faxes); Moser v. Federal Communications Commission, 46 F.3d 970 (9th Cir. 1995), *cert. denied*, 515 U.S. 1161 (1995) (prerecorded telemarketing calls); Missouri, ex rel. Nixon v. American Blast Fax, Inc., 323 F.3d 649 (8th Cir. 2003), *cert. denied*, 540 U.S. 1104 (2004) (unsolicited faxes).

[32] 47 C.F.R. § 64.1 200(a)(2)(iv).

[33] See CRS Report RS2 1647, *Facsimile Advertising Rules Under the Junk Fax Prevention Act of 2005*, by Patricia Moloney Figliola.

[34] 15 U.S.C. §§ 6101 *et seq*. P.L. 107-56 (2001) amended the statute to cover, in addition to calls "to induce purchases of goods or services," calls soliciting "a charitable contribution, donation, or gift of money or other thing of value."

[35] 16 C.F.R. § 3 10.4(c).

[36] 16 C.F.R. § 310.4(b)(iii).

[37] U.S. Security v. Federal Trade Commission, 282 F. Supp. 2d 1285 (W.D. Okla. 2003).

[38] Mainstream Marketing Services, Inc. v. Federal Trade Commission, 283 F. Supp. 2d 1151 (D. Colo. 2003), *stay granted*, 345 F.3d 850 (10th Cir. 2003), *rev'd*, 358 F.3d 1228 (10th Cir. 2004), *cert. denied*, 543 U.S. 812 (2004).

[39] 358 F.3d at 1246.

[40] 47 C.F.R. § 64.1200(e)(2).

[41] For additional information on federal and state do-not-call registries, and on the court cases mentioned above, see CRS Report RL31642, *Regulation of the Telemarketing Industry: State and National Do Not Call Registries*, by Angie Welborn. See also CRS Report RL30763, *Telemarketing: Dealing with Unwanted Telemarketing Calls*, by James R. Riehl.

[42] 15 U.S.C. §§ 5711 *et seq.* The FTC rules appear at 16 C.F.R. Part 308.

[43] "CAN-SPAM" is an acronym for "Controlling the Assault of Non-Solicited Pornography and Marketing." For additional information on the CAN-SPAM Act of 2003, see CRS Report RL31953, *"Spam": An Overview of Issues Concerning Commercial Electronic Mail*, by Patricia Moloney Figliola; and CRS Report RL3 1488, *Regulation of Unsolicited Commercial E-Mail*, by Angie A. Welborn.

[44] 69 Fed. Reg. 21204 (2004), 16 C.F.R. Part 316; [http://www.ftc.gov/opa/2004/04/ adultlabel.htm].

In: Advertising: Developments and Issues in the Digital Age   ISBN: 978-1-61761-783-6
Editor: William L. Poulsen   © 2011 Nova Science Publishers, Inc.

Chapter 5

STATEMENT OF THE FEDERAL TRADE COMMISSION ON BEHAVIORAL ADVERTISING, BEFORE THE SENATE COMMITTEE ON COMMERCE, SCIENCE AND TRANSPORTATION

William L. Poulsen

I. INTRODUCTION

Chairman Inouye, Vice Chainnan Stevens, and Members of Committee, I am Lydia Pames,[1] Director of the Bureau of Consumer Protection at the Federal Trade Commission (the "FTC" or "Commission"). I appreciate the opportunity to appear before you today to discuss the Commission's activities regarding online behavioral advertising, the practice of collecting information about an individual's online activities in order to serve advertisements that are tailored to that individual's interests. Over the past year or so, the Commission has undertaken a comprehensive effort to educate itself and the public about this practice and its implications for consumer privacy. This testimony will describe the Commission's efforts, which have included hosting a "Town Hall" meeting and issuing for public comment FTC staff's proposed online behavioral advertising principles.[2]

The Commission's examination of behavioral advertising has shown that the issues surrounding this practice are complex, that the business models are diverse and constantly evolving, and that behavioral advertising may provide benefits to consumers even as it raises concerns about consumer privacy. At this time, the Commission is cautiously optimistic that the privacy concerns raised by behavioral advertising can be addressed effectively by industry self- regulation.[3]

II. BEHAVIORAL ADVERTISING

Many businesses use online behavioral advertising in an attempt to increase the effectiveness of their advertising by targeting advertisements more closely to the interests of their audience. The practice generally involves the use of "cookies" to track consumers' activities online and associate those activities with a particular computer or device. In many cases, the information collected is not personally identifiable in the traditional sense — that is, the information does not include the consumer's name, physical address, or similar identifier that could be used to identify the consumer in the offline world. Many of the companies engaged in behavioral advertising are so-called "network advertisers," companies that serve advertisements across the Internet at websites that participate in their networks.[4]

An example of how behavioral advertising might work is as follows: a consumer visits a travel website and searches for airline flights to New York City. The consumer does not purchase any tickets, but later visits the website of a local newspaper to read about the Washington Nationals baseball team. While on the newspaper's website, the consumer receives an advertisement from an airline featuring flights to New York City.

In this simple example, the travel website where the consumer conducted his research might have an arrangement with a network advertiser to provide advertising to its visitors. The network advertiser places on the consumer's computer a cookie, which stores non-personally identifiable information such as the web pages the consumer has visited, the advertisements that the consumer has been shown, and how frequently each advertisement has been shown. Because the newspaper's website is also part of the advertising network, when the consumer visits the newspaper website, the network advertiser recognizes the cookie from the travel website as its own and identifies the consumer as likely having an interest in traveling to New York. It then serves the corresponding advertisement for airline flights to New York.

In a slightly more sophisticated example, the information about the content that the consumer had selected from the travel website could be combined with information about the consumer's activities on the newspaper's website. The advertisement served could then be tailored to the consumer's interest in, not just New York City, but also baseball *(e.g.,* an advertisement referring to the New York Yankees).

As these examples illustrate, behavioral advertising may provide benefits to consumers in the form of advertising that is more relevant to their interests. Consumer research has shown that many online consumers value more personalized ads, which may facilitate shopping for the specific products that consumers want.[5] Further, by providing advertisements that are likely to be of interest to the consumer, behavioral advertising also may reduce the number of unwanted, and potentially unwelcome, advertisements consumers receive online

More broadly, the revenue model for the Internet is, to a large extent, advertising-based, and using behavioral techniques can increase the cost-effectiveness of online advertising. Thus, behavioral advertising may help subsidize and support a diverse range of free online content and services that otherwise might not be available or that consumers would otherwise have to pay for — content and services such as blogging, search engines, social networking, and instant access to newspapers and information from around the world.

At the same time, however, behavioral advertising raises consumer privacy concerns. As described below, many consumers express discomfort about the privacy implications of being tracked, as well as the specific harms that could result. In particular, without adequate safeguards in place, consumer tracking data may fall into the wrong hands or be used for unanticipated purposes.[6] These concerns are exacerbated when the tracking involves sensitive information about, for example, children, health, or a consumer's finances.

Recent high-profile incidents where tracking data has been released have magnified consumers' concerns. In August 2006, for example, an employee of internet service provider and web services company AOL made public the search records of approximately 658,000 customers.[7] The search records were not identified by name, and, in fact, the company had taken steps to anonymize the data. By combining the highly particularized and often personal searches, however, several newspapers, including the New York Times,[8] and consumer groups were able to identify some individual AOL users and their queries, challenging traditional notions about what data is or is not personally identifiable.

Another incident involved the social networking site Facebook. In November 2007, Facebook released a program called Beacon, which allowed users to share infolination about their online activities, such as the purchases they had made or the videos they had viewed. The Beacon service tracked the activities of logged-in users on websites that had partnered with Facebook. If a user did not opt out of this tracking, Facebook's partner sites would send to Facebook information about the user's purchases at the partner sites. Facebook then published this information on the user's profile page and sent it to the user's Facebook "friends."

The Beacon program raised significant concerns among Facebook users.[9] Approximately 30 groups formed on Facebook to protest Beacon, with one of the groups representing over 4,700 members,[10] and over 50,000 Facebook users signed a petition objecting to the new program.[11] Within a few weeks, Facebook changed its program by adding more user controls over what information is shared with "friends" and by improving notifications to users before sharing their information with others on Facebook.[12]

Surveys confirm that consumers are concerned about the privacy of their activities as they navigate online For example, in two recent surveys, a majority of consumers expressed some degree of discomfort with having information about their online activities collected and used to serve advertising.[13] Similarly, only 20 percent of consumers in a third survey stated that they would allow a marketer to share information about them in order to track their purchasing behaviors and to help predict future purchasing decisions.[14] Another survey found that 45 percent of consumers believe that online tracking should be banned, and another 47 percent would allow such tracking, but only with some form of consumer control.[15] These surveys underscore the importance of online privacy to consumers and highlight the fundamental importance of maintaining trust in the online marketplace.

III. FTC INITIATIVES CONCERNING CONSUMER PRIVACY AND BEHAVIORAL ADVERTISING

Since privacy first emerged as a significant consumer protection issue in the mid 1990s, it has been one of the Commission's highest priorities. The Commission has worked to address privacy issues through consumer and business education, law enforcement, and policy initiatives. For example, the FTC has promulgated and enforced the Do Not Call Rule to respond to consumer complaints about unsolicited and unwanted telemarketing;[16] has waged a multi-faceted war on identity theft;[17] has encouraged better data security practices by businesses through educational initiatives[18] and a robust enforcement program;[19] has brought numerous enforcement actions to reduce the incidence of spun and spyware;[20] and has held numerous workshops to examine emerging technologies and business practices, and the privacy and other issues they raise for consumers.[21] In early 2006, recognizing the ever-increasing importance of privacy to consumers and to a healthy marketplace, the Commission established the Division of Privacy and Identity Protection, a division devoted exclusively to privacy-related issues.

In developing and implementing its privacy program, the FTC has been mindful of the need for flexibility and balance — that is, the need to address consumer concerns and harms without stifling innovation or imposing needless costs on consumers and businesses.

A. 1999 Workshop on Online Profiling

The Commission first examined the issue of behavioral advertising in 1999, when it held a joint public workshop with the Department of Commerce on the practice — then called "online profiling." The workshop examined the practice of tracking consumers' activities online, as well as the role of self-regulation in this area.

In response to the concerns highlighted at the workshop, industry members formed the Network Advertising Initiative ("NAI"), a self-regulatory organization addressing behavioral advertising by network advertisers. Shortly thereafter, the NAI issued the NAI Self-Regulatory Principles ("NAI Principles") governing collection of information for online advertising by network advertisers.[22] In the early 2000s, however, with the "burst" of the dot coin bubble, many network advertisers — including most of the NAI membership — went out of business.

Emblematic of the highly dynamic nature of the online enviromnent, by the time the FTC held its public hearings on Protecting Consumers in the Next Tech-ade ("Tech-ade") only a few years later,[23] the issue of online tracking and advertising had reemerged. In the intervening years, behavioral advertising had become a highly successful business practice, and a number of Tech-ade participants raised concerns about its effects on consumer privacy.

B. The FTC Town Hall on Online Behavioral Advertising

Beginning in Fall 2006, the Commission staff held a series of meetings with numerous industry representatives, technology experts, consumer and privacy advocates, and academics to learn more about the practice of behavioral advertising. The purpose of these meetings was to explore further the issues raised at Tech-ade, learn about developments since the FTC's 1999 Workshop, and examine concerns about behavioral advertising that had been raised by privacy advocates and others.[24] Seeking a broader forum in which to examine and discuss these issues, and particularly the privacy issues raised by the practice, the FTC held a two-day Town Hall meeting on behavioral advertising in November 2007.

From the Town Hall, as well as the meetings preceding it, several key points emerged. First, as discussed above, online behavioral advertising may provide many valuable benefits to consumers in the form of free content, personalization that many consumers value, and a potential reduction in unwanted advertising. Second, the invisibility of the practice to consumers raises privacy concerns, as does the risk that data collected for behavioral advertising — including sensitive data about children, health, or finances — could be misused. Third, business and consumer groups alike expressed support for transparency and consumer control in the online marketplace.

Many participants at the Town Hall also criticized the self-regulatory efforts that had been implemented to date. In particular, these participants stated that the NAI Principles had not been sufficiently effective in addressing the privacy concerns raised by behavioral advertising because of the NAI's limited membership, the limited scope of the NAI Principles (which apply to network advertisers but not to other companies engaged in behavioral advertising), and the NAI Principles' lack of enforcement and cumbersome opt-out system.[25] Further, while other industry associations had promulgated online self-regulatory schemes to address privacy issues, these schemes had not generally focused on behavioral advertising.[26]

C. The FTC's Proposed Self-Regulatory Principles

In December 2007, in response to the issues discussed at the Town Hall and in public comments received in connection with that event, Commission staff issued and requested comment on a set of proposed principles titled, "Behavioral Advertising: Moving the Discussion Forward to Possible Self-Regulatory Principles" (the "Principles"). The proposed Principles address the central concerns about online behavioral advertising expressed by interested parties; they also build upon existing "best practices" in the area of privacy, as well as (in some cases) previous FTC guidance and/or law enforcement actions. At the same time, the Principles reflect FTC staffs recognition of the potential benefits provided by online behavioral advertising and the need to maintain vigorous competition in this area.

The purpose of the proposed Principles is to encourage more meaningful and enforceable self-regulation. At this time, the Commission believes that self-regulation may be the preferable approach for this dynamic marketplace because it affords the flexibility that is needed as business models continue to evolve.

In brief, the staff proposal identifies four governing principles for behavioral advertising.[27] The first is transparency and consumer control: companies that collect information for behavioral advertising should provide meaningful disclosures to consumers about the practices, as well as choice about whether their information is collected for this purpose.[28] The second principle is reasonable security: companies should provide reasonable security for behavioral data so that it does not fall into the wrong hands, and should retain data only as long as necessary to fulfill a legitimate business or law enforcement need.[29] The third principle governs material changes to privacy policies: before a company uses behavioral data in a manner that is materially different from promises made when the data was collected, it should obtain affirmative express consent from the consumer.[30] This principle ensures that consumers can rely on promises made about how their infoimation will be used, and can prevent contrary uses if they so choose. The fourth principle states that companies should obtain affirmative express consent before they use sensitive data — for example, data about children, health, or finances — for behavioral advertising.[31]

IV. Next Steps

In response to the request for public comment, Commission staff received over 60 comments on the Principles, representing many thoughtful and constructive views from diverse business sectors, industry self-regulatory bodies, privacy advocates, technologists, academics, and consumers. The comment period for the Principles has closed, and Commission staff is carefully evaluating the comments received.

Included in the comments were a number of specific proposals for how self-regulation could be implemented, as well as reports regarding steps taken to address privacy concerns since the Town Hall. The FTC is encouraged by the efforts that have already been made by the NAT[32] and some other organizations and companies[33] and believes that the self-regulatory process that has been initiated is a promising one. Although there is more work to be done in this area, the Commission is cautiously optimistic that the privacy issues raised by online behavioral advertising can be effectively addressed through meaningful, enforceable self-regulation. The dynamic and diverse online environment demands workable and adaptable approaches to privacy that will be responsive to the evolving marketplace. Nevertheless, the Commission will continue to closely monitor the marketplace so that it can take appropriate action to protect consumers as the circumstances warrant.

V. Conclusion

The Commission appreciates this opportunity to discuss its work on behavioral advertising. The Commission is committed to addressing new and emerging privacy issues such as online behavioral advertising and looks forward to working further with the Committee on this important consumer issue.

End Notes

[1] The views expressed in this statement represent the views of the Commission. My oral presentation and responses to any questions are my own, however, and do not necessarily reflect the views of the Commission or any individual Commissioner.

[2] *See* Federal Trade Commission, "Ehavioral Advertising: Tracking, Targeting, & Technology," *available at* http://www.ftc.gov/bcu/workshops/ehavioral/index.shtml.

[3] Although FTC staff has proposed self-regulation to address the general privacy concerns raised by behavioral advertising, the Commission will of course continue to bring enforcement actions to challenge law violations in appropriate cases.

[4] The advertisements are typically based upon data collected about a given consumer as he or she travels across the different websites in the advertising network. A website may belong to multiple networks.

[5] *See* Larry Ponemon, "FTC Presentation on Cookies and Consumer Permissions," presented at the FTC's Town Hall "Ehavioral Advertising: Tracking, Targeting, and Technology" (Nov. 1, 2007), at *7, available at* http://www.ftc.aov/bcp/workshops/ehavioral/presentations/31ponemon.pdf (survey found that 55 percent of respondents believed that an online ad that targeted their individual preferences or interests improved, to some degree, their online experience). *See also* TRUSTe/TNS Presentation, TRUSTe and TNS Global, "Consumer

Attitudes about Behavioral Advertising" at 10 (March 28, 2008) (72 percent of respondents found online advertising annoying when it was not relevant to their interests or needs). *But see infra* note 13 and accompanying text.

[6] As a result of these concerns, a number of consumer groups and others have asked the Commission to take action in this area. *See, e.g.,* Center for Digital Democracy and U.S. Public Interest Research Group Complaint and Request for Inquiry and Injunctive Relief Concerning Unfair and Deceptive Online Marketing Practices (Nov. 1, 2006), *available at* http://www.democraticmedia.org/files/pdf/FTCadprivacy.pdf; Ari Schwartz and Alissa Cooper, Center for Democracy and Technology, "CDT Letter to Commissioner Rosch," (Jan. 19, 2007), *available at* http ://www. cdt.org/privacy/20070119rosch-b ehavioral-letter. p df; Mindy B ockstein, "Letter to Chairman Majoras Re: DoubleClick, Inc. and Google, Inc. Merger," New York State Consumer Protection Board (May 1, 2007), *available at* http ://epic.org/privacy/ftc/t400gle/cpb .pdf.

[7] *See, e.g.,* Jeremy Kirk, "AOL Search Data Reportedly Released," Computerworld (Aug. 6, 2007), *available at* http ://computerworld. com/action/article. do ?c ornmand=viewArticleB asic&taxonomyName=priva cy&articleId=9002234&taxonomvId=84.

[8] *See* Michael Barbaro and Tom Zeller, "A Face Is Exposed for AOL Searcher No. 4417749," www.nytimes.com, Aug. 9, 2006, *available at* http://www.nvtimes.com/2006/08/09/technology/09aol.html.

[9] In one now-famous example, a man had bought a ring for his wife as a surprise; the surprise was ruined when his wife read about his purchase on the man's user profile page. *See, e.g.,* Ellen Nakashima, "Feeling Betrayed, Facebook Users Force Site to Honor Privacy," Washingtonpost.com, (Nov. 30, 2007), *available at* http://wvvw.washingtonpost.com/wp-dvn/content/article/2007/11/29/AR2007112902503 palm'

[10] *See* Facebook home page, http://www.facebook.com, viewed on March 21, 2008.

[11] MoveOn.org Civic Action[TM] created an online petition for consumers to express their objection to Facebook's Beacon program. The petition stated, "Sites like Facebook must respect my privacy. They should not tell my friends what I buy on other sites — or let companies use my name to endorse their products — without my explicit permission." MoveOn.org Civic Action Petition, *available at* http://ww̃w.civic.moveon.org/ facebookprivacy/, viewed June 9, 2008.

[12] *See* Reuters News, "Facebook Makes Tweak After Privacy Protest," RedHerring.com, Nov. 30, 2007, *available at* http://www.redherring.com/Home/23224.

[13] *See* Alan Westin, "Online Users, Behavioral Marketing and Privacy: Results of a National Harris/Westin Survey" (March 2008) (almost 60 percent of respondents were "not comfortable" to some degree with online behavioral marketing); TRUSTe/TNS Presentation, "Behavioral Advertising: Privacy, Consumer Attitudes and Best Practices," at 10 (April 23, 2008) (57 percent of respondents were not comfortable with advertisers using browsing history to serve ads, even if the information is not connected to personally identifiable information).

[14] *See* Ponemon Presentation, *supra* note 5, at 11.

[15] *See* George R Milne, "Information Exchange Expectations of Consumers, Marketing Managers and Direct Marketers," University of Massachusetts Amherst (presented on Nov. 1, 2007), *available at* http://www.ftc. ov/b cp/workshops/ehavioral/pres entations/3 gmilne pdf.

[16] Telemarketing Sales Rule: Final Rule, 16 C.F.R. Part 310 (2003), *available at* http ://www.ftc.gov/os/2003/01/tsrfin.pdf.

[17] *See, e.g.,* FTC ID theft website, *available at* www.ftc.aov/idtheft. In one recent effort, the FTC coordinated with the U.S. Postal Service to send a letter to every American household containing information about how to protect against identity theft. *See* Press Release, "Postmaster General Sends Advice to Prevent ID Theft," U.S. Postal Service (Feb. 19, 2008), *available at* http://www.usps.com/connnunications /newsroom/2008/pr08_014.htm.

[18] *See, e.g.,* Federal Trade Commission, "Protecting Personal Information: A Guide for Business," *available at* http://www.ftc.gov/infosecurity/; *see also* http://onguardonline gov/index.html.

[19] Since 2001, the Commission has obtained twenty consent orders against companies that allegedly failed to provide reasonable protections for sensitive consumer information. *See In the Matter of The TJX Companies,* FTC File No. 072-3055 (Mar. 27, 2008, settlement accepted for public comment); *In the Matter of Reed Elsevier Inc. and Seisint Inc.,* FTC File No. 052-3094 (Mar. 27, 2008, settlement accepted for public comment); *United States v. ValueClick, Inc.,* No. CV08-01711 (C.D. Cal. Mar. 13, 2008); *In the Matter of Goal Financial, LLC,* FTC Docket No. C-4216 (April 15, 2008); *In the Matter of Life is Good, Inc.,* FTC Docket No. C4218 (Apr. 18, 2008); *United States v. American United Mortgage,* No. CV07C 7064, (N.D. Ill. Dec. 18, 2007); *In the Matter of Guidance Software, Inc.,* FTC Docket No. C-4187 (Apr. 3, 2007); *In the Matter of CardSystems Solutions, Inc.,* FTC Docket No. C-4168 (Sept. 5, 2006); *In the Matter of Nations Title Agency, Inc.,* FTC Docket No. C-4161 (June 19, 2006); *In the Matter of DSW, Inc.,* FTC Docket No. C-4157 (Mar. 7, 2006); *United States v. ChoicePoint, Inc.,* No. 106-CV-0198 (N.D. Ga. Feb. 15, 2006); *In the Matter of Superior Mortgage Corp.,* FTC Docket No. C-4153 (Dec. 14, 2005); *In the Matter of BJ's Wholesale Club, Inc.,* FTC Docket No. C4148 (Sept. 20, 2005); *In the Matter of Nationwide Mortgage Group, Inc.,* FTC Docket No. 9319 (Apr. 12, 2005); *In the Matter of Petco Animal Supplies, Inc.,* FTC Docket No. C-4133 (Mar. 4, 2005); *In the Matter of Sunbelt Lending Services,* FTC Docket No. C-4129 (Jan. 3, 2005); *In the Matter of MTS Inc., d/b/a Tower Records/Books/Video,* FTC Docket No. C-4110 (May 28, 2004); *In the Matter of*

Guess?, Inc., FTC Docket No. C-4091 (July 30, 2003); *In the Matter of Microsoft Corp.,* FTC Docket No. C-4069 (Dec. 20, 2002); *In the Matter of Eli Lilly & Co.,* FTC Docket No. C-4047 (May 8, 2002).

[20] Since 2004, the Commission has initiated eleven spyware-related law enforcement actions. Detailed information regarding each of these law enforcement actions is available at http://www.ftc.aov/bcp/edu/microsites/spyware/law_enfor.htm. Since 1997, when the FTC brought its first enforcement action targeting unsolicited commercial email, or "spam," the FTC has brought 94 law enforcement actions. *See generally* Report on "Spain Summit: The Next Generation of Threats and Solutions" (Nov. 2007), *available at* http://www.ftc.gov/os/2007/12/071220spamsummitreport.pdf.

[21] *See* discussion *infra* pp. 9-12.

[22] Briefly, the NAI Principles set forth guidelines for online network advertisers and provide a means by which consumers can opt out of behavioral advertising at a centralized website. For more information on the FTC workshop and NAI, *see* Online Profiling: A Report to Congress (June 2000) at 22 and Online Profiling A Report Congress Part 2 Recommendations (July 2000), *available at* http://www.ftc.gov/os/2000/06/onlineprofilinueportjune2000.pdf and http://www.networkadvertising.org. As discussed further below, NAI recently proposed for public comment revised NAI Principles.

[23] The purpose of the Tech-ade hearings, held in November 2006, was to examine the technological and consumer protection developments anticipated over the next decade. *See generally* http://www.ftc.gov/bcp/workshops/techade/index.html.

[24] *See* CDD *et al.,* Complaint and Request for Inquiry and Injunctive Relief, *supra* note 6. Many of these concerns were amplified by the announcement of the proposed merger between Google and DoubleClick in April 2007. The Commission approved the merger on December 20, 2007, at the same time that it issued FTC staff's proposed self-regulatory guidelines. *See* "Staff Proposes Online Behavioral Advertising Policy Principles," Federal Trade Commission (Dec. 20, 2008), *available at* http://www.ftc.g,ov/opa/2007/12/principles.shtm. The Principles are discussed *infra* at 13.

[25] According to critics, the NAI Principles' opt-out mechanism is difficult to locate and use because it is located on the NAI website, where consumers would be unlikely to find it. As noted above, in April of this year, the NAI issued a proposed revised set of self-regulatory principles designed to address criticisms of the original NAI Principles and to respond to the FTC staff's call for stronger self-regulation. The NAI has sought comment on its proposed revised principles, and comments were due June 12, 2008. *See* "Self-Regulatory Principles for Online Preference Marketing By Network Advertisers," Network Advertising Initiative (issued April 10, 2008), *available at* http://www.networkadvertisina.org/pdfs/NAI_principles.pdf.

[26] Since the Town Hall, some of these industry groups, as well as several online companies and privacy groups, have sought to address the concerns raised about behavioral advertising. *See, e.g.,* Interactive Advertising Bureau, "Privacy Principles," (adopted Feb. 24, 2008), *available at* http://www.iab .net/iabpro ducts and industry services/1421/1443/1464; Comment "Online Behavioral Advertising: Moving the Discussion Forward to Possible Self- Regulatory Principles," Microsoft Corp. (April 11, 2008), *available at* http://www.ftc.aov/os/comments/behavioraladprinciples/080411 microsoft.pdf; Comment "FTC Staff Proposed Online Behavioral Advertising Principles: Comments of AOL, LLC," AOL, LLC (April 11, 2008), *available at* http://www.ftc.gov/con'nnents/behavioraladprinciples/080411aol.pdf; Ari Schwartz, Center for Democracy and Technology, *et al.,* "Consumer Rights and Protections in the Behavioral Advertising Sector," (Oct. 31, 2007) (proposing a "Do Not Track List" designed to increase consumers' control over tracking of their activities online), *available at* http://www.cdt.org/privacy/20071031consumerprotectionsbehavioral.pdf.

[27] Recent news reports have highlighted concerns about behavioral advertising involving Internet Service Providers ("ISPs"). The ISP-based model for delivering behaviorally-targeted advertising may raise heightened privacy concerns because it could involve the tracking of subscribers wherever they go online and the accumulation of vast stores of data about their online activities. Further, information about the subscriber's activities potentially could be combined with the personally identifiable information that ISPs possess about their subscribers. In issuing the proposed Principles for public comment, FTC staff intended the Principles to apply to ISPs.

[28] For more information and guidance on the use of disclosures in online advertising, see *Dot Com Disclosures, Information About Online Advertising,* http://www.ftc.2ov/bcp/conline/pubs/buspubs/dotcom/index.shtml (May 2000).

[29] The FTC has highlighted the need for reasonable security in numerous educational materials and enforcement actions to date. *See supra* notes 18-19.

[30] *See, e.g., Gateway Learning Corp.,* Docket No. C-4120 (Sept. 10, 2004), http://www.ftc.gov/opa/2004/07/2ateway.shtm (company made material changes to its privacy policy and allegedly applied such changes to data collected under the old policy; opt-in consent required for future such changes).

[31] Commission staff also sought comment on the potential uses of tracking data beyond behavioral advertising.

[32] Current NAI members include DoubleClick, Yahoo! Inc., TACODA, Inc., Acerno, AlmondNet, BlueLithium, Mindset Media, Revenue Science, Inc., 24/7 Real Media Inc., and Undertone Networks.

[33] *See supra* note 26. Although many organizations and consumer groups have undertaken efforts to address FTC staff's proposed Principles, a few organizations have expressed concern that implementing the Principles would be too costly and would undermine continued development of the online marketplace. FTC staff is evaluating all of these comments as it considers next steps in this area.

In: Advertising: Developments and Issues in the Digital Age   ISBN: 978-1-61761-783-6
Editor: William L. Poulsen   © 2011 Nova Science Publishers, Inc.

Chapter 6

STATEMENT OF LESLIE HARRIS, PRESIDENT/CEO, CENTER FOR DEMOCRACY AND TECHNOLOGY, BEFORE THE SENATE COMMITTEE ON COMMERCE, SCIENCE AND TRANSPORTATION, HEARING ON "PRIVACY IMPLICATIONS OF ONLINE ADVERTISING"

I. SUMMARY

Chairman Inouye and Members of the Committee:

On behalf of the Center for Democracy & Technology ("CDT"), I thank you for the opportunity to testify today. We applaud the Committee's leadership in examining the privacy impact of new online advertising models.

CDT recognizes that advertising is an important engine of Internet growth. Consumers benefit from a rich diversity of content, services and applications that are provided without charge and supported by advertising revenue. However, as sophisticated new behavioral advertising models are deployed, it is vital that consumer privacy be protected. Massive increases in data processing and storage capabilities have allowed advertisers to track, collect and aggregate information about consumers' Web browsing activities, compiling individual profiles used to match advertisements to consumers' interests. All of this is happening in the context of an online environment where more data is collected – and retained for longer periods – than ever before and existing privacy protections have been far outpaced by technological innovation.

Behavioral advertising represents a small but rapidly growing part of the online advertising market. Market research firm eMarketer reported last year that spending on behaviorally targeted online advertising is expected to reach $1 billion this year and to quadruple by 2011.[1] The recent spate of acquisitions of the online advertising industry's largest players by major Internet companies is powerful evidence that the online advertising marketplace is headed toward more data aggregation tied to a single profile – and one that may be more readily tied to a person's identity.[2] And while we have yet to see evidence that this new advertising model will reap the promised rewards, it is already migrating from individual Web sites to the infrastructure of the Internet itself: In the last year, Internet

Service Providers ("ISPs") have begun to form partnerships with ad networks to mine information from individual Web data streams for behavioral advertising. Ad networks that partner with ISPs could potentially collect and record every aspect of a consumer's Web browsing, including every Web page visited, the content of those pages, how long each page is viewed, and what links are clicked. Emails, chats, file transfers and many other kinds of data could all be collected and recorded.

The ISP model raises particularly serious questions. Thus far, implementations appear to defy reasonable consumer expectations, could interfere with Internet functionality, and may violate communications privacy laws.

Notwithstanding the recent growth of behavioral advertising, most Internet users today do not know that their browsing information may be tracked, aggregated and sold. After almost a decade of self-regulation, there is still a profound lack of transparency associated with these practices and an absence of meaningful consumer controls.

There are several efforts underway to respond to the new online advertising environment. First, the Federal Trade Commission staff recently released a draft of proposed principles for self-regulation, which represent a solid step forward. However, it is not clear whether the FTC will formally adopt the principles or put its enforcement power behind them.

The Network Advertising Initiative ("NAI") is also in the process of revising its guidelines. This is a welcome but long-overdue development. Unfortunately, self-regulation has not worked to date and, even if strengthened, will never by itself fully protect consumers' privacy interests.

Congress needs to take a comprehensive look at the current and emerging practices associated with behavioral advertising and the risks those practices pose to consumer privacy and control. We recommend that Congress take the following steps to address the significant privacy concerns raised by behavioral advertising:

- The Committee should hold a series of hearings to examine specific aspects of behavioral advertising, in particular the growing involvement of ISPs, the use of sensitive information, and secondary uses of behavioral profiles.
- The Committee should set a goal of enacting in the next year a simple, flexible baseline consumer privacy law that would protect consumers from inappropriate collection and misuse of their personal information, both online and offline.
- The Committee should strongly urge the Federal Trade Commission to exercise its full enforcement authority over online advertising practices.
- Congress should examine and strengthen existing communications privacy laws to cover new services, technologies and business models with consistent rules. The Electronic Communications Privacy Act ("ECPA") is decades old, and its application in today's online world is often unclear.
- Congress should encourage the FTC to investigate how technology can be harnessed to give consumers better control over their online information. Simple tools that put consumers in controls of their information, such as a "Do Not Track" list, deserve consideration.

II. Understanding Online Advertising Practices

Commercial Web sites that supply content to consumers free of charge are often supported by online advertising. These sites – known as "publishers" in the advertising world – make available certain portions of space on their pages to display ads. That space is sold to advertisers, ad agencies, or online ad intermediaries that find and place advertisements into the space. These intermediaries may also make arrangements to collect information about user visits to the publisher pages. Since very few publishers supply their own advertising, it is common that when a consumer visits a publisher site, the consumer's computer also connects to one or more advertisers, ad agencies, or ad intermediaries to send data about the consumer's visit to the site and receive the advertising on the site.

One type of ad intermediary is known as an "advertising network." At their most basic level, ad networks contract with many different publishers on one side and many different advertisers on the other. Armed with a pool of space in which to display ads on publisher sites, and a pool of ads to display, ad networks are in the business of matching up the two by using the data they collect about consumers' site visits.

A. Contextual Advertising

There are many different ways for an ad network to determine which advertisement should be placed in which space. The two most often discussed are "contextual" advertising and "behavioral" advertising. Contextual advertising, which is often used to generate ads alongside search results, matches advertisements to the content of the page that a consumer is currently viewing – a consumer who visits a sports site may see advertisements for golf clubs or baseball tickets on that site.

The privacy risks associated with contextual advertising vary. If the practice is transparent to the user and data collection and retention is minimal, the practice poses little risk. By contrast, privacy concerns are heightened if the user data is retained in an identifiable or pseudonymous form (i.e., linked to a user identifier) for long periods of time even if it is not immediately used to create advertising profiles.

B. Behavioral Advertising

By contrast, behavioral advertising matches advertisements to the interests of the consumer as determined over time. If a consumer visits several different travel sites before viewing a news site, he or she might see a behaviorally targeted travel advertisement displayed on the news page, even if the news page contains no travel content. A traditional behavioral ad network builds up profiles of individual consumers by tracking their activities on publisher sites in the network (although this model is evolving, as we discuss below). When the consumer visits a site where the ad network has purchased ad space, the ad network collects data about that visit and serves an advertisement based on the consumer's profile. Diagrams illustrating this process are included in Appendix A.

Consumers' behavioral advertising profiles may incorporate many different kinds of data that are in and of themselves not personally identifiable. Many networks avoid linking profiles to what has traditionally been considered "personally identifiable information" ("PII"): names, addresses, telephone numbers, email addresses, and other identifiers. But as the comprehensiveness of consumer advertising profiles increases, the ability of marketers and others to link specific individuals to profiles is also growing. In 2006, for example, AOL released three months' worth of search queries generated by half a million users; in the interest of preserving users' anonymity, AOL replaced individuals' screen names with numbers. Based solely on search terms associated with one number, reporters at the New York Times were able to pinpoint the identity of the user who generated them.[3] The risk of supposedly non-personally identifying data being used to identify individuals has spurred several ad networks to take extra steps to de-identify or remove personal information from their data storage.[4]

Profiles may also be intentionally tied to PII. For example, data collected online by a merchant or by a service provider may permit an advertising profile to be tied to an individual's email account. Offline data may also be merged with online profiles. For years, data service companies have maintained profiles about consumers based on information gleaned from public sources such as property and motor vehicle records, as well as records from sources like catalog sales and magazine subscriptions. These data companies are now also entering the online advertising business, potentially allowing the linking of online and offline profiles.[5]

C. The Evolution of Behavioral Advertising – More Data, More Data Sources

As noted above, recent market consolidation facilitates more comprehensive data collection. Companies that run consumers' favorite Web-based services – Web search, Web mail, maps, calendars, office applications, and social networks – have all purchased behavioral advertising networks within the last year. In the past, major Internet companies could gather information about how an individual used its services and applications such as search, but did not have direct access to information about the user's other Web browsing habits. With the acquisition of behavioral advertising networks, these companies could potentially marry the rich data about an individual's use of one site with a broad view of his or her activities across the Web. The concerns about this aggregation of consumer data are heightened because many online companies retain data for months or years on end in identifiable or pseudonymous form, creating a host of privacy risks.

Finally, ad networks are now turning to the most comprehensive and concentrated source of information about Internet use: the individual Web data streams that flow through ISPs.[6] In this emerging model, the ISP intercepts or allows an ad network to intercept the content of each individual's Web data stream. The ad network then uses this traffic data for behavioral advertising, serving targeted ads to the ISP's customers on publisher sites as the customers surf the Web. We address the unique issues posed by this advertising model in detail below.

III. THE PRIVACY RISKS OF BEHAVIORAL ADVERTISING

Behavioral advertising poses a growing risk to consumer privacy; consumers are largely unaware of the practice and are thus ill equipped to take protective action. They have no expectation that their browsing information may be tracked and sold, and they are rarely provided sufficient information about the practices of advertisers or others in the advertising value chain to gauge the privacy risks and make meaningful decisions about whether and how their information may be used. In a recently released Harris Interactive/Alan F. Westin study, 59% of respondents said they were not comfortable with online companies using their browsing behavior to tailor ads and content to their interests even when they were told that such advertising supports free services.[7] A recent TRUSTe survey produced similar results.[8] It is highly unlikely that these respondents understood that this type of ad targeting is already taking place online every day.

In most cases, data collection for behavioral advertising operates on an opt-out basis. Opt-out mechanisms for online advertising are often buried in fine print, difficult to understand, hard to execute and technically inadequate. Only the most sophisticated and technically savvy consumers are likely to be able to successfully negotiate such opt-out processes. Moreover, in most cases, opt-out mechanisms offered for behavioral advertising only opt the user out of receiving targeted ads, but do not opt the user out of data collection about his or her Internet usage.

For behavioral advertising to operate in a truly privacy-protective way, data collection needs to be limited and data retention limits should be tied to the original purposes for collecting the data. Consumers need to be informed about what data is being collected about their Internet activities, how the information will be used, whether the information will be shared with others, and what measures are being taken to ensure that any transfer of data remains secure. They should be presented with this information in a manner that supports informed choice over their information and that choice should honored persistently over time. Consumers must also have opportunities for legal redress for misuse of the data. As a recent D.C. District Court opinion established, data leakage and the concern for potential abuses of that data are recognizable harms standing alone, without any need to show misuse of the data.[9] Consumers do not need to become victims of identity theft to suffer from an invasion of privacy.

There is also a risk that profiles for behavioral advertising may be used for purposes other than advertising. For example, ad networks that focus on "re-targeting" ads may already be using profiles to help marketers engage in differential pricing.[10] Behavioral profiles, particularly those that can be tied to an individual, may also be a tempting source of information in making decisions about credit, insurance, and employment. While the lack of transparency makes it almost impossible to know whether behavioral profiles are being used for other purposes, the lack of enforceable rules around the collection and use of most personal information leaves the door wide open for a myriad of secondary uses.

Finally, because the legal standards for government access to personal information held by third parties are extraordinarily low, these comprehensive consumer profiles are available to government officials by mere subpoena, without notice to the individual or an opportunity for the individual to object.[11]

IV. THE USE OF SENSITIVE INFORMATION FOR BEHAVIORAL ADVERTISING

The concerns about behavioral advertising practices are heightened because of the increasingly sensitive nature of the information that consumers are providing online in order to take advantage of new services and applications. Two data types of particular concern are health information and location information.

A. Personal Health Information – Increasingly Available Online

Personal health data is migrating online through an ever-expanding array of health information and search sites, online support groups, and personal health record sites. Federal privacy rules under the Health Information Portability and Accountability Act ("HIPAA") do not cover personal health information once it moves online and out of the control of HIPAA-covered entities. Once it is posted online, it may have no more legal protection than any other piece of consumer information. In addition, information provided by consumers that is not part of a "medical record" – such as search terms – may nevertheless reveal highly sensitive information. We do not know the full extent to which personal health data is being collected for behavioral advertising. We do know that the limits placed on its collection by the industry are inadequate and that there is an urgent need to develop a definition for personal health information in the Internet context that is robust enough to protect privacy.

B. Location Information – Not Always Protected By Current Law

As technologies converge and Internet services are provided over cellular phones and other mobile devices, the ability to physically locate consumers is spurring location-based advertising, targeted to where a user is at any given moment. Plans to incorporate location information into behavioral advertising are still in development. Although laws exist to protect location information collected by telecommunications carriers, applications providers are increasingly offering location-based services that fall completely out of that legal framework. Standards for government access to location information are also unclear, even as law enforcement has shown a greater interest in such information.[12]

V. THE EMERGING USE OF ISP DATA FOR BEHAVIORAL ADVERTISING

The use of ISP data for behavioral advertising is one area that requires close scrutiny from lawmakers. The interception and sharing of Internet traffic content for behavioral advertising defies reasonable user expectations, can be disruptive to Internet and Web functionality, and may run afoul of communications privacy laws.

A. How ISP Data is Used for Behavioral Advertising

In this new model, an ad network strikes a deal with an ISP that allows the network to receive the contents of the individual Web traffic streams of each of the ISP's customers. The ad network analyzes the content of the traffic in order to create a record of the individual's online behaviors and interests. As customers of the ISP surf the Web and visit sites where the ad network has purchased ad space, they see advertisements targeted based on their previous Internet behavior. While the model as it exists today involves an ISP contracting with a third party that operates such an ad network, it would also be possible for ISPs to do the traffic content inspection, categorization, and advertising delivery themselves.

B. Privacy Implications of the Use of ISP Data for Behavioral Advertising

The privacy implications of behavioral advertising at large are amplified in this ISP model. Ad networks that partner with ISPs may potentially gain access to all or substantially all of an individual's Web traffic as it traverses the ISP's infrastructure, including traffic to all political, religious, and other non-commercial sites. While traditional ad networks may be large, few if any provide the opportunity to collect information about an individual's online activities as comprehensively as in the ISP model, particularly with respect to activities involving non-commercial content. And although these ad networks currently inspect predominantly Web traffic, ISPs carry emails, chats, file transfers and many other kinds of data that they could decide to pass on to behavioral ad networks in the future.

Moreover, the use of Internet traffic content for behavioral advertising defies user expectations about what happens when they surf the Web and communicate online. Absent unmistakable notice, consumers simply do not expect their ISP or its partners to be looking into the content of their Internet communications. Finding out that there is a middleman lurking between consumers and the Web sites they visit would come as a unwelcome surprise to most Internet users. ISPs are a critical part of the chain of trust that undergirds the Internet. Giving an unknown third party broad access to all or most consumer communications may undermine that trust.

C. Current Implementations May Interfere with Normal Internet Use

Despite these concerns, several ad network companies are moving forward with plans to use ISP data for behavioral advertising. The two most prominent ad networks engaged in this practice are NebuAd in the United States and Phorm in the UK. Charter Communications, a cable broadband ISP, recently announced – and then delayed – a plan to conduct trials of the NebuAd behavioral advertising technology.[13] Several other ISPs, such as Wide Open West (WOW!), CenturyTel, Embarq and Knology also announced plans with NebuAd to trial or deploy its behavioral advertising technology. Although a number of these ISPs have put their plans on hold in the wake of a firestorm of criticism, NebuAd continues to work with U.S. ISPs and seek new ISP partners. Phorm, which originally announced deals with three of the

UK's largest ISPs and has sought partnerships with U.S. ISPs, is also now encountering hesitation from some of its partners.[14]

Independent analyses of both companies' systems have revealed that by virtue of their ability to intercept Internet traffic in the middle of the network – and based on their desire to track individual Internet users – they engage in an array of practices that are inconsistent with the usual flow of Internet traffic. NebuAd reportedly injects computer code into Web traffic streams that causes numerous cookies to be placed on users' computers for behavioral tracking, none of which are related to or sanctioned by the Web sites the users visit.[15] When a user navigates to a particular Web site, Phorm reportedly pretends to be that Web site so that it can plant a behavioral tracking cookie linked to that site on the user's computer.[16] In addition to the privacy implications of tracking all of an individual's Web activities, this kind of conduct has the potential to create serious security vulnerabilities in the network,[17] hamper the speed of users' Internet connections, and interfere with ordinary Web functionality. At a time when many different kinds of companies are working to build a trusted computing platform for the Internet, having ISPs work with partners whose practices undermine trust raises future cyber-security concerns.

D. Current Implementations May Violate Federal Law

Depending on how this advertising model is implemented, it may also run afoul of existing communications privacy laws. The federal Wiretap Act, as amended by the Electronic Communications Privacy Act ("ECPA"), prohibits the interception and disclosure of electronic communications – including Internet traffic content – without consent.[18] Although exceptions to this rule permit interception and disclosure without consent, we seriously doubt that any of them apply to the interception or disclosure of Internet traffic content for behavioral advertising purposes. Accordingly, we believe that the Wiretap Act requires unavoidable notice and affirmative opt-in consent before Internet traffic content may be used from ISPs for behavioral advertising purposes. Certain state laws may take this one step further, requiring consent from both parties to the communication: the consumer and the Web site he or she is visiting. A detailed CDT legal memorandum on the application of the Wiretap Act, ECPA and relevant state wiretap laws to the use of ISP data for behavioral advertising is attached as Appendix B.

As several members of Congress have noted, the Cable Communications Policy Act also applies here.[19] The law prohibits cable operators from collecting or disclosing personally identifiable information without prior consent.[20] While the term "personally identifiable information" in the law is defined by what it does not include – "any record of aggregate data which does not identify particular persons"[21] – we doubt that a user's entire Web traffic stream, unique to that individual, often containing both PII and non-PII, would be considered aggregate data as that term is commonly understood.

We do not believe that it is possible to shoehorn the collection and disclosure of a subscriber's entire browsing history for advertising purposes into the statute's exception for collection or disclosure of information that is necessary to render service.[22] Thus, we conclude that cable-based ISPs that wish to disclose customer information to advertising networks would also have to meet the consent requirements of the Cable Communications Policy Act.

The ISP models that have been deployed thus far have failed to obtain affirmative, express opt-in consent required by law. Several small U.S. ISPs, for example, have failed to meet this threshold requirement, burying vague information about their deals with NebuAd in the ISPs' terms of service.[23] Charter Communications, the largest U.S. ISP that had planned to partner with NebuAd, notified its subscribers that they would be receiving more relevant ads, but did not explain its plans to intercept subscribers' traffic data, and did not provide a way for subscribers to give or withhold consent. Charter has since suspended its plans.

Designing a robust opt-in consent system for ISP-based behavioral advertising presents a formidable challenge. We are less than sanguine that such a system can be easily designed, particularly since it must not only provide a way for consumers to give affirmative consent, but it must also provide a method for them to revoke that consent. The burden is on those who wish to move forward with the model to demonstrate that an express notice and consent regime can work in this context.

VI. THE LIMITS OF SELF-REGULATION

For almost a decade, the primary privacy framework for the behavioral advertising industry has been provided by the Network Advertising Initiative, a self-regulatory group of online advertising networks formed in response to pressure from the Federal Trade Commission and consumer advocates in the wake of privacy concerns over the merger of ad network DoubleClick and Abacus, an offline data broker. NAI members agree to provide consumers with notice and, at minimum, a method to opt out of behavioral advertising. They further pledged to use information collected for only for marketing purposes. While at the time of their release CDT welcomed the NAI principles as an important first step, we also noted then that there were flaws in the approach that needed to be addressed and that self-regulation was not a complete solution. The FTC agreed, concluding in its July 2000 report to Congress that "backstop legislation addressing online profiling is still required to fully ensure that consumers' privacy is protected online."[24] That remains true today.

Eight years after the creation of the principles, few consumers are aware of behavioral advertising and fewer still have been able to successfully navigate the confusing and complex opt-out process.[25] Although individual NAI companies have launched their own consumer awareness initiatives, more work remains to be done.[26] For those consumers who successfully opt out, the NAI's reliance on flawed opt-out cookies means that user preferences are often not persistently honored.

In addition, the NAI's guidelines for the use of sensitive information have never been adequate to guard consumer privacy. Until recently, the definition was limited to a narrowly defined set of PII. While the definition is being revised, it still falls far short of what is needed to address the increasingly sensitive nature of consumer information online.[27]

Finally, the NAI principles only apply to companies that voluntarily join the initiative. The NAI has no way to force companies to join; the current membership is missing numerous behavioral advertising firms, including some key industry players. In addition, measures to ensure compliance and transparency have withered on the vine.[28] The original NAI principles provided for independent audits and enforcement against noncompliant members, but the audit results were never made public, and reporting on compliance with the principles has been inconsistent.[29]

For all these reasons, while we encourage more robust self-regulatory efforts, we continue to have doubts about the effectiveness of the self-regulatory framework. As online advertising becomes increasingly complex and data collection becomes more pervasive, Congress and the FTC must step in to ensure that consumer interests are fully protected.

VII. THE ROLE OF CONGRESS

Congress should take action to address the significant privacy concerns raised by behavioral advertising:

- As a first step, we urge the Committee to hold a series of hearings to examine specific aspects of behavioral advertising. In particular, we believe that further investigation of new models of behavioral advertising using ISP data is warranted, and that the Committee should explore how current laws such as ECPA, the Wiretap Act and the Cable Communications Policy Act apply. Secondary uses of behavioral advertising profiles for purposes other than marketing also deserve additional investigation and scrutiny, as does the use of sensitive information.
- This Committee should set a goal of enacting in the next year general privacy legislation covering both the online and offline worlds. CDT has long argued for simple, flexible baseline consumer privacy legislation that would protect consumers from inappropriate collection and misuse of their personal information while enabling legitimate business use to promote economic and social value. In principle, such legislation would codify the fundamentals of fair information practices, requiring transparency and notice of data collection practices, providing consumers with meaningful choice regarding the use and disclosure of that information, allowing consumers reasonable access to personal information they have provided, providing remedies for misuse or unauthorized access, and setting standards to limit data collection and ensure data security.
- The Federal Trade Commission has played a helpful role in consumer education efforts around behavioral advertising. But it also must exercise its authority under its deception and unfairness jurisdiction to issue enforceable guidelines for behavioral advertising. We ask the Committee to strongly urge the Commission to exercise the full measure of its enforcement authority over online advertising practices.
- Congress should also examine and strengthen existing communications privacy laws to cover new services, technologies and business models with consistent rules. ECPA was passed more than 20 years ago, long before there was a World Wide Web and the Internet became integrated into Americans' daily lives. The application of the law to common online activities including Web search remains unclear and the legal protections it provides for the enormous amounts of personal data stored online are far too low.

- Finally, Congress should encourage the FTC to investigate how technology can be harnessed to give consumers better control over their online information. The lack of effective controls and the difficulty that consumers have in exercising choice about their participation in online tracking and targeting was the motivation behind the "Do Not Track" list idea proposed by CDT and nine other consumer and privacy groups.[30] Although the proposal has been controversial, the idea behind Do Not Track is both simple and important: provide consumers with an easy-to-use, technology-neutral, persistent way to opt out of behavioral advertising. Congress should promote further study of this idea and other innovative ways to put consumers in control of their information.

VIII. CONCLUSION

I would like to thank the Committee again for holding this important hearing. We believe that Congress has a critical role to play in ensuring that privacy is protected in an increasingly complex online advertising environment. CDT looks forward to working with the Committee as it pursues these issues further.

APPENDIX A: SIMPLIFIED ILLUSTRATION OF A TRADITIONAL ONLINE AD NETWORK

Figure 1 below shows a simplified version of a traditional online ad network. Ad networks contract with advertisers on one side and publishers on the other. They take the ads they receive from advertisers and match them to open ad spaces on publisher sites.

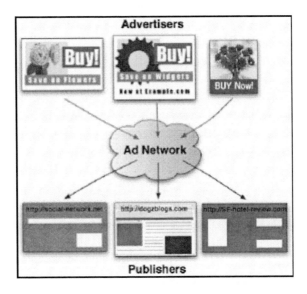

Figure 1.

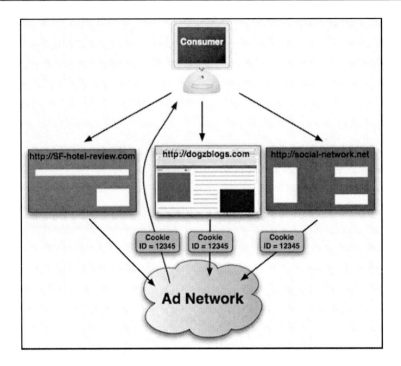

Figure 2.

Figure 2 shows how an ad network collects data about a consumer's Web activities. When the consumer first visits a publisher site in the network (SF-hotel-review.com), the ad network places a cookie with a unique ID (12345) on the consumer's computer. When the user subsequently visits other publisher sites in the network (including dogzblogs.com and social-network.net), the cookie containing the ID is automatically transmitted to the ad network. This allows the ad network to keep track of what sites the consumer has visited and build a behavioral profile based on that information, linked to the cookie ID.

APPENDIX B: AN OVERVIEW OF THE FEDERAL WIRETAP ACT, ELECTRONIC COMMUNICATIONS PRIVACY ACT, AND STATE TWO-PARTY CONSENT LAWS OF RELEVANCE TO THE NEBUAD SYSTEM AND OTHER USES OF INTERNET TRAFFIC CONTENT FROM ISPS FOR BEHAVIORAL ADVERTISING

Much of the content on the Internet (just like content in newspapers, broadcast TV, radio and cable) is supported in whole or part by advertising revenue. The Internet offers special opportunities to target ads based on the expressed or inferred interests of the individual user. There are various models for delivering targeted ads online. These range from the purely contextual (everyone who visits a travel site sees the same airline ad) to models that involve compiling information about the online behavior of individual Internet users, to be used in serving them advertisements. For years, Web sites have entered into agreements with advertising networks to use "cookies" to track individual users across Web sites in order to compile profiles. This approach has always been, and remains, a source of privacy concern, in part because the conduct usually occurs unbeknownst to most Internet users. Recent developments, including the mergers between online service providers and some of the largest online advertising networks, have heightened these concerns. The Center for Democracy & Technology has been conducting a major project on behavioral advertising, in which we have been researching behavioral advertising practices, consulting with Internet companies and privacy advocates, developing policy proposals, filing extensive comments at the FTC, and analyzing industry self-regulatory guidelines.

This memo focuses on the implications of a specific approach to behavioral advertising being considered by Internet advertising networks and Internet Service Providers (ISPs). This new approach involves copying and inspecting the content of each individual's Internet activity with the cooperation of his or her ISP.[31] Under this new model, an advertising network strikes a deal with an ISP, and the ISP allows the network to copy the contents of the individual Web traffic streams of each of the ISP's customers. The advertising network analyzes the content of these traffic streams in order to create a record of each individual's online behaviors and interests. Later, as customers of the ISP surf the Web and visit sites where the advertising network has purchased advertising space, they see ads targeted based on their previous Internet behavior.

NebuAd is one such advertising network company operating in the United States. In the past few months, it has come to light that NebuAd was planning to partner with Charter Communications, a cable broadband ISP, to conduct trials of the NebuAd behavioral advertising technology. Several other smaller ISPs, such as Wide Open West (WOW!), CenturyTel, Embarq, and Knology, have also announced plans with NebuAd to trial or deploy its behavioral advertising technology. In response to concerns raised by subscribers, privacy advocates, and policymakers, Charter, CenturyTel and Embarq have delayed these plans, but NebuAd and other similar companies are continuing to seek new ISP partners.

The use of Internet traffic content from ISPs for behavioral advertising is different from the "cookie"-based model in significant ways and raises unique concerns.[32] Among other differences, it copies all or substantially all Web transactions, including visits to sites that do not use cookies. Thus, it may capture not only commercial activity, but also visits to political, advocacy, or religious sites or other non-commercial sites that do not use cookies.

In this memo, we conclude that the use of Internet traffic content from ISPs may run afoul of federal wiretap laws unless the activity is conducted with the consent of the subscriber.[33] To be effective, such consent should not be buried in terms of service and should not be inferred from a mailed notice. We recommend prior, express consent, but we do not offer here any detailed recommendations on how to obtain such consent in an ISP context. Also, we note that that the California law requiring consent of all the parties to a communication has been applied by the state Supreme Court to the monitoring of telephone calls when the monitoring is done at a facility outside California. The California law so far has not been applied to Internet communications and it is unclear whether it would apply specifically to the copying of communications as conducted for behavioral monitoring purposes, but if it or another state's all-party consent rule were applied to use of Internet traffic for behavioral profiling, it would seem to pose an insurmountable barrier to the practice.

I. Wiretap Act

A. Service Providers Cannot "Divulge" The Contents of Subscriber Communications, Except Pursuant to Limited Exceptions

The federal Wiretap Act, as amended by the Electronic Communications Privacy Act, protects the privacy of wire, oral, and electronic communications.[34] "[E]lectronic communication" is defined as "any transfer of signs, signals, writing, images, sounds, data, or intelligence of any nature transmitted in whole or in part by a wire, radio, electromagnetic, photoelectronic or photooptical system . . . ."[35] Web browsing and other Internet communications are clearly electronic communications protected by the Wiretap Act.

In language pertinent to the model under consideration, § 2511(3) of the Act states that "a person or entity providing an electronic communication service to the pubic shall not intentionally divulge the contents of any communications . . . while in transmission on that service to any person or entity other than an addressee or intended recipient . . . ."[36]

There are exceptions to this prohibition on disclosure, two of which may be relevant here. One exception specifies that "[i]t shall not be unlawful under this chapter for an . . . electronic communication service, whose facilities are used in the transmission of a[n] . . . electronic communication, to intercept, disclose, or use that communication in the normal course of his employment while engaged in any activity which is a *necessary incident to the rendition of his service* or to the protection of the rights or property of the provider of that service."[37] We will refer to this as the "necessary incident" exception. The second exception is for disclosures with the consent of one of the parties.[38] We will discuss both exceptions below. We conclude that only the consent exception applies to the disclosure of subscriber content for behavioral advertising, and we will discuss preliminarily what "consent" would mean in this context.

B. With Limited Exceptions, Interception Is Also Prohibited

The Wiretap Act regulates the "interception" of electronic communications. The Act defines "intercept" as the "acquisition of the contents of any . . . electronic . . . communication through the use of any electronic, mechanical, or other device."[39]

The Wiretap Act broadly bars all intentional interception of electronic communications.[40] The Act enumerates specific exceptions to this prohibition.[41] Law enforcement officers, for example, are authorized to conduct interceptions pursuant to a court order. For ISPs and other service providers, there are three exceptions that might be relevant. Two we have mentioned already: the "necessary incident" exception and a consent exception.[42]

A third exception, applicable to interception but not to disclosure, arises from the definition of "intercept," which is defined as acquisition by an "electronic, mechanical, or other device," which in turn is defined as "any device or apparatus which can be used to intercept a[n] . . . electronic communication *other than*—(a) any telephone or telegraph instrument, equipment or facility, or any component thereof . . . (ii) being used by a provider of . . . electronic communication service in the *ordinary course of its business* . . . ."[43] This provision thus serves to limit the definition of "intercept," providing what is sometimes called the "telephone extension" exception, but which we will call the "business use" exception.

C. The Copying of Internet Content for Disclosure to Advertising Networks Constitutes Interception

When an ISP copies a customer's communications or allows them to be copied by an advertising network, those communications have undoubtedly been "intercept[ed]."[44] Therefore, unless an exception applies, it seems likely that placing a device on an ISP's network and using it to copy communications for use in developing advertising profiles would constitute illegal interception under § 2511(1)(a); similarly, the disclosure or use of the intercepted communications would run afoul of § 2511(1)(c) or § 2511(1)(d), respectively.

D. The "Necessary Incident" Exception Probably Does Not Permit the Interception or Disclosure of Communications for Behavioral Advertising Purposes

The Wiretap Act permits interception of electronic communications when the activity takes place as "a necessary incident to the rendition of [the ISP's] service or to the protection of the rights or property of the provider of that service."[45] The latter prong covers anti-spam and anti-virus monitoring and filtering and various anti-fraud activities, but cannot be extended to advertising activities, which, while they may enhance the service provider's revenue, do not "protect" its rights. Courts have construed the "necessary incident" prong quite strictly, requiring a service provider to show that it *must* engage in the activity in order to carry out its business.[46] It is unlikely that the copying, diversion, or disclosure of Internet traffic content for behavioral advertising would be construed as a "necessary incident" to an ISP's business. Conceivably, an ISP could argue that its business included copying its subscribers communications and providing them to third parties for purposes of placing advertisements on Web sites unaffiliated with the ISP, but the ISP would probably have to state that that business existed and get the express agreement of its customers that they were subscribing to that business as well as the basic business of Internet access, which leads anyhow to the consent model that we conclude is necessary.

E. While It Is Unclear Whether the "Business Use" Exception Would Apply to the Use of a Device Installed or Controlled by a Party Other than the Service Provider, the Exception Does Not Apply to the Prohibition Against Divulging a Subscriber's Communications

The "business use" exception, § 2510(5)(a), constricts the definition of "device" and thereby narrows the definition of "intercept" in the Wiretap Act. There are two questions involved in assessing applicability of this exception to the use of Internet traffic content for behavioral advertising: (1) whether the device that copies the content for delivery to the advertising network constitutes a "telephone or telegraph instrument, equipment or facility, or any component thereof," and (2) whether an ISP's use of the device would be within the "ordinary course of its business."

We will discuss the "business use" exception at some length, because there has been considerable discussion already about whether copying of an ISP subscriber's communications for behavioral advertising is an "interception" under § 2511(1) of the Wiretap Act. However, even if the business use exception applied, an ISP would only avoid liability for the *interception* of electronic communications. It would still be prohibited from divulging the communications of its customers to an advertising network under the separate section of the Wiretap Act, § 2511(3), which states that a service provider "shall not intentionally divulge the contents of any communication . . . while in transmission on that service to any person or entity other than an addressee or intended recipient . . . ."[47] The business use exception does not apply to this prohibition against divulging.[48]

At first glance, it would seem that the business use exception is inapplicable to the facilities of an ISP because the exception applies only to a "telephone or telegraph instrument, equipment or facility, or any component thereof." However, the courts have recognized that ECPA was motivated in part by the "dramatic changes in new computer and telecommunications technologies"[49] and therefore was intended to make the Wiretap Act largely neutral with respect to its treatment of various communications technologies. The Second Circuit, for example, concluded in a related context that the term "telephone" should broadly include the "instruments, equipment and facilities that ISPs use to transmit e-mail."[50] Therefore, as a general matter, it should be assumed that the business use exception is available to ISPs.

However, it is not certain that the device used to copy and divert content for behavioral advertising would be considered to be a component of the service provider's equipment or facilities. In some of the behavioral advertising implementations that have been described, the monitoring device or process is not developed or controlled by the ISP but rather by the advertising network.

The second question is whether an ISP's use of a device to copy traffic content for behavioral advertising falls within the "ordinary course of its business." There are a number of cases interpreting this exception, but none of them clearly addresses a situation where a service provider is copying all of the communications of its customers. Many of the cases arise in situations where employers are monitoring the calls of their employees for purposes of supervision and quality assurance. "These cases have narrowly construed the phrase 'ordinary course of business.'"[51] Often such cases also involve notice to the employees and implied consent.[52] One court has stated that, even if an entity could satisfy the business use exception, notice to one of the parties being monitored would be required.[53] Other cases involve the monitoring of prisoners.

Some cases have interpreted "ordinary course" to mean anything that is used in "normal" operations. The D.C. Circuit, for instance, has suggested that monitoring "undertaken normally" qualifies as being within the "ordinary course of business."[54] In the context of law enforcement taping of the phone calls of prisoners, the Ninth and Tenth Circuits have concluded that something is in the "ordinary course" if it is done routinely and consistently.[55] It might be that courts would give equal or greater latitude to service providers in monitoring their networks than they would give to mere subscribers or users.

Other circuit courts have used a more limited interpretation, concluding that "ordinary course" only applies if the device is being used to intercept communications for "legitimate business reasons."[56] Although the courts have not been entirely clear as to what that means, some have suggested that it is much closer to necessity than to mere profit motive.[57] One frequently-cited case explicitly holds that the business use exception does not broadly encompass a company's financial or other motivations: "The phrase 'in the ordinary course of business' cannot be expanded to mean anything that interests a company."[58]

Normal principles of statutory interpretation would require that some independent weight be given to the word "ordinary," so that the exception does not encompass anything done for business purposes. It is unclear, however, how much weight courts would give to the word "ordinary" in a rapidly changing market. It does not seem that the phrase "ordinary course of business" should preclude innovation, but courts might refer to past practices and normal expectations surrounding a line of business and specifically might look to what customers have come to expect.

Viewed one way, it is hard to see how the copying of content for behavioral advertising is part of the "ordinary course of business" of an ISP. After all, the ISP is not the one that will be using the content to develop profiles of its customers; the profiling is done by the advertising network, which does not even disclose to the ISP the profiles of its own subscribers. (The profiles are proprietary to the advertising network and it is careful not to disclose them to anyone.) Very few (if any) of the ads that are placed using the profiles will be ads for the ISP's services; they will be ads for products and services completely unrelated to the ISP's "ordinary course of business." Moreover, the ads will be placed on Web sites having no affiliation with the ISP. On the other hand, the ISP could argue that part of its business model—part of what keeps its rates low—is deriving revenue from its partnership with advertising networks.

The legislative histories of the Wiretap Act and ECPA weigh against a broad reading of the business use exception. Through these laws, Congress intended to create a statutory regime generally affording strong protection to electronic communications. Congress included limited, specific and detailed exceptions for law enforcement access to communications, and other limited, specific and detailed exceptions to allow companies providing electronic communications service to conduct ordinary system maintenance and operational activities. Congress gave especially high protection to communications content. If the business use exception can apply any time an ISP identifies a new revenue stream that can be tapped though use of its customers' communications, this careful statutory scheme would be seriously undermined.

F. The Consent Exception: The Context Weighs Heavily in Favor of Affirmative, Opt-In Consent from ISP Subscribers

Consent is an explicit exception both to the prohibition against intercepting electronic communications under the Wiretap Act and to the Act's prohibition against disclosing subscriber communications. The key question is: How should consent be obtained for use of Internet traffic content for behavioral advertising? Courts have held in telephone monitoring cases under the Wiretap Act that consent can be implied, but there are relatively few cases specifically addressing consent and electronic communications. However, in cases involving telephone monitoring, one circuit court has stated that consent under the Wiretap Act "is not to be cavalierly implied."[59] Another circuit court has noted that consent "should not casually be inferred"[60] and that consent must be "actual," not "constructive."[61] Yet another circuit court has stated: "Without actual notice, consent can only be implied when the surrounding circumstances *convincingly* show that the party knew about and consented to the interception."[62] Furthermore, "knowledge of the *capability* of monitoring alone cannot be considered implied consent."[63] The cases where consent has been implied involve very explicit notice; many of them involve the monitoring of prisoners' phone calls.[64]

Consent is context-based. It is one thing to imply consent in the context of a prison or a workplace, where notice may be presented as part of the daily log-in process. It is quite another to imply it in the context of ordinary Internet usage by residential subscribers, who, by definition, are using the service for personal and often highly sensitive communications.

Continued use of a service after a mailed notice might not be enough to constitute consent. Certainly, mailing notification to the bill payer is probably insufficient to put all members of the household who share the Internet connection on notice.

Thus, it seems that an assertion of implied consent, whether or not users are provided an opportunity to opt out of the system, would most likely not satisfy the consent exception for the type of interception or disclosure under consideration here. Express prior consent (opt-in consent) is clearly preferable and may be required. While meaningful opt-in consent would be sufficient, courts would likely be skeptical of an opt-in consisting merely of a click-through agreement—i.e., a set of terms that a user agrees to by clicking an on-screen button—if it displays characteristics typical of such agreements, such as a large amount of text displayed in a small box, no requirement that the user scroll through the entire agreement, or the opt-in provision buried among other terms of service.[65]

In regards to consent, the model under discussion here is distinguishable from the use of "cookies," which were found to be permissible by a federal district court in a 2001 case involving DoubleClick.[66] In that case, the Web sites participating in the DoubleClick advertising network were found to be parties to the communications of the Internet users who visited those sites. As parties to the communications, the Web sites could consent to the use of the cookies to collect information about those communications. Here, of course, the ISPs are not parties to the communications being monitored and the interception or disclosure encompasses communications with sites that are not members of the advertising network. Therefore, the source of consent must be the IPS's individual subscribers, as it would be impossible to obtain consent from every single Web site that every subscriber may conceivably visit.

II. State Laws Requiring Two-Party Consent to Communication Interception

A. Summary

In addition to the federal Wiretap Act, a majority of states have their own wiretap laws, which can be more stringent than the federal law. Most significantly, twelve states[67] require all parties to consent to the interception or recording of certain types of communications when such interception is done by a private party not under the color of law.

In several of these states—for example, Connecticut—the all-party consent requirement applies only to the recording of oral conversations. In others, the all-party consent rule extends to both voice and data communications. For example, Florida's Security of Communications Act makes it a felony for any individual to intercept, disclose, or use any wire, oral, or electronic communication, unless that person has obtained the prior consent of all parties.[68] Similarly, the Illinois statute on criminal eavesdropping prohibits a person from "intercept[ing], retain[ing], or transcrib[ing an] electronic communication unless he does so . . . with the consent of all of the parties to such . . . electronic communication."[69]

The most important all-party consent law may be California's, because the California Supreme Court held in 2006 that the law can be applied to activity occurring outside the state.

B. California

The 1967 California Invasion of Privacy Act makes criminally liable any individual who "intentionally taps, or makes any unauthorized connection . . . or who willfully and without the consent of all parties to the communication . . . reads, or attempts to read, or to learn the contents or meaning of any message . . . or communication while the same is in transit or passing over any wire, line, or cable, or is being sent from, or received at any place" in California.[70] It also establishes liability for any individual "who uses, or attempts to use, in any manner . . . any information so obtained" or who aids any person in doing the same.[71] The law has a separate section creating liability for any person eavesdropping upon or recording a confidential communication "intentionally and without the consent of all parties," whether the parties are present in the same location or communicating over telegraph, telephone, or other device (except a radio).[72]

Consent can be implied only in very limited circumstances. The California state Court of Appeals held in *People v. Garber* that a subscriber to a telephone system is deemed to have consented to the telephone company's monitoring of his calls if he uses the system in a manner that reasonably justifies the company's belief that he is violating his subscription rights, and even then the company may only monitor his calls to the extent necessary for the investigation.[73] An individual can maintain an objectively reasonable expectation of privacy by explicitly withholding consent for a tape recording, even if the other party has indicated an intention to record the communication.[74]

In *Kearney v. Salomon Smith Barney, Inc.*, the state Supreme Court addressed the conflict between the California all-party consent standard and Georgia's wiretap law, which is modeled after the federal one-party standard.[75] It held that, where a Georgia firm recorded calls made from its Georgia office to residents in California, the California law applied. The court said that it would be unfair to impose damages on the Georgia firm, but prospectively the case effectively required out-of-state firms having telephone communications with people in California to announce to all parties at the outset their intent to record a communication. Clear notice and implied consent are sufficient. "If, after being so advised, another party does not wish to participate in the conversation, he or she simply may decline to continue the communication."[76]

C. The Implications of Kearney

The Kearney case arose in the context of telephone monitoring, and there is a remarkable lack of case law addressing whether the California statute applies to Internet communications. If it does, or if there is one other state that applies its all-party consent rule to conduct affecting Internet communications across state lines, then no practical form of opt-in, no matter how robust, would save the practice of copying Internet content for behavioral advertising. That is, even if the ISP only copies the communications of those subscribers that consent, and the monitoring occurs only inside a one-party consent state, as soon as one of those customers has a communication with a non-consenting person (or Web site) in an all-party consent state that applies its rule to interceptions occurring outside the state, the ISP would seem to be in jeopardy. The ISP could not conceivably obtain consent from every person and Web site in the all-party consent state. Nor could it identify (for the purpose of obtaining consent) which people or Web sites its opted-in subscribers would want to communicate with in advance of those communications occurring.

A countervailing argument could be made that an all-party consent rule is not applicable to the behavioral advertising model, since the process only copies or divulges one half of the communication, namely the half from the consenting subscriber.

Conclusion

The practice that has been described to us, whereby an ISP may enter into an agreement with an advertising network to copy and analyze the traffic content of the ISP's customers, poses serious questions under the federal Wiretap Act. It seems that the disclosure of a subscriber's communications is prohibited without consent. In addition, especially where the copying is achieved by a device owned or controlled by the advertising network, the copying of the contents of subscriber communications seems to be, in the absence of consent, a prohibited interception. Affirmative express consent, and a cessation of copying upon withdrawal of consent, would probably save such practices under federal law, but there may be state laws requiring all-party consent that would be more difficult to satisfy.

End Notes

[1] "Behavioral Advertising on Target … to Explode Online," *eMarketer* (Jun. 2007), http://www.emarketer.com/Article.aspx?id=1004989.

[2] No fewer than five major mergers and acquisitions have been completed in the last 18 months: Google purchased online advertising company DoubleClick, Inc.; WPP Group, a large ad agency, acquired the online ad company 24/7 Real Media; Yahoo! acquired ad firm RightMedia; Microsoft acquired online ad service provider aQuantive; AOL purchased Tacoda, a pioneering firm in the area of behavioral advertising.

[3] Michael Barbaro and Tom Zeller, Jr., "A Face Is Exposed for AOL Searcher No. 4417749," *The New York Times* (Aug.   2006), http://www.nytimes.com/2006/08/09/technology/09aol.html?_r=1&ex=1312776000&adxnnl=1&oref=slogin&adxnnlx=1215021816-j7kbrLxHU1hCdcMyNqHEbA.

[4] See, e.g., Microsoft, *Privacy Protections in Microsoft's Ad Serving System and the Process of "De-identification"* (Oct.   2007),   http://download.microsoft.com/download/3/1/d/31df6942-ed99-4024-a0e0-594b9d27a31a/Privacy%20Protections%20in%20Microsoft%27s%20Ad%20Serving%20System%20and%20the%20Process%20of%20De-Identification.pdf.

[5] Acxiom runs Relevance-X, an online ad network. Last year Experian acquired the online data analysis company Hitwise. *See* Acxiom, *Acxiom: Relevance-X* (last visited Jul. 2008), http://www.acxiom.com/Relevance-X; Experian,   "Acquisition   of   Hitwise"   (Apr.   2007),   http://www.experiangroup.com/corporate/news/releases/2007/2007-04-17b/.

[6] *See, e.g.,* Peter Whoriskey, "Every Click You Make," *The Washington Post* (Apr. 2008), http://www.washingtonpost.com/wp-dyn/content/article/2008/04/03/AR2008040304052.html?nav=hcmodule;   Saul Hansell, "I.S.P. Tracking: The Mother of All Privacy Battles," *The New York Times: Bits Blog* (Mar. 2008) at http://bits.blogs.nytimes.com/2008/03/20/isp-tracking-the-mother-of-all-privacy-battles/?scp=1-b&sq=the+mother+of+all+privacy+battles&st=nyt.

[7] Alan F. Westin, *How Online Users Feel About Behavioral Marketing and How Adoption of Privacy and Security Policies Could Affect Their Feelings* (Mar. 2008).

[8] TRUSTe, "TRUSTe Report Reveals Consumer Awareness and Attitudes About Behavioral Targeting" (Mar. 2008),   http://www.marketwire.com/mw/release.do?id=837437&sourceType=1   ("71   percent   of   online consumers are aware that their browsing information may be collected by a third party for advertising purposes . . .. 57 percent of respondents say they are not comfortable with advertisers using that browsing history to serve relevant ads, even when that information cannot be tied to their names or any other personal information.").

[9] *Am. Fed'n of Gov't Employees v. Hawley*, D.D.C., No. 07-00855, 3/31/08 (ruling, *inter alia*, that concerns about identity theft, embarrassment, inconvenience, and damage to financial suitability requirements after an

apparent data breach constituted a recognizable "adverse effect" under the Privacy Act, 5 U.S.C. § 552(a) (citing *Kreiger v. Dep't of Justice*, 529 F.Supp.2d 29, 53 (D.D.C. 2008)).

[10] *See* Louise Story, "Online Pitches Made Just For You," *The New York Times* (Mar. 2008), http://www.nytimes.com/2008/03/06/business/media/06adco.html.

[11] *See* Center for Democracy & Technology, *Digital Search and Seizure: Updating Privacy Protections to Keep Pace with Technology* (2006), http://www.cdt.org/publications/digital-search-and-seizure.pdf at 7-9; Deirdre K. Mulligan, "Reasonable Expectations in Electronic Communications: A Critical Perspective on the Electronic Communications Privacy Act," 72 Geo. Wash. L. Rev. 1557 (Aug. 2004); Daniel J. Solove, "Digital Dossiers and the Dissipation of Fourth Amendment Privacy," 75 S. Cal. L. Rev. 1083, 1135 (2002).

[12] *See* Center for Democracy & Technology, *Digital Search & Seizure: Updating Privacy Protections to Keep Pace with Technology* (2006), http://www.cdt.org/publications/digital-search-and-seizure.pdf at 23-29.

[13] Saul Hansell, "Charter Suspends Plan to Sell Customer Data to Advertisers," *The New York Times: Bits Blog* (Jun. 2008), http://bits.blogs.nytimes.com/2008/06/24/charter-suspends-plan-to-sell-customer-data-to-advertisers/?scp=3-b&sq=charter+nebuad&st=nyt.

[14] Chris Williams, "CPW builds wall between customers and Phorm," *The Register* (Mar. 2008), http://www.theregister.co.uk/2008/03/11/phorm_shares_plummet/

[15] Robert M. Topolski, *NebuAd and Partner ISPs: Wiretapping, Forgery and Browser Hijacking*, Free Press and Public Knowledge (Jun 2008), http://www.publicknowledge.org/pdf/nebuad-report-20080618.pdf.

[16] Richard Clayton, *The Phorm "Webwise" System* (May 2008), http://www.cl.cam.ac.uk/~rnc1/080518-phorm.pdf.

[17] These types of behaviors have much in common with well-understood online security threats, and parts of the Internet security community are already investigating how to respond. *See* Anti-Spyware Coalition, "Anti-Spyware Coalition Aims to Address Behavioral Targeting" (Apr. 2008), http://antispywarecoalition.org/newsroom/20080425press.htm.

[18] 18 U.S.C. § 2511.

[19] House Representative Edward Markey and House Representative Joe Barton, *Letter to Charter Communications CEO in Regards to the Charter-NebuAd Data Collection Scheme* (May 2008) http://markey.house.gov/docs/telecomm/letter_charter_comm_privacy.pdf. A 1992 amendment adding the phrase "other services" to the Cable Act's privacy provision made it clear that the law covers Internet services provided by cable operators.

[20] 47 U.S.C. § 551(b)-(c).

[21] *Id.* § 551(a)(2)(A).

[22] *Id.* § 551(a)(2)(B).

[23] *See* Mike Masnick, "Where's The Line Between Personalized Advertising And Creeping People Out?," *TechDirt* (Mar. 2008), http://www.techdirt.com/articles/20080311/121305499.shtml; Peter Whoriskey, "Every Click You Make," *The Washington Post* (Apr. 2008), http://www.washingtonpost.com/wp-dyn/content/article/2008/04/03/AR2008040304052.html?nav=hcmodule.

[24] Federal Trade Commission, *Online Profiling: A Report to Congress* (Jul. 2000), http://www.ftc.gov/os/2000/07/onlineprofiling.htm.

[25] The drawbacks of opt-out cookies have been well documented: they are confusing for the majority of consumers who do not understand the technology and counter-intuitive to those who are accustomed to deleting their cookies to protect their privacy. Cookies are susceptible to accidental deletion and file corruption. While the NAI is in the process of updating the principles, it has not proposed changes to the opt-out regime. *See* Center for Democracy & Technology, *Applying the FTC's Spyware Principles to Behavioral Advertising: Comments of the Center for Democracy & Technology in regards to the FTC Town Hall, "Ehavioral Advertising: Tracking, Targeting, and Technology"* (Oct. 2007), http://www.cdt.org/privacy/20071019CDTcomments.pdf at 8.

[26] *See, e.g.,* AOL, *Mr. Penguin* (last visited Jul. 2008), http://corp.aol.com/o/mr-penguin/; Yahoo!, *Customized Advertising* (last visited Jul. 2008), http://info.yahoo.com/relevantads/; Google, *The Google Privacy Channel* (last visited Jul. 2008), http://youtube.com/user/googleprivacy.

[27] Center for Democracy & Technology, *Comments Regarding the NAI Principles 2008: The Network Advertising Initiative's Self-Regulatory Code of Conduct for Online Behavioral Advertising* (June 2008), http://www.cdt.org/privacy/20080612_NAI_comments.pdf at 6-9.

[28] CDT testing has revealed that only a tiny fraction of companies that collect data that could be used for behavioral advertising are NAI members. *See* Center for Democracy & Technology, *Statement of The Center for Democracy & Technology before The Antitrust, Competition Policy and Consumer Rights Subcommittee of the Senate Committee on the Judiciary on "An Examination of the Google-DoubleClick Merger and the Online Advertising Industry: What Are the Risks for Competition and Privacy?"* (Sept. 2007), http://www.cdt.org/privacy/20070927committee-statement.pdf.

[29] *See* Pam Dixon, *The Network Advertising Initiative: Failing at Consumer Protection and at Self-Regulation* (Nov. 2007), http://www.worldprivacyforum.org/pdf/WPF_NAI_report_Nov2_2007fs.pdf at 16-17.

[30] *See* Pam Dixon et al, *Consumer Rights and Protections in the Behavioral Advertising Sector* (Oct. 2007), http://www.cdt.org/privacy/20071031consumerprotectionsbehavioral.pdf.

[31] *See, e.g.,* Peter Whoriskey, *Every Click You Make*, WASH. POST (Apr. 3, 2008), http://www. washingtonpost.com/wp-dyn/content/article/2008/04/03/AR2008040304052.html?nav=hcmodule; Saul Hansell, *I.S.P. Tracking: The Mother of All Privacy Battles*, N.Y. TIMES: BITS BLOG (Mar. 20, 2008), http://bits.blogs.nytimes.com/2008/03/20/isp-tracking-the-mother-of-all-privacy-battles/?scp=1-b&sq=the+mother+of+all+privacy+battles&st=nyt.

[32] Privacy concerns also apply to advertising-based models that have been developed for services, such as email, that ride over ISP networks. *See* CDT Policy Post 10.6, *Google GMail Highlights General Privacy Concerns*, (Apr. 12, 2004), http://www.cdt.org/publications/policyposts/2004/6 (recommending express prior opt-in for advertising-based email service).

[33] Additional questions have been raised under the Cable Communications Policy Act. *See* Rep. Edward Markey and Rep. Joe Barton, *Letter to Charter Communications CEO in Regards to the Charter-NebuAd Data Collection Scheme* (May 2008), http://markey.house.gov/docs/telecomm/letter_charter_comm_privacy.pdf. In this memo, we focus on issues arising under the federal Wiretap Act, as amended by the Electronic Communications Privacy Act.

[34] 18 U.S.C. §§ 2510-2522.

[35] *Id.* § 2510(12).

[36] *Id.* § 2511(3)(a). Lest there be any argument that the disclosure does not occur while the communications are "in transmission," we note that the Stored Communications Act (SCA) states that "a person or entity providing an electronic communication service to the public shall not knowingly divulge to any person or entity the contents of a communication while in electronic storage by that service." *Id.* § 2702(a)(1). We do not comment further here on the SCA because, in our judgment, the approach that has been described so far clearly involves the divulging of communications "while in transmission."

[37] *Id.* § 2511(2)(a)(i) (emphasis added). This analysis focuses on the capture of electronic communications and definitions are abridged accordingly.

[38] *Id.* § 2511(3)(b)(ii).

[39] *Id.* § 2510(4).

[40] *Id.* § 2511(1).

[41] *Id.* § 2511(2).

[42] Separate from the consent provision for disclosure, the consent exception for interception is set forth in 18 U.S.C. § 2511(2)(d): "It shall not be unlawful under this chapter for a person not acting under color of law to intercept a[n] . . . electronic communication where such person is a party to the communication or where one of the parties to the communication has given prior consent to such interception . . . ."

[43] *Id.* § 2510(5) (emphasis added).

[44] *See, e.g.,* United States v. Rodriguez, 968 F.2d 130, 136 (2d Cir. 1992) (holding in context of telephone communications that "when the contents of a wire communication are captured or redirected in any way, an interception occurs at that time" and that "[r]edirection presupposes interception"); *In re* State Police Litig., 888 F. Supp. 1235, 1267 (D. Conn. 1995) (stating in context of telephone communications that "it is the act of diverting, and not the act of listening, that constitutes an 'interception'").

[45] 18 U.S.C. § 2511(2)(a)(i).

[46] *See* United States v. Councilman, 418 F.3d 67, 82 (1st Cir. 2005) (en banc) (holding that service provider's capture of emails to gain commercial advantage "clearly" was not within service provider exception); Berry v. Funk, 146 F.3d 1003, 1010 (D.C. Cir. 1998) (holding in context of telephone communications that switchboard operators' overhearing of a few moments of phone call to ensure call went through is a "necessary incident," but anything more is outside service provider exception).

[47] 18 U.S.C. § 2511(3)(a).

[48] By adopting two different exceptions—"necessary incident" and "ordinary course"—Congress apparently meant them to have different meanings. Based on our reading of the cases, the necessary incident exception is narrower than the ordinary course exception. It is significant that the "necessary incident" exception applies to both interception and disclosure while the "ordinary course" exception is applicable only to interception. This suggests that Congress meant to allow service providers broader latitude in examining (that is, "intercepting" or "using") subscriber communications so long as they did not disclose the communications to third parties. This permits providers to conduct a range of in-house maintenance and service quality functions that do not involve disclosing communications to third parties.

[49] S. Rep. No. 99-541, at 1 (1986), *reprinted in* 1986 U.S.C.C.A.N. 3555.

[50] Hall v. Earthlink Network, Inc., 396 F.3d 500, 505 (2d Cir. 2005) (quoting S. Rep. No. 99-541 at 8).

[51] United States v. Murdock, 63 F.3d 1391. 1396 (6th Cir 1995).

[52] *E.g.,* James v. Newspaper Agency Corp., 591 F.2d 579 (10th Cir. 1979).

[53] *See, e.g.,* Adams v. City of Battle Creek, 250 F.3d 980, 984 (6th Cir. 2001).

[54] Berry v. Funk, 146 F.3d 1003, 1009 (D.C. Cir. 1998) (workplace monitoring).

[55] *See* United States v. Van Poyck, 77 F.3d 285, 292 (9th Cir. 1996); United States v. Gangi, 57 Fed. Appx. 809, 814 (10th Cir. 2003).

[56] *See* Arias v. Mutual Central Alarm Serv., Inc., 202 F.3d 553, 560 (2d Cir. 2000) (monitoring calls to an central alarm monitoring service).

[57] *See id.* (concluding that alarm company had legitimate reasons to tap all calls because such businesses "are the repositories of extremely sensitive security information, including information that could facilitate access to their customers' premises"); *see also* First v. Stark County Board of Comm'rs, 234 F.3d 1268, at *4 (6th Cir. 2000) (table disposition).

[58] Watkins v. L.M. Berry & Co., 704 F.2d 577, 582 (11th Cir. 1983). Watkins states: "We hold that a personal call may not be intercepted in the ordinary course of business under the exemption in section 2510(5)(a)(i), except to the extent necessary to guard against unauthorized use of the telephone or to determine whether a call is personal or not. In other words, a personal call may be intercepted in the ordinary course of business to determine its nature but never its contents." 704 F.2d at 583. This language supports the conclusion that the business use exception could not cover wholesale interception of ISP traffic, no more than switchboard operators can perform wholesale monitoring of telephone traffic.

[59] Watkins. 704 F.2d at 581 ("Consent under title III is not to be cavalierly implied. Title III expresses a strong purpose to protect individual privacy by strictly limiting the occasions on which interception may lawfully take place.").

[60] Griggs-Ryan v. Smith, 904 F.2d 112, 117 (1st Cir. 1990).

[61] *In re* Pharmatrak, Inc. Privacy Litig., 329 F.3d 9, 20 (1st Cir. 2003); *see also* United States v. Corona-Chavez, 328 F.3d 974, 978 (8th Cir. 2003).

[62] Berry v. Funk, 146 F.3d 1003, 1011 (D.C. Cir. 1998) (internal quotation omitted).

[63] Watkins, 704 F.2d at 581; *see also* Deal v. Spears, 980 F.2d 1153, 1157 (8th Cir. 1992) (holding that consent not implied when individual is aware only that monitoring might occur, rather than knowing monitoring is occurring).

[64] "The circumstances relevant to an implication of consent will vary from case to case, but the compendium will ordinarily include language or acts which tend to prove (or disprove) that a party knows of, or assents to, encroachments on the routine expectation that conversations are private. And the ultimate determination must proceed in light of the prophylactic purpose of Title III-a purpose which suggests that consent should not casually be inferred." Griggs-Ryan, 904 F.2d at 117.

[65] *See, e.g.,* Specht v. Netscape Commc'ns Corp., 306 F.3d 17 (2d Cir. 2002) (rejecting online arbitration agreement because, among other things, site permitted customer to download product without having scrolled down to arbitration clause and agreement button said only "Download"); United States v. Lanoue, 71 F.3d 966, 981 (1st Cir. 1995) ("Deficient notice will almost always defeat a claim of implied consent.").

[66] *In re* DoubleClick Inc. Privacy Litig., 154 F.Supp.2d 497 (S.D.N.Y. 2001).

[67] The twelve states are California, Connecticut, Florida, Illinois, Maryland, Massachusetts, Michigan, Montana, Nevada, New Hampshire, Pennsylvania, and Washington.

[68] Fla. Stat. § 934.03(1).

[69] Ill. Comp Stat. 5/14-1(a)(1).

[70] Cal. Pen. Code § 631(a).

[71] *Id.*

[72] *Id.* § 632(a). The statute explicitly excludes radio communications from the category of confidential communications.

[73] 275 Cal. App. 2d 119 (Cal. App. 1st Dist. 1969).

[74] Nissan Motor Co. v. Nissan Computer Corp., 180 F. Supp. 2d 1089 (C.D. Cal. 2002).

[75] 39 Cal. 4th 95 (2006).

[76] Id. at 118.

In: Advertising: Developments and Issues in the Digital Age   ISBN: 978-1-61761-783-6
Editor: William L. Poulsen   © 2011 Nova Science Publishers, Inc.

Chapter 7

GUIDES CONCERNING THE USE OF ENDORSEMENTS AND TESTIMONIALS IN ADVERTISING

Federal Trade Commission

This document includes only the text of the Revised Endorsement and Testimonial Guides. To learn more, read the Federal Register Notice at www.ftc.gov/opa/2009/10/endortest.shtm.

§ 255.0 PURPOSE AND DEFINITIONS

(a) The Guides in this part represent administrative interpretations of laws enforced by the Federal Trade Commission for the guidance of the public in conducting its affairs in conformity with legal requirements. Specifically, the Guides address the application of Section 5 of the FTC Act (15 U.S.C. 45) to the use of endorsements and testimonials in advertising. The Guides provide the basis for voluntary compliance with the law by advertisers and endorsers. Practices inconsistent with these Guides may result in corrective action by the Commission under Section 5 if, after investigation, the Commission has reason to believe that the practices fall within the scope of conduct declared unlawful by the statute.

The Guides set forth the general principles that the Commission will use in evaluating endorsements and testimonials, together with examples illustrating the application of those principles. The Guides do not purport to cover every possible use of endorsements in advertising. Whether a particular endorsement or testimonial is deceptive will depend on the specific factual circumstances of the advertisement at issue.

(b) For purposes of this part, an endorsement means any advertising message (including verbal statements, demonstrations, or depictions of the name, signature, likeness or other identifying personal characteristics of an individual or the name or seal of an organization) that consumers are likely to believe reflects the opinions, beliefs, findings, or experiences of a party other than the sponsoring advertiser, even if the views expressed by that party are identical to those of the sponsoring advertiser. The party whose opinions, beliefs, findings, or experience the message appears to reflect will be called the endorser and may be an individual, group, or institution.

(c) The Commission intends to treat endorsements and testimonials identically in the context of its enforcement of the Federal Trade Commission Act and for purposes of this part. The term endorsements is therefore generally used hereinafter to cover both terms and situations.

(d) For purposes of this part, the term product includes any product, service, company or industry.

(e) For purposes of this part, an expert is an individual, group, or institution possessing, as a result of experience, study, or training, knowledge of a particular subject, which knowledge is superior to what ordinary individuals generally acquire.

Example 1: A film critic's review of a movie is excerpted in an advertisement. When so used, the review meets the definition of an endorsement because it is viewed by readers as a statement of the critic's own opinions and not those of the film producer, distributor, or exhibitor. Any alteration in or quotation from the text of the review that does not fairly reflect its substance would be a violation of the standards set by this part because it would distort the endorser's opinion. [*See* § 255.1(b).]

Example 2: A TV commercial depicts two women in a supermarket buying a laundry detergent. The women are not identified outside the context of the advertisement. One comments to the other how clean her brand makes her family's clothes, and the other then comments that she will try it because she has not been fully satisfied with her own brand. This obvious fictional dramatization of a real life situation would not be an endorsement.

Example 3: In an advertisement for a pain remedy, an announcer who is not familiar to consumers except as a spokesman for the advertising drug company praises the drug's ability to deliver fast and lasting pain relief. He purports to speak, not on the basis of his own opinions, but rather in the place of and on behalf of the drug company. The announcer's statements would not be considered an endorsement.

Example 4: A manufacturer of automobile tires hires a well-known professional automobile racing driver to deliver its advertising message in television commercials. In these commercials, the driver speaks of the smooth ride, strength, and long life of the tires. Even though the message is not expressly declared to be the personal opinion of the driver, it may nevertheless constitute an endorsement of the tires. Many consumers will recognize this individual as being primarily a racing driver and not merely a spokesperson or announcer for the advertiser. Accordingly, they may well believe the driver would not speak for an automotive product unless he actually believed in what he was saying and had personal knowledge sufficient to form that belief. Hence, they would think that the advertising message reflects the driver's personal views. This attribution of the underlying views to the driver brings the advertisement within the definition of an endorsement for purposes of this part.

Example 5: A television advertisement for a particular brand of golf balls shows a prominent and well-recognized professional golfer practicing numerous drives off the tee. This would be an endorsement by the golfer even though she makes no verbal statement in the advertisement.

Example 6: An infomercial for a home fitness system is hosted by a well-known entertainer. During the infomercial, the entertainer demonstrates the machine and states that it is the most effective and easy-to-use home exercise machine that she has ever tried. Even if she is reading from a script, this statement would be an endorsement, because consumers are likely to believe it reflects the entertainer's views.

Example 7: A television advertisement for a housewares store features a well-known female comedian and a well-known male baseball player engaging in light-hearted banter about products each one intends to purchase for the other. The comedian says that she will buy him a Brand X, portable, high-definition television so he can finally see the strike zone. He says that he will get her a Brand Y juicer so she can make juice with all the fruit and vegetables thrown at her during her performances. The comedian and baseball player are not likely to be deemed endorsers because consumers will likely realize that the individuals are not expressing their own views.

Example 8: A consumer who regularly purchases a particular brand of dog food decides one day to purchase a new, more expensive brand made by the same manufacturer. She writes in her personal blog that the change in diet has made her dog's fur noticeably softer and shinier, and that in her opinion, the new food definitely is worth the extra money. This posting would not be deemed an endorsement under the Guides.

Assume that rather than purchase the dog food with her own money, the consumer gets it for free because the store routinely tracks her purchases and its computer has generated a coupon for a free trial bag of this new brand. Again, her posting would not be deemed an endorsement under the Guides.

Assume now that the consumer joins a network marketing program under which she periodically receives various products about which she can write reviews if she wants to do so. If she receives a free bag of the new dog food through this program, her positive review would be considered an endorsement under the Guides.

§ 255.1 GENERAL CONSIDERATIONS

(a) Endorsements must reflect the honest opinions, findings, beliefs, or experience of the endorser. Furthermore, an endorsement may not convey any express or implied representation that would be deceptive if made directly by the advertiser. [*See* §§ 255.2(a) and (b) regarding substantiation of representations conveyed by consumer endorsements.

(b) The endorsement message need not be phrased in the exact words of the endorser, unless the advertisement affirmatively so represents. However, the endorsement may not be presented out of context or reworded so as to distort in any way the endorser's opinion or experience with the product. An advertiser may use an endorsement of an expert or celebrity only so long as it has good reason to believe that the endorser continues to subscribe to the views presented. An advertiser may satisfy this obligation by securing the endorser's views at reasonable intervals where reasonableness will be determined by such factors as new information on the performance or effectiveness of the product, a material alteration in the product, changes in the performance of competitors' products, and the advertiser's contract commitments.

(c) When the advertisement represents that the endorser uses the endorsed product, the endorser must have been a bona fide user of it at the time the endorsement was given. Additionally, the advertiser may continue to run the advertisement only so long as it has good reason to believe that the endorser remains a bona fide user of the product. [*See* § 255.1(b) regarding the "good reason to believe" requirement.]

(d) Advertisers are subject to liability for false or unsubstantiated statements made through endorsements, or for failing to disclose material connections between themselves and their endorsers [*see* § 255.5]. Endorsers also may be liable for statements made in the course of their endorsements.

Example 1: A building contractor states in an advertisement that he uses the advertiser's exterior house paint because of its remarkable quick drying properties and durability. This endorsement must comply with the pertinent requirements of Section 255.3 (Expert Endorsements). Subsequently, the advertiser reformulates its paint to enable it to cover exterior surfaces with only one coat. Prior to continued use of the contractor's endorsement, the advertiser must contact the contractor in order to determine whether the contractor would continue to specify the paint and to subscribe to the views presented previously.

Example 2: A television advertisement portrays a woman seated at a desk on which rest five unmarked computer keyboards. An announcer says, "We asked X, an administrative assistant for over ten years, to try these five unmarked keyboards and tell us which one she liked best." The advertisement portrays X typing on each keyboard and then picking the advertiser's brand. The announcer asks her why, and X gives her reasons. This endorsement would probably not represent that X actually uses the advertiser's keyboard at work. In addition, the endorsement also may be required to meet the standards of Section 255.3 (expert endorsements).

Example 3: An ad for an acne treatment features a dermatologist who claims that the product is "clinically proven" to work. Before giving the endorsement, she received a write-up of the clinical study in question, which indicates flaws in the design and conduct of the study that are so serious that they preclude any conclusions about the efficacy of the product. The dermatologist is subject to liability for the false statements she made in the advertisement. The advertiser is also liable for misrepresentations made through the endorsement. [*See* Section 255.3 regarding the product evaluation that an expert endorser must conduct.]

Example 4: A well-known celebrity appears in an infomercial for an oven roasting bag that purportedly cooks every chicken perfectly in thirty minutes. During the shooting of the infomercial, the celebrity watches five attempts to cook chickens using the bag. In each attempt, the chicken is undercooked after thirty minutes and requires sixty minutes of cooking time. In the commercial, the celebrity places an uncooked chicken in the oven roasting bag and places the bag in one oven. He then takes a chicken roasting bag from a second oven, removes from the bag what appears to be a perfectly cooked chicken, tastes the chicken, and says that if you want perfect chicken every time, in just thirty minutes, this is the product you need. A significant percentage of consumers are likely to believe the celebrity's statements represent his own views even though he is reading from a script. The celebrity is subject to liability for his statement about the product. The advertiser is also liable for misrepresentations made through the endorsement.

Example 5: A skin care products advertiser participates in a blog advertising service. The service matches up advertisers with bloggers who will promote the advertiser's products on their personal blogs. The advertiser requests that a blogger try a new body lotion and write a review of the product on her blog. Although the advertiser does not make any specific claims about the lotion's ability to cure skin conditions and the blogger does not ask the advertiser whether there is substantiation for the claim, in her review the blogger writes that the lotion cures eczema and recommends the product to her blog readers who suffer from this condition. The advertiser is subject to liability for misleading or unsubstantiated representations made through the blogger's endorsement. The blogger also is subject to liability for misleading or unsubstantiated representations made in the course of her endorsement. The blogger is also liable if she fails to disclose clearly and conspicuously that she is being paid for her services. [*See* § 255.5.]

In order to limit its potential liability, the advertiser should ensure that the advertising service provides guidance and training to its bloggers concerning the need to ensure that statements they make are truthful and substantiated. The advertiser should also monitor bloggers who are being paid to promote its products and take steps necessary to halt the continued publication of deceptive representations when they are discovered.

§ 255.2 Consumer Endorsements

(a) An advertisement employing endorsements by one or more consumers about the performance of an advertised product or service will be interpreted as representing that the product or service is effective for the purpose depicted in the advertisement. Therefore, the advertiser must possess and rely upon adequate substantiation, including, when appropriate, competent and reliable scientific evidence, to support such claims made through endorsements in the same manner the advertiser would be required to do if it had made the representation directly, *i.e.*, without using endorsements. Consumer endorsements themselves are not competent and reliable scientific evidence.

(b) An advertisement containing an endorsement relating the experience of one or more consumers on a central or key attribute of the product or service also will likely be interpreted as representing that the endorser's experience is representative of what consumers will generally achieve with the advertised product or service in actual, albeit variable, conditions of use. Therefore, an advertiser should possess and rely upon adequate substantiation for this representation. If the advertiser does not have substantiation that the endorser's experience is representative of what consumers will generally achieve, the advertisement should clearly and conspicuously disclose the generally expected performance in the depicted circumstances, and the advertiser must possess and rely on adequate substantiation for that representation.[1]

(c) Advertisements presenting endorsements by what are represented, directly or by implication, to be "actual consumers" should utilize actual consumers in both the audio and video, or clearly and conspicuously disclose that the persons in such advertisements are not actual consumers of the advertised product.

Example 1: A brochure for a baldness treatment consists entirely of testimonials from satisfied customers who say that after using the product, they had amazing hair growth and their hair is as thick and strong as it was when they were teenagers. The advertiser must have competent and reliable scientific evidence that its product is effective in producing new hair growth.

The ad will also likely communicate that the endorsers' experiences are representative of what new users of the product can generally expect. Therefore, even if the advertiser includes a disclaimer such as, "Notice: These testimonials do not prove our product works. You should not expect to have similar results," the ad is likely to be deceptive unless the advertiser has adequate substantiation that new users typically will experience results similar to those experienced by the testimonialists.

Example 2: An advertisement disseminated by a company that sells heat pumps presents endorsements from three individuals who state that after installing the company's heat pump in their homes, their monthly utility bills went down by $100, $125, and $150, respectively. The ad will likely be interpreted as conveying that such savings are representative of what consumers who buy the company's heat pump can generally expect. The advertiser does not have substantiation for that representation because, in fact, less than 20% of purchasers will save $100 or more. A disclosure such as, "Results not typical" or, "These testimonials are based on the experiences of a few people and you are not likely to have similar results" is insufficient to prevent this ad from being deceptive because consumers will still interpret the ad as conveying that the specified savings are representative of what consumers can generally expect. The ad is less likely to be deceptive if it clearly and conspicuously discloses the generally expected savings and the advertiser has adequate substantiation that homeowners can achieve those results. There are multiple ways that such a disclosure could be phrased, *e.g.*, "the average homeowner saves $35 per month," "the typical family saves $50 per month during cold months and $20 per month in warm months," or "most families save 10% on their utility bills."

Example 3: An advertisement for a cholesterol-lowering product features an individual who claims that his serum cholesterol went down by 120 points and does not mention having made any lifestyle changes. A well-conducted clinical study shows that the product reduces the cholesterol levels of individuals with elevated cholesterol by an average of 15% and the advertisement clearly and conspicuously discloses this fact. Despite the presence of this disclosure, the advertisement would be deceptive if the advertiser does not have adequate substantiation that the product can produce the specific results claimed by the endorser (*i.e.*, a 120-point drop in serum cholesterol without any lifestyle changes).

Example 4: An advertisement for a weight-loss product features a formerly obese woman. She says in the ad, "Every day, I drank 2 WeightAway shakes, ate only raw vegetables, and exercised vigorously for six hours at the gym. By the end of six months, I had gone from 250 pounds to 140 pounds." The advertisement accurately describes the woman's experience, and such a result is within the range that would be generally experienced by an extremely overweight individual who consumed WeightAway shakes, only ate raw vegetables, and exercised as the endorser did. Because the endorser clearly describes the limited and truly exceptional circumstances under which she achieved her results, the ad is not likely to convey that consumers who weigh substantially less or use WeightAway under less extreme circumstances will lose 110 pounds in six months. (If the advertisement simply says that the endorser lost 110 pounds in six months using WeightAway together with diet and exercise, however, this description would not adequately alert consumers to the truly remarkable circumstances leading to her weight loss.) The advertiser must have substantiation, however, for any performance claims conveyed by the endorsement (*e.g.*, that WeightAway is an effective weight loss product).

If, in the alternative, the advertisement simply features "before" and "after" pictures of a woman who says "I lost 50 pounds in 6 months with WeightAway," the ad is likely to convey that her experience is representative of what consumers will generally achieve. Therefore, if consumers cannot generally expect to achieve such results, the ad should clearly and conspicuously disclose what they can expect to lose in the depicted circumstances (*e.g.*, "most women who use WeightAway for six months lose at least 15 pounds").

If the ad features the same pictures but the testimonialist simply says, "I lost 50 pounds with WeightAway," and WeightAway users generally do not lose 50 pounds, the ad should disclose what results they do generally achieve (*e.g.*, "most women who use WeightAway lose 15 pounds").

Example 5: An advertisement presents the results of a poll of consumers who have used the advertiser's cake mixes as well as their own recipes. The results purport to show that the majority believed that their families could not tell the difference between the advertised mix and their own cakes baked from scratch. Many of the consumers are actually pictured in the advertisement along with relevant, quoted portions of their statements endorsing the product. This use of the results of a poll or survey of consumers represents that this is the typical result that ordinary consumers can expect from the advertiser's cake mix.

Example 6: An advertisement purports to portray a "hidden camera" situation in a crowded cafeteria at breakfast time. A spokesperson for the advertiser asks a series of actual patrons of the cafeteria for their spontaneous, honest opinions of the advertiser's recently introduced breakfast cereal. Even though the words "hidden camera" are not displayed on the screen, and even though none of the actual patrons is specifically identified during the advertisement, the net impression conveyed to consumers may well be that these are actual customers, and not actors. If actors have been employed, this fact should be clearly and conspicuously disclosed.

Example 7: An advertisement for a recently released motion picture shows three individuals coming out of a theater, each of whom gives a positive statement about the movie. These individuals are actual consumers expressing their personal views about the movie. The advertiser does not need to have substantiation that their views are representative of the opinions that most consumers will have about the movie. Because the consumers' statements would be understood to be the subjective opinions of only three people, this advertisement is not likely to convey a typicality message.

If the motion picture studio had approached these individuals outside the theater and offered them free tickets if they would talk about the movie on camera afterwards, that arrangement should be clearly and conspicuously disclosed. [*See* § 255.5.]

§ 255.3 EXPERT ENDORSEMENTS

(a) Whenever an advertisement represents, directly or by implication, that the endorser is an expert with respect to the endorsement message, then the endorser's qualifications must in fact give the endorser the expertise that he or she is represented as possessing with respect to the endorsement.

(b) Although the expert may, in endorsing a product, take into account factors not within his or her expertise (*e.g.*, matters of taste or price), the endorsement must be supported by an actual exercise of that expertise in evaluating product features or characteristics with respect to which he or she is expert and which are relevant to an ordinary consumer's use of or experience with the product and are available to the ordinary consumer. This evaluation must have included an examination or testing of the product at least as extensive as someone with the same degree of expertise would normally need to conduct in order to support the conclusions presented in the endorsement. To the extent that the advertisement implies that the endorsement was based upon a comparison, such comparison must have been included in the expert's evaluation; and as a result of such comparison, the expert must have concluded that, with respect to those features on which he or she is expert and which are relevant and available to an ordinary consumer, the endorsed product is at least equal overall to the competitors' products. Moreover, where the net impression created by the endorsement is that the advertised product is superior to other products with respect to any such feature or features, then the expert must in fact have found such superiority. [*See* § 255.1(d) regarding the liability of endorsers.]

Example 1: An endorsement of a particular automobile by one described as an "engineer" implies that the endorser's professional training and experience are such that he is well acquainted with the design and performance of automobiles. If the endorser's field is, for example, chemical engineering, the endorsement would be deceptive.

Example 2: An endorser of a hearing aid is simply referred to as "Doctor" during the course of an advertisement. The ad likely implies that the endorser is a medical doctor with substantial experience in the area of hearing. If the endorser is not a medical doctor with substantial experience in audiology, the endorsement would likely be deceptive. A nonmedical "doctor" (*e.g.*, an individual with a Ph.D. in exercise physiology) or a physician without substantial experience in the area of hearing can endorse the product, but if the endorser is referred to as "doctor," the advertisement must make clear the nature and limits of the endorser's expertise.

Example 3: A manufacturer of automobile parts advertises that its products are approved by the "American Institute of Science." From its name, consumers would infer that the "American Institute of Science" is a bona fide independent testing organization with expertise in judging automobile parts and that, as such, it would not approve any automobile part without first testing its efficacy by means of valid scientific methods. If the American Institute of Science is not such a bona fide independent testing organization (*e.g.*, if it was established and operated by an automotive parts manufacturer), the endorsement would be deceptive. Even if the American Institute of Science is an independent bona fide expert testing organization, the endorsement may nevertheless be deceptive unless the Institute has conducted valid scientific tests of the advertised products and the test results support the endorsement message.

Example 4: A manufacturer of a non-prescription drug product represents that its product has been selected over competing products by a large metropolitan hospital. The hospital has selected the product because the manufacturer, unlike its competitors, has packaged each dose of the product separately. This package form is not generally available to the public. Under the circumstances, the endorsement would be deceptive because the basis for the hospital's choice – convenience of packaging – is neither relevant nor available to consumers, and the basis for the hospital's decision is not disclosed to consumers.

Example 5: A woman who is identified as the president of a commercial "home cleaning service" states in a television advertisement that the service uses a particular brand of cleanser, instead of leading competitors it has tried, because of this brand's performance. Because cleaning services extensively use cleansers in the course of their business, the ad likely conveys that the president has knowledge superior to that of ordinary consumers. Accordingly, the president's statement will be deemed to be an expert endorsement. The service must, of course, actually use the endorsed cleanser. In addition, because the advertisement implies that the cleaning service has experience with a reasonable number of leading competitors to the advertised cleanser, the service must, in fact, have such experience, and, on the basis of its expertise, it must have determined that the cleaning ability of the endorsed cleanser is at least equal (or superior, if such is the net impression conveyed by the advertisement) to that of leading competitors' products with which the service has had experience and which remain reasonably available to it. Because in this example the cleaning service's president makes no mention that the endorsed cleanser was "chosen," "selected," or otherwise evaluated in side-by-side comparisons against its competitors, it is sufficient if the service has relied solely upon its accumulated experience in evaluating cleansers without having performed side-by-side or scientific comparisons.

Example 6: A medical doctor states in an advertisement for a drug that the product will safely allow consumers to lower their cholesterol by 50 points. If the materials the doctor reviewed were merely letters from satisfied consumers or the results of a rodent study, the endorsement would likely be deceptive because those materials are not what others with the same degree of expertise would consider adequate to support this conclusion about the product's safety and efficacy.

§ 255.4 ENDORSEMENTS BY ORGANIZATIONS

Endorsements by organizations, especially expert ones, are viewed as representing the judgment of a group whose collective experience exceeds that of any individual member, and whose judgments are generally free of the sort of subjective factors that vary from individual to individual. Therefore, an organization's endorsement must be reached by a process sufficient to ensure that the endorsement fairly reflects the collective judgment of the organization. Moreover, if an organization is represented as being expert, then, in conjunction with a proper exercise of its expertise in evaluating the product under § 255.3 (expert endorsements), it must utilize an expert or experts recognized as such by the organization or standards previously adopted by the organization and suitable for judging the relevant merits of such products. [*See* § 255.1(d) regarding the liability of endorsers.]

Example: A mattress seller advertises that its product is endorsed by a chiropractic association. Because the association would be regarded as expert with respect to judging mattresses, its endorsement must be supported by an evaluation by an expert or experts recognized as such by the organization, or by compliance with standards previously adopted by the organization and aimed at measuring the performance of mattresses in general and not designed with the unique features of the advertised mattress in mind.

§ 255.5 DISCLOSURE OF MATERIAL CONNECTIONS

When there exists a connection between the endorser and the seller of the advertised product that might materially affect the weight or credibility of the endorsement (*i.e.*, the connection is not reasonably expected by the audience), such connection must be fully disclosed. For example, when an endorser who appears in a television commercial is neither represented in the advertisement as an expert nor is known to a significant portion of the viewing public, then the advertiser should clearly and conspicuously disclose either the payment or promise of compensation prior to and in exchange for the endorsement or the fact that the endorser knew or had reason to know or to believe that if the endorsement favored the advertised product some benefit, such as an appearance on television, would be extended to the endorser. Additional guidance, including guidance concerning endorsements made through other media, is provided by the examples below.

Example 1: A drug company commissions research on its product by an outside organization. The drug company determines the overall subject of the research (*e.g.*, to test the efficacy of a newly developed product) and pays a substantial share of the expenses of the research project, but the research organization determines the protocol for the study and is responsible for conducting it. A subsequent advertisement by the drug company mentions the research results as the "findings" of that research organization. Although the design and conduct of the research project are controlled by the outside research organization, the weight consumers place on the reported results could be materially affected by knowing that the advertiser had funded the project. Therefore, the advertiser's payment of expenses to the research organization should be disclosed in this advertisement.

Example 2: A film star endorses a particular food product. The endorsement regards only points of taste and individual preference. This endorsement must, of course, comply with § 255.1; but regardless of whether the star's compensation for the commercial is a $1 million cash payment or a royalty for each product sold by the advertiser during the next year, no disclosure is required because such payments likely are ordinarily expected by viewers.

Example 3: During an appearance by a well-known professional tennis player on a television talk show, the host comments that the past few months have been the best of her career and during this time she has risen to her highest level ever in the rankings. She responds by attributing the improvement in her game to the fact that she is seeing the ball better than she used to, ever since having laser vision correction surgery at a clinic that she identifies by name. She continues talking about the ease of the procedure, the kindness of the clinic's doctors, her speedy recovery, and how she can now engage in a variety of activities without glasses, including driving at night. The athlete does not disclose that, even though she does not appear in commercials for the clinic, she has a contractual relationship with it, and her contract pays her for speaking publicly about her surgery when she can do so. Consumers might not realize that a celebrity discussing a medical procedure in a television interview has been paid for doing so, and knowledge of such payments would likely affect the weight or credibility consumers give to the celebrity's endorsement. Without a clear and conspicuous disclosure that the athlete has been engaged as a spokesperson for the clinic, this endorsement is likely to be deceptive. Furthermore, if consumers are likely to take away from her story that her experience was typical of those who undergo the same procedure at the clinic, the advertiser must have substantiation for that claim.

Assume that instead of speaking about the clinic in a television interview, the tennis player touts the results of her surgery – mentioning the clinic by name – on a social networking site that allows her fans to read in real time what is happening in her life. Given the nature of the medium in which her endorsement is disseminated, consumers might not realize that she is a paid endorser. Because that information might affect the weight consumers give to her endorsement, her relationship with the clinic should be disclosed.

Assume that during that same television interview, the tennis player is wearing clothes bearing the insignia of an athletic wear company with whom she also has an endorsement contract. Although this contract requires that she wear the company's clothes not only on the court but also in public appearances, when possible, she does not mention them or the company during her appearance on the show. No disclosure is required because no representation is being made about the clothes in this context.

Example 4: An ad for an anti-snoring product features a physician who says that he has seen dozens of products come on the market over the years and, in his opinion, this is the best ever. Consumers would expect the physician to be reasonably compensated for his appearance in the ad. Consumers are unlikely, however, to expect that the physician receives a percentage of gross product sales or that he owns part of the company, and either of these facts would likely materially affect the credibility that consumers attach to the endorsement. Accordingly, the advertisement should clearly and conspicuously disclose such a connection between the company and the physician.

Example 5: An actual patron of a restaurant, who is neither known to the public nor presented as an expert, is shown seated at the counter. He is asked for his "spontaneous" opinion of a new food product served in the restaurant. Assume, first, that the advertiser had posted a sign on the door of the restaurant informing all who entered that day that patrons would be interviewed by the advertiser as part of its TV promotion of its new soy protein "steak." This notification would materially affect the weight or credibility of the patron's endorsement, and, therefore, viewers of the advertisement should be clearly and conspicuously informed of the circumstances under which the endorsement was obtained.

Assume, in the alternative, that the advertiser had not posted a sign on the door of the restaurant, but had informed all interviewed customers of the "hidden camera" only after interviews were completed and the customers had no reason to know or believe that their response was being recorded for use in an advertisement. Even if patrons were also told that they would be paid for allowing the use of their opinions in advertising, these facts need not be disclosed.

Example 6: An infomercial producer wants to include consumer endorsements for an automotive additive product featured in her commercial, but because the product has not yet been sold, there are no consumer users. The producer's staff reviews the profiles of individuals interested in working as "extras" in commercials and identifies several who are interested in automobiles. The extras are asked to use the product for several weeks and then report back to the producer. They are told that if they are selected to endorse the product in the producer's infomercial, they will receive a small payment. Viewers would not expect that these "consumer endorsers" are actors who were asked to use the product so that they could appear in the commercial or that they were compensated. Because the advertisement fails to disclose these facts, it is deceptive.

Example 7: A college student who has earned a reputation as a video game expert maintains a personal weblog or "blog" where he posts entries about his gaming experiences. Readers of his blog frequently seek his opinions about video game hardware and software. As it has done in the past, the manufacturer of a newly released video game system sends the student a free copy of the system and asks him to write about it on his blog. He tests the new gaming system and writes a favorable review. Because his review is disseminated via a form of consumer-generated media in which his relationship to the advertiser is not inherently obvious, readers are unlikely to know that he has received the video game system free of charge in exchange for his review of the product, and given the value of the video game system, this fact likely would materially affect the credibility they attach to his endorsement. Accordingly, the blogger should clearly and conspicuously disclose that he received the gaming system free of charge. The manufacturer should advise him at the time it provides the gaming system that this connection should be disclosed, and it should have procedures in place to try to monitor his postings for compliance.

Example 8: An online message board designated for discussions of new music download technology is frequented by MP3 player enthusiasts. They exchange information about new products, utilities, and the functionality of numerous playback devices. Unbeknownst to the message board community, an employee of a leading playback device manufacturer has been posting messages on the discussion board promoting the manufacturer's product. Knowledge of this poster's employment likely would affect the weight or credibility of her endorsement. Therefore, the poster should clearly and conspicuously disclose her relationship to the manufacturer to members and readers of the message board.

Example 9: A young man signs up to be part of a "street team" program in which points are awarded each time a team member talks to his or her friends about a particular advertiser's products. Team members can then exchange their points for prizes, such as concert tickets or electronics. These incentives would materially affect the weight or credibility of the team member's endorsements. They should be clearly and conspicuously disclosed, and the advertiser should take steps to ensure that these disclosures are being provided.

End Notes

[1] The Commission tested the communication of advertisements containing testimonials that clearly and prominently disclosed either "Results not typical" or the stronger "These testimonials are based on the experiences of a few people and you are not likely to have similar results." Neither disclosure adequately reduced the communication that the experiences depicted are generally representative. Based upon this research, the Commission believes that similar disclaimers regarding the limited applicability of an endorser's experience to what consumers may generally expect to achieve are unlikely to be effective.

Nonetheless, the Commission cannot rule out the possibility that a strong disclaimer of typicality could be effective in the context of a particular advertisement. Although the Commission would have the burden of proof in a law enforcement action, the Commission notes that an advertiser possessing reliable empirical testing demonstrating that the net impression of its advertisement with such a disclaimer is non-deceptive will avoid the risk of the initiation of such an action in the first instance.

CHAPTER SOURCES

The following chapters have been previously published:

Chapter 1 – This is an edited, excerpted and augmented edition of a United States Congressional Research Service publication, Report Order Code R40908, dated November 9, 2009.

Chapter 2 – This is an edited, excerpted and augmented edition of a United States Congressional Research Service publication, Report Order Code RL34693, dated January 20, 2010.

Chapter 3 – This is an edited, excerpted and augmented edition of a United States Congressional Research Service publication, Report Order Code R40590, dated May 20, 2009.

Chapter 4 – This is an edited, excerpted and augmented edition of a United States Congressional Research Service publication, Report Order Code RL32177, dated April 10, 2008.

Chapter 5 – These remarks were delivered as Statement of the Federal Trade Commission given before the Senate Committee on Commerce, Science and Transportation on June 18, 2008.

Chapter 6 – These remarks were delivered as Statement of Leslie Harris given before the Senate Commerce, Science and Transportation Committee on July 9, 2008.

Chapter 7 – This is an edited, excerpted and augmented edition of a United States Federal Trade Commission publication, Report Number 16 CFR Part 255.

INDEX

D

E

F